THE HIDDEN POWER OF NAMES

THE HIDDEN POWER OF NAMES

ANGELA ROBYINSON

Copyright © 2024 by Angela Robyinson

Edited by: Gina Casto
Illustrations: Thetiana Gushchyna, Trinity Sage Burke
Cover Design: Erika Alyana Duran (easduran.myportfolio.com)
Book Design, Tyepesetting, and Formatting: Judy Sery

angelarobyinson@gmail.com
www.nomenumerics.com

ISBN: 979-8-9913282-4-1 (Paperback)
ISBN: 979-8-9913282-1-0 (eBook)
ISBN: 979-8-9913282-3-4 (Hardcover)

THE HIDDEN POWER OF NAMES

Using the Ancient Science of Nameology to Understand Yourself, Discover Your Life's Destiny, and Unlock Your Full Potential

---

ANGELA ROBYINSON

I dedicate this book with deep love and great respect to my children, Judy, Rona, and Shlomi, who have always been the source of my strength and motivation, and from their very existence, I drew the strength to move forward. The book is also dedicated to my beloved grandchildren, Lia, Emma, and Adam.
I love you all very much.

I also dedicate this book to my twin flame, whose spirit I have always felt next to me. The strength of my love for you, my dear, has awakened me from a long and deep slumber.

CONTENTS

ACKNOWLEDGMENTS

First, lastly, and always, I wish to express my deep love and appreciation for God and the sacred Hebrew alphabet, from which all the writing in this book emanates. Secondly, I want to express my gratitude to my spiritual teachers from every religion, who have accompanied me in the past and continue to do so today, as well as those with whom I was lucky enough to learn and those whom I did not have the opportunity to meet in person, but their wisdom and writings have profoundly influenced me. I am immensely grateful to them with all my heart and soul.

Among my earliest spiritual teachers was Menachem Mendel Morgensztern, known as "The Holy Flame from Kotzk." At the age of fourteen, he awakened in me a profound longing for divinity, with his writings serving as a beacon on my journey. The author Ayn Rand, whose work introduced me to the teachings of Socrates, Plato, and Aristotle at a very young age, enlightened me about the importance of "staying true to the origin." Osho, a philosopher, author, and spiritual teacher, has been a source of wisdom I cherish for over thirty years. And Rabbi Philip S. Berg, the founder of "The National Institute for the Research in Kabbalah," played a crucial role in acquainting me with the world of Kabbalah.

I extend my sincere gratitude to Nassim Haramein, a revolutionary physicist and cosmologist who developed "The Connected Universe" theory, based on quantum field theory. Gregg Braden, a researcher, author, and one of the foremost scientists of our era, bridges science, spirituality, and reality. My appreciation also extends to biologist and thinker Dr. Bruce Lipton, scientist and author Dr. Joe Dispenza, mythology scholar Joseph Campbell, and philosophers Alan Watts and Ram Dass. I am equally grateful to great poets Rumi, Shams Tabrizi, Kahlil Gibran, and Hafiz, whose poetry has offered inspiration and helped me to appreciate the beauty of language and love. Their wisdom and writings have helped me to simplify the highly complex concepts of *Sefer Yetzirah: The Book of Creation* into language that is both simpler and more accessible, enabling a wider audience to grasp its profound teachings.

Lastly, I want to give thanks to my divine guidance, to my "I AM" presence, and to that strong and unwavering inner voice that has accompanied and guided me throughout my life, from the earliest stages of my childhood. The voice that I heard in my heart, the voice that accompanied me and gave me a feeling of warmth, security, love, and support. I want to express my gratitude to the divine and sacred spirit within me. I love you, God.

PREFACE

Since my early childhood, I have sought an explanation for my existence in this earthly realm. For as long as I can remember, I have searched for answers to fundamental questions such as: Who am I? Why am I here? What are the lessons I am supposed to learn here, and what is the unique gift I have come to offer the world? I yearned to find the meaning of my life on Earth and have discovered these answers in the wisdom of the Hebrew alphabet.

My journey with the Hebrew letters began in the 1970s. Back then, I immigrated from the Soviet Union to Israel with my parents and siblings, and that is when I began to learn the Hebrew language. The love for the Hebrew letters awakened within me immediately.

Late at night, when everyone else in the house was asleep, I would find myself sitting and drawing the graphic forms of the Hebrew letters. It was love at first sight, and I felt an inexplicable connection to them. However, I only discovered the reason behind this connection much later in life during my Holistic Psychotherapy studies and through in-depth personal development processes, such as reincarnation, which I will discuss further in my writings.

In the late 1980s, my parents and siblings left for America. I was already a wife and mother and decided to stay in Israel. Over time, this decision became clear to me. I felt a soulful need to deepen my knowledge of the Hebrew language.

From a young age, I loved to read, and I read a lot. I speak, read, and write in several languages, but reading in Hebrew has always held a special place in my heart. I love to read Hebrew more than any other language.

The subjects that interested me the most included spirituality, mysticism, esotericism, Kabbalah, philosophy, psychology, sociology, and mythology. However, my primary fascination was with the Bible and writings associated with ancient texts and scriptures.

When reading the Bible, I sensed that a great part of it stores immense wisdom and an encrypted truth, presented to us humans in the form of ciphers and codes in a cryptic and mystical language. I felt this wisdom deep in my heart, but I could not yet translate it into words and into tangible concepts that others could easily understand.

My love for writing in Hebrew became a constant in my life. From the time I was a child until today, I have spent hours writing to God, expressing everything on my mind. Through writing, I feel a deep connection with God, as if I am in constant communication with Him through the Hebrew letters. Sometimes, in moments of silence, contemplation, or writing, I see in my mind's eye the energetic dance of the letters and the forms they create as they connect.

The first significant turning point in my life, which brought me closer to my soul's path, occurred in the 1990s when my eldest daughter started experiencing strong eye twitches. Conventional medicine recommended neurological medication. I felt uneasy about this approach and turned to God in search of a solution. The answer I received was to pay closer attention to the signs around me.

The very next day, I encountered an old friend I had not seen in years, a former colleague who had previously suffered from severe eye twitches. As we spoke, I noticed that her eyes were no longer twitching. When I asked her how she had resolved the issue, she shared that she had learned **Reiki**[1], which turned out to be the solution.

---

[1] Reiki is a holistic healing technique that fosters relaxation and alleviates stress and anxiety by using gentle touch to channel universal life energy through the practitioner's hands. Reiki aids in healing by helping people become energetically balanced physically, emotionally, mentally and spiritually and is often used as a complementary therapy to support overall well-being.

Three days after that encounter, I found myself immersed in Reiki studies. As part of my studies, I needed to undergo Reiki treatments myself. When I returned home after the first treatment, I noticed that my daughter's eye twitches had stopped. This powerful and thrilling experience opened the door to a new and unfamiliar world, prompting me to study alternative medicine.

I embarked on the journey of studying alternative medicine, delving into various therapeutic methods and techniques, including meditation, guided imagery, Reiki at all levels, Bach flower remedies, Aromatherapy, Electro-Magnetic Field balancing technique (EMF), conscious breathing (Prana-Yama), Holistic Psychotherapy, Theta Healing, Light Language, Yoga, and Vipassana meditation. Alongside these, I also delved into the study of Kabbalah, Astrology, Numerology, the "72 Names of God," and the ancient study of the secret power of the Hebrew letters. These studies extended over many years, paving the way for my later exploration of the mysteries of Kabbalah knowledge.

In the early 2000s, after completing my Master's Reiki studies and seven years of studying numerology and the secret of the Hebrew letters, I began teaching in private and public self-awareness centers and various colleges during my spare time. I conducted courses and workshops in Reiki, self-awareness, numerology, and the power of the Hebrew letters. Around that time, I also started receiving information in the form of images, words and sounds through telepathic communication. In my mind's eye, I saw visual patterns of letters moving slowly or quickly and heard sentences and biblical verses within me.

The initial draft of this book began approximately twenty-one years ago, in 2002. It commenced with a gentle tapping on my heart chakra, followed by a tickling sensation behind my ears and a deep, clear, and distinct inner voice inviting me to sit in a quiet meditative position, take slow and deep breaths, and be present and attentive. Initially, for a while, I ignored the voice, although it was not a stranger to me; it had always been with me for as long as I could remember. I used to listen to it frequently during my early childhood, particularly during my morning runs at 5:00 a.m. However, it was only after it repeated itself many times that it managed to capture my attention.

One day, during a morning meditation, I responded to the call and said, "Here I am." I was asked to be attentive and relaxed, to be in a state of openness, receptivity, and, above all, readiness to wake up in the early hours of the night, around three or four in the morning, and dedicate time to writing the information that would be conveyed to me. And I surrendered without knowing where this surrender would lead me.

This continued for over a year. I would wake up without any prior intention, between three and four in the morning, feeling a warm and gentle tingling sensation in my earlobes. The deep and tranquil voice invited me to sit and write down the information that flowed through me.

In this way, the first draft of this book was written.

At first, the information was delivered in somewhat of a "biblical" language, which I could not always decipher. The information contained symbols and signs, some of which are known to us today as "Sacred Geometry." The familiar, deep, and beloved voice, who identified as "I Am That I Am," invited me to establish a theoretical foundation for my writing. A theory that would unite the secrets of the holy Hebrew alphabet, as well as the symbols of Sacred Geometry associated with the letters and the psychological, physiological, and biological processes they speak of so that eventually, the theory would make the connection between spirituality, science, and reality.

When I reviewed the material I had written, I noticed that the language in which the information was conveyed to me bore a striking resemblance to that used in the *Sefer Yetzirah*. This ancient mystical Hebrew text, which explores the creation and formation of our world, has long fascinated me and has been a subject of my study for many years.

Ever since I first read it, I have been driven to delve deeper into its profound meanings. I felt a strong desire to understand the codes and magical clues within the book. However, as my earthly life demanded a significant portion of my time—raising children, pursuing both an alternative and academic education, working, and establishing a vast professional career, I left little room to process the information that was delivered to me. As a result, my writings ended up tucked away in a drawer.

In the mid-2010s, after reaching the peak of my professional career as a Finance and Human Resources Manager, I experienced a significant turning point in my life. On the surface, everything seemed fine. I was promoted to a senior position as a Human Resources Manager, a promotion that brought with it an increased salary and benefits, but I felt that something was missing and that I was not fulfilling my full spiritual potential. During this period, I also began experiencing pain and numbing in my left arm, which gradually intensified and at times I could barely move it.

On a bright, sunny day, I received a spiritual calling to rise and embark on a journey. Somewhat thrillingly, this calling started with the words "go forth" (לכי לך), echoing the biblical words spoken to Abraham, the Father of Many Nations: *"And the Lord said to Abram, 'Go forth from your land and from your birthplace and from your father's house to the land that I will show you.'"* (Genesis Chapter 12, Verse 1)

Following this call, I left Israel and embarked on a journey, accompanied by my beloved son and equipped with only two suitcases.

Leaving Israel, my home for forty years, was not an easy decision, as it meant that I had to leave behind my beloved daughters and grandchildren. The beginning of the journey, like any journey, was accompanied by uncertainty, doubts, apprehensions, anxiety, and fears. But my unwavering faith in God and the hope within me gave me the strength to rise and move forward. I decided to surrender to God and allow Him to guide me to my destined path.

After several months of traveling through various lands, each with its own unique spiritual gifts, I arrived at a small in Northern California known as "Mount Shasta." While I was on the plane heading to Mount Shasta, I felt an overwhelming excitement in my heart that I could not quite comprehend. Tears welled up in my eyes, my body trembled, and I could not help but cry upon hearing that familiar, strong, and clear voice say, "Welcome home, my beloved daughter of light."

With every fiber of my being, I felt I had arrived home.

The story of how the locals in Mount Shasta received my son and me is like a fairy tale. Mother Shasta welcomed us with immense love. From the moment we arrived, a group of residents took it upon themselves to care for us. They arranged an apartment, furnished it, provided bedding and kitchen utensils, invited us for meals, and enveloped us in a sense of home and family. Some said the place had been waiting for us.

Shortly after our arrival, I felt a calling to go to the mountain. The calling came from the depths of the mountain directly into the depths of my heart. I responded to the call, and since then, I have completely devoted myself to this journey, to the extensive soul family that resides in higher dimensions, to my "I AM" presence, and to God and Mother Earth.

While Mount Shasta may not be directly related to the Hebrew letters, the unique energy of the mountain—its clear air, lush forests, serene lakes, and profound silence—coupled with the high vibrational frequencies of the area—profoundly influenced my spiritual journey. It provided the clarity and peace of mind that was necessary for me to deeply connect with the divine voice within.

Diagram 1: Mount Shasta

Mount Shasta is no ordinary mountain; it is a magical peak located on the northern side of the Sierra Nevada Mountain range. This mountain serves as a source of mystical power for Earth's inhabitants and a focal point for both material and non-material entities, including angels, spiritual guides, and extraterrestrial spacecraft. Rising over four thousand meters above sea level, Mount Shasta is considered one of the planet's sacred places. The mountain also functions as an energetic portal, representing the entry point for the planet's networks of light. It is a holy place that vibrates at the frequency of the fifth dimension, providing individuals with the potential for spiritual acceleration and a strong connection to higher dimensions, where they can receive communicated messages.

Mount Shasta is one of the few places in the world where local water comes directly from the Earth's depths. This water is pure, cold, and crystal clear, of high quality, refreshing, and quenching both the soul and spirit.

When sitting at the base of the mountain, one often observes that its summit is crowned with a kind of white halo. Above the peak, rare and exceptionally beautiful cloud formations are visible. The air around the mountain is crisp and cool, and the entire area is adorned with ancient oak and cedar trees covered in vibrant green moss. In this place, one can hear unique sounds and feel the presence of the beings surrounding them with love, healing energies, and tranquility. Most importantly, it provides access to higher dimensions in the galaxy in both body and consciousness.

It is believed that Mount Shasta was the ancient dwelling place of the Lemurians, an advanced civilization of highly developed beings. They possessed sophisticated technology and profound spiritual knowledge, living on Earth in unity consciousness and in harmony with nature and the world until around thirteen thousand years ago. Following a catastrophic event, they are said to have retreated underground beneath the earth of Mount Shasta. This theory has been supported by some researchers and authors in their writings.

INTRODUCTION

As I sat at the base of Mount Shasta, the sacred Hebrew letters began to whisper to me once more. In the serene stillness of the mountain, I heard their voices urging me to redeem them and bring forth the information that was given to me years ago, alongside additional knowledge they wished to convey. I once again began to receive information telepathically, in the form of images, words, and sounds, experiencing flashes that filled me with understanding and wisdom.

All the messages I received came to me in the Hebrew language. The sacred letters taught me that the Hebrew language is the source of all languages and that in the process of human evolution, the Hebrew language was embedded in human DNA as an ancient Hebrew word-image.

When I began to inscribe the profound wisdom of the Hebrew letters into writing, I was asked to write with my left hand so that I could serve as a channel connected to the right hemisphere, the intuitive and non-verbal hemisphere. Being right-handed since childhood, I never thought I had the ability to write with my left hand. I was surprised to discover that I am, in fact, ambidextrous.

But this was only the first in a series of discoveries that awaited me. As the information flowed to me and I delved into their understanding and wisdom, a growing compassion developed within me, both for myself and those around me. I cannot claim that self-judgment and judgment of others completely disappeared; it would be presumptuous of me to do so. However, I changed my approach to my inner dialogue. I learned to understand it and its language, and over time, I found that my inner dialogue became more considerate, kind, gentle, compassionate, and loving, both toward myself and those around me.

As I delved deeper into the various aspects of each letter, I found myself and my path. And as I delved into their collective wisdom and the biological, psychological, and physiological processes linked to them, the pieces of information began to form a framework. The previous books I wrote emerged from the drawer and underwent fresh processing, and "The 22 Codes of Creation" method that I developed began to take shape and write itself. And this is just the tip of the iceberg.

The sacred Hebrew letters provide us with profound, abstract, and practical insights. In them lies the ability to foster deep self-awareness and increase levels of love, compassion, and self-acceptance, which, in turn, enable the individual to develop emotional resilience and well-being. To truly free ourselves and have the freedom to choose the right path in our earthly journey, it is essential that we learn about the forces that work within us and upon us through the letters of our birth name.

The twenty-two sacred letters symbolize the path that the human soul undergoes throughout its earthly journey, reflecting the ups, downs, and personal lessons that each of us encounters.

The purpose of the letters is to prepare us, human beings, for the current times, during which Mother Earth undergoes her ascension, and we, her children, ascend with her. This process enables us to develop self-awareness, sharpen our senses, and evolve into multidimensional beings. Their role is to provide the knowledge and tools needed to awaken from a slumbering consciousness, recalling our divine essence to help remove the veil of illusion that has blinded our eyes for thousands of years, leaving us trapped in false beliefs of separateness and disconnected from the divine aspect within us.

When you learn to identify and connect with the hidden power within the letters of your name, you will be able to attract divine abundance into your life, manifesting health, love, satisfaction, and joy. These are just a few of the benefits.

Many people remain disconnected from their true potential simply because they are unaware of its existence. The information in this book will reveal to each reader their potential. You will discover that the letters of your name hold unique power, strength, and wisdom necessary for success in this earthly life and for fulfilling your potential.

As you recognize these hidden powers lying dormant within your soul, they will come to life and manifest in your external world as well.

So far, dozens of books, if not more, have been written on the subject of the Hebrew letters. What sets this book apart is not only the understanding of the letters of your name but also its practical aspect. I have strived to explain the essential truths communicated to me by the sacred Hebrew letters in a concise, clear, and straightforward manner, while maintaining their profound essence.

This book will speak to your heart, not only because it provides deep and empowering self-awareness but also because it offers practical tools to identify your true potential and that of your loved ones, thereby supporting personal development.

I hope this knowledge will create miracles in your life and provide you with a profound understanding of your true self, sparing you from misery and mental and emotional enslavement. Above all, I hope this information will give you the courage to follow your inner calling, to follow your heart, and to rise and move forward toward your destiny instead of waiting for it to knock at your door.

This book is the first in a series that delves into the wisdom and the power of Hebrew letters, and it is presented to you with much light and love.

It is written from the heart and speaks to the heart. I am thrilled to embark on this journey of self-discovery with you.

THE THIRST FOR TRUTH

He who thirsts for truth is the one who thirsts for God.

Among all people and across all times, there always exists someone who thirsts for the absolute. The smallness and meanness, the betrayal, and the baseness that surround him from all sides inflict pain on his heart. Yet, with confidence and tranquility, he marches toward the truth, and his soul, like a torch, illuminates his path.

The one who thirsts for the absolute, at all times, sees the mountain before his eyes and longs to climb it. Between him and the mountain flows the river of tears. To reach the mountain, he must cross this river, and one cannot cross the river of tears without bringing a gift: tears of blood, the blood of a heart that feels the pain of the world.

He who thirsts for the absolute infuriates people against him. They secretly love him, for they wish to be like him, yet they openly hate him for their inability to emulate him. He who thirsts for the absolute loves all people but must remain apart from them. He can offer them the gold of his heart from afar, but up close, the people would exchange this gold for pennies.

He who thirsts for the absolute finds happiness only in communion with God. He is indifferent to all things for which the majority of people yearn and joyously chooses the life that others resent. The disaster of mankind stems from its lack of understanding, as for the absolute one must seek and for the absolute one must aspire in his daily life.

The holy flame from Kotzk

RECONNECTING WITH
THE SACRED HEART

The information you are about to uncover will profoundly impact your lives. You are about to get a glimpse behind the scenes of reality, a glimpse that will expand your consciousness, trigger a significant shift in your perception, and accelerate your spiritual awakening.

The information presented in this book will help you understand, both easily and clearly, the forces operating on you and within you. It will provide you with an elevated and broad perspective on life. As you immerse yourself in the mysteries, secrets and the powers of the Hebrew letters, your life will be irrevocably transformed. Your perception of reality will undergo a transformation, enabling you to grasp new insights and definitions. This journey will connect you with your true purpose, the very reason for your existence, leading you toward a profound awakening.

The forthcoming information is not new. Rather, it has been concealed, waiting for us for hundreds and thousands of years. The religions that have held spiritual authority for generations have not only claimed exclusive access to spiritual knowledge but also diligently withheld significant portions of it from us, driven by control-oriented motives and vested interests. I believe that some of the information found in the Bible and the New Testament has been distorted and altered to block our access to divine wisdom and our true power and potential. It is far simpler to control and manipulate a slumbering individual toward the precipice than one who is awake and aware.

The truth, which has been hidden from humanity for millennia, is gradually beginning to be revealed in the form of ancient texts that aid us in connecting and assembling the various puzzle pieces. Examples of this are the "Dead Sea Scrolls" and other ancient discoveries.

It is important to understand that everything comes from God, both light and darkness and we, the human beings on our mother planet, have been bestowed with the gift of choice, coupled with the capacity for experiential learning. This profound capability was granted to us through the wisdom of our ancestral mother, Eve. In the Hebrew language, the name "Eve" (חוה) also carries the connotation of experience, signifying our innate ability to acquire wisdom through personal experiences.

This innate ability enables us to experience, perceive and interact with the divine creation. This interaction involves navigating through a range of emotional, experiential trials that encompass positive and negative aspects, symbolically represented as light and darkness or good and evil. Through these diverse experiences, which can be likened to a testing ground, we have the opportunity to choose our path. This path involves developing an understanding of both the positive and negative elements of life, akin to striving toward a godlike comprehension of good and evil.

The primary objective of this book, above all else, is to guide us in the rediscovery of our sacred heart—a heart from which we have been disconnected since the fall of ancient Lemuria, an event that transpired approximately thirteen thousand years ago. This disconnection has sown seeds of fear and forgetfulness deep within us, leading to the loss of our connection to love, compassion, and the divine wellspring residing within us. Consequently, this has propelled us further into the realms of materiality, duality, and separation.

Gradually, this forgetfulness has ensnared humanity in a collective **amnesia**[1] so profound that we have entirely forfeited our

---

[2] Amnesia refers to a condition characterized by significant memory loss, impacting a person's ability to remember information and experiences. This forgetfulness goes beyond normal everyday lapses, often impairing various aspects of an individual's life and functioning.

awareness of our true essence, origin, and innate creative abilities. We have completely forgotten who we are, what our origins are, and the fact that we are creators ourselves. This pervasive forgetfulness has plunged humanity into a profound state of unconsciousness, which, in turn, has given rise to considerable suffering and anguish.

I hold the belief that had this knowledge been imparted to us millennia ago, we would have had the opportunity to comprehend the suppressed and lost aspects of our personal and collective subconscious. As a result, the prevalence of psychiatry and chemical interventions might have been significantly diminished.

READER'S GUIDE

The original version of this book was written in Hebrew and has since been translated into English. Due to inherent language differences, the English version of this book is slightly different. This adaptation was undertaken with the goal of ensuring that English-speaking readers can more easily access the insights provided. It was a nuanced task that involved maintaining the integrity and depth of the original Hebrew content while making it accessible and meaningful to an English-speaking audience. My aim was to bridge the linguistic and cultural gap, delivering the valuable insights of this book to a broader audience without compromising its essence.

As you progress through the text, you will encounter biblical verses whose interpretations are based on the original Hebrew scriptures. It is important to acknowledge the differences between the original Hebrew Bible and its English translations. No translation can fully encapsulate the breadth of ideas, cultural contexts, and linguistic nuances present in the Hebrew original. The Hebrew language, characterized by its rich vocabulary, distinctive grammatical structures, and profound layers of meaning, belongs to a different language family than English. This disparity poses significant challenges in translation, where a direct word-for-word translation may result in inaccuracies and misunderstandings.

Over centuries, scholars, translators, and religious figures have endeavored to translate the profound depth and nuanced meanings of the Hebrew scriptures for English-speaking audiences. This effort has yielded hundreds of distinct English Bible versions, each aiming to make the Hebrew scriptures comprehensible to English readers. The English verses cited in this book are taken from the New American Standard Bible.

To ensure that English-speaking readers can access the insights provided in this book through the study of Hebrew letters, I have included charts at the end of the book that draw parallels between the Hebrew letters and their English counterparts. These charts are designed to help English-speaking readers not only understand the essence and wisdom carried by each Hebrew letter but also to navigate the insights contained within the letters, despite the inherent differences between the two languages.

CHAPTER 1

Tracing the Origins of the Letters

The source from which I gained much wisdom and understanding regarding the secret of the letters and the wisdom contained within them is Kabbalah, also known as "the Secret Doctrine" or the theory of Kabbalah. However, the source that provided the inspiration and framework for my writing is *Sefer Yetzirah: The Book of Creation.*

The theory of Kabbalah is entirely based on *Sefer Yetzirah* and is essentially its development and expansion. According to Kabbalistic tradition, the Secret Doctrine has existed since the dawn of mankind. Kabalistic practitioners assert that the knowledge found in *Sefer Yetzirah* has its origins in advanced extraterrestrial civilizations whose purpose is to aid in humanity's development. I strongly resonate with this assertion.

Sefer Yetzirah constitutes the human expression of the soul. It presents humans as the origin of divine creation and deals with the cosmological aspects of creation. The book is written as a meditative text and contains magical clues of great significance. A text that fills the reader with wonder, mystery, and insights.

Throughout generations, *Sefer Yetzirah* has been subject to various interpretations by philosophers, Jewish sages, Christian theologians, and numerous others. Some sources suggest that this philosophical and mystical text was also known to the Essenes, members of a Jewish philosophical sect from the Second Temple period, who studied The Torah and its secrets meticulously.

Certain sources even suggest that *Sefer Yetzirah* was familiar to the Pythagoreans, adherents of the school founded by the illustrious mathematician and philosopher Pythagoras, who utilized the numerical part of this knowledge. Moreover, some sources imply that certain parts of *Sefer Yetzirah* were interpreted in the ancient Hindu scriptures known as the Vedas, written in Sanskrit.

The book *Sefer Yetzirah* is not easy to comprehend. It is written like a cryptic scroll, and deciphering its content requires seriousness, deep insight, and much meditation. What helped me understand this secretive scroll was the training I received over approximately three decades, which included various spiritual techniques. However, more than anything else, it was my numerous meditations with these sacred letters that aided me in connecting with their profound wisdom.

Sefer Yetzirah indicates that in order to create the world, the Supreme Creator harnessed the gematrical, phonetic, graphic, and geometric properties of the Hebrew letters. In essence, these twenty-two sacred letters encapsulate the divine energies and principles that brought the world into existence. They also serve as the means by which we shape the reality of our lives on the earthly plane.

The theory of Kabbalah extends this understanding, indicating that the genetic coding of the human DNA comprises twenty-two distinct codes of various light ciphers that operate within humans as **seeds of consciousness**[2]. Through understanding and deciphering these seeds, one gains access to higher states of consciousness and spiritual awakening.

Sefer Yetzirah was written with the intention of providing mankind with principles that would lead them to evolutionary development. I hypothesize that to make it easier for us to understand, the author of *Sefer Yetzirah* linked the forces of

---

[2] Seeds of consciousness is a term used in spiritual and philosophical contexts to describe the fundamental and unmanifested level of awareness from which all thoughts, emotions, and experiences emerge. Seed consciousness symbolizes the core of awareness before it takes specific forms in our conscious experience. These seeds of consciousness are encoded within the human DNA and serve as the fundamental patterns for the development of human consciousness and spiritual awareness. They represent the potential for inner growth and enlightenment, akin to the idea that through understanding and unlocking these codes, individuals can access higher states of consciousness and spiritual awakening.

nature acting upon us with the inner soul forces acting within us by correlating the letters to the elements, planets, and zodiac signs. This correlation facilitates a more accessible understanding of the distinctive character and attributes associated with each Hebrew letter.

What the theory of Kabbalah revealed to humankind thousands of years ago is only now being substantiated through advanced science, particularly within the realm of quantum physics, where mathematical and empirical evidence is emerging to support these ancient insights.

As I underscore throughout my writings, while the physical body is temporary, the soul is eternal. When the soul chooses to manifest itself in earthly existence, it constructs a personal blueprint, often referred to as the "soul contract." Within this contract, the soul delineates its "soul script"—a narrative of what it aspires to achieve during its earthly journey, including who it intends to meet, the wisdom it aims to acquire, and the souls it will engage in the intricate dance of life.

These souls, also known as soulmates and twin flames, often incarnate as family members, lovers, partners, friends, colleagues, and more. The soul contract specifies the junctures in time when it will encounter these soul members, as well as the scenarios or catalysts that will guide it toward actions that bring it closer to learning its personal lessons and fulfilling its spiritual purpose. Although this soul contract is initially predetermined, we are in a process of spiritual evolution. Therefore, we can consciously evolve and either rewrite or change parts of our soul contract, making a sort of "script correction."

Invitation to a Journey

Our journey will commence by delving into the essence of Hebrew letters, unraveling their origins, understanding their uniqueness, and the pivotal role they play in the creation process. From there, we will embark on an exploration of the significance harbored within our given name and surname, understanding the inherent power it holds and the multifaceted intellectual, emotional, spiritual, and practical potential it carries. We will learn to comprehend the structure of our name and the strengths and weaknesses attributed to each letter.

Additionally, we will focus on the various subdivisions of the letters, each offering a wealth of information and insights. These insights will furnish you with the tools needed to harness the letters of your name for the purpose of personal development, thereby allowing you to manifest your highest and most benevolent potential. Through this process, you will not only align yourself with the reality you aspire to inhabit but also summon forth miracles and wonders in your earthly journey.

As we traverse this journey, you will unveil your unique temperament, the inner driving force that propels you, and the authentic desires nestled within your heart. You will learn to recognize the constructive and inhibiting aspects of your personality, along with the way you tend to unconsciously perceive the world, thereby gaining a deeper understanding of your life experiences. Moreover, you will unearth the latent powers of your soul, a revelation that will equip you with the insight necessary to effectively and precisely employ these powers. This, in turn, will enable you to foster loving, compassionate, and harmonious relationships, not only with others but also within yourself.

The information presented in this book will reveal to you your inherent tendencies, the bedrock of your fundamental beliefs, and the energetic forces that influence and drive you hypnotically and subconsciously. By learning the power embedded within the letters of your name, you will come to recognize the extent to which your name provides you with roots, anchors, and grounding, as well as with wings that enable you to soar, elevate, and move forward toward the realization of your dreams.

We are the ones we have been waiting for. Each and every one of us carries within the consciousness of the Messiah. Let us embark on this exploration together. And just like any journey, we will begin with the first step: understanding the true and profound essence of the letters.

CHAPTER 2

The Essence of the Letters

"With thirty-two mystical paths of wisdom, engraved Yah, the lord of hosts, his universe with three books: text, number and communication."
Sefer Yetzirah, Chapter 1, Verse 1

The secret power of letters and names is rooted in the ancient Hebrew text known as *Sefer Yetzirah: The Book of Creation* or *The Book of Formation*. *Sefer Yetzirah* begins with a verse narrating the story of the creation of the universe and its existence. It reveals that the formation of our universe was accomplished through thirty-two paths of wondrous wisdom, which are the twenty-two Hebrew letters and the ten divine spheres. These pathways constitute the building blocks of the universe and the foundation for its essential components of divine creation.

Sefer Yetzirah delves deeply into these remarkable paths of wisdom and the various ways through which God, the supreme divinity, is revealed to us. According to it, our reality is composed of a system of numerical numbers and Hebrew letters, their inherent qualities, their gematrical value, their energetic light frequencies, and the resonant sounds they create.

In order to create the different worlds, the supreme creator first formed *energetic vessels* possessing both spiritual and physical power. These vessels contain within them light frequencies, vibrations, sounds, and numerical-mathematical values. Through the energetic blueprint of these vessels, it is possible to create anything in the universe and existence and to impart life to it. These vessels are none other than the constituent letters from which the Hebrew language, known as "The Holy Language," is composed. A language that is considered to be the original language of humanity.

The Hebrew language is called "The Holy Language," as the Hebrew letters constitute the building blocks of the physical world in which we live and exist. They contain the spiritual root of all possibilities of creation and have the ability to create different realities through the encoded ciphers encrypted in them.

The Hebrew language is a coded language. Each letter signifies a specific amount of light that penetrates it based on its graphic pattern. It also embodies a certain quality according to its gematrical value and emits a vibrational frequency that resonates with its sound when pronounced. Moreover, each letter carries unique energy and its distinct fortune, which it radiates outward (from inside to outside) or magnetically attracts toward itself, drawing in equivalent energy in return (from outside to inside). This coded light information provides us with insights into our physics, genetics, and **morphogenetics**[3].

Since the mysterious story of the Tower of Babel, where the original language was distorted and different languages emerged, the wisdom and profundity of the Hebrew letters have been forgotten. This hidden wisdom, which remained dormant for thousands of years, is being gradually rediscovered in recent times by those on a spiritual path.

One way to understand how the vibrational frequencies of these letters operate within a person is by exploring the fields of natural science. In physics, for instance, the structure of every atom consists of a central nucleus surrounded by rapidly moving electrons, creating intense internal activity. Similarly, in the context of the

---

[3] Morphogenetics is a term derived from the field of developmental biology, which deals with the development of biological systems in various organisms, including humans. It denotes the process by which order is established in a developing organism, where differentiated cells organize into tissues, organs, and organ systems and ultimately form the entire organism.

Holy language, when one letter connects with another, it forms a word and an energetic vibrational frequency. When these words combine to form sentences, they create a vibrational resonance.

In the **metaphysics**[4] of the universe, nothing is random, including the selection of an individual's birth name. The act of naming a child is not just a formality; it marks the initial step in embracing the self-identity that the child will carry throughout their life journey. It also signifies the spiritual and practical role they are destined to fulfill.

In the **Talmud**[5], it is said, "To every person, there is a name," and this assertion is not in vain. A name is one of the most important tools a person has. It functions as a tool that grants the individual an insight into their human essence, similar to an ID card that can be deciphered by interpreting the hidden code within its constituent letters. The purpose of a name is to provide the individual with an understanding of their spiritual potential, including their talents, abilities, and the energetic power at their disposal to realize this spiritual potential.

However, before delving into a deep understanding of the uniqueness and power of the Hebrew letters in the creation process, it is important to first understand what a letter is.

---

[4]   Metaphysics is a branch of philosophy that explores concepts beyond physics and utilizes abstract concepts such as existence, knowledge, substance, cause, time, and space to help define reality and our understanding of it.

[5]   Talmud is a central text in Judaism, comprising a comprehensive collection of ancient teachings, laws, and interpretations based on the Torah.

What is a Letter?

A letter is an energetic pulse and electromagnetic frequency. Each letter operates within us similarly to our heartbeat (the expansion and contraction) and our breathing (inhalation and exhalation).

Each letter encapsulates the energy of an event and a corresponding response. Thus, the letters in our names describe the internal processes we undergo, from the moment we encounter an event triggered by internal or external stimuli to our eventual response.

In Hebrew, the term for "letter" (אות), composed of the letters Alef (A), Vav (V), and Tav (T), carries a meaningful interpretation. The letter Alef represents the initial energy of the event, Vav symbolizes the interpretive energy that judges the event, and Tav signifies the resultant response energy. So, in fact, this interpretative judgment within the human **mind**[6] is what creates the psycho-physiological response.

---

[6] The mind is the seat where human consciousness is formed. It contains a collection of psychological forces involved in perception, evaluation, and decision-making. It encompasses the "self" reflected in thoughts, emotions, sensations, perceptions, memory, unconscious desires, and motivations.

Diagram 2: Letter-Action

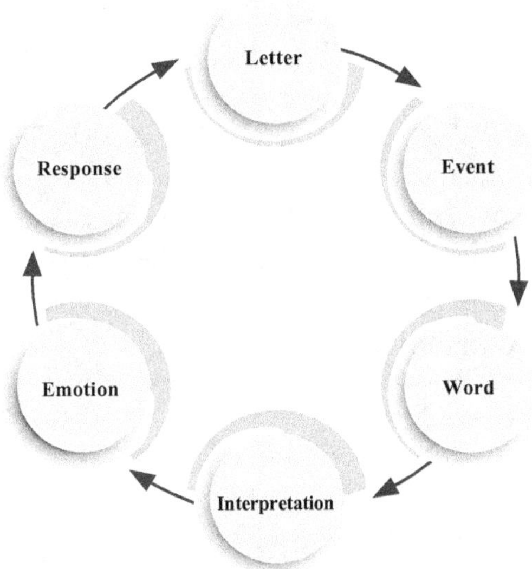

A letter and another letter create an **energetic pulse** that activates both the internal and external environment, producing an **event.** This event, sparks the emergence of **words** within us, leading to **thoughts.** As we think in words, these lead to judgmental **interpretations,** which in turn trigger **emotions.** These emotions drive our **responses,** whether as physical actions or verbal expressions. Once initiated, this response stimulates further events, creating a continuous cycle, until we develop a deeper personal awareness and understanding of this process.

The spoken word possesses immense power. In the Genesis creation stories, divine creation began with the words *"Let there be light."*

Within the Hebrew word "letter" (אות), the word "you" (את) is concealed. Reversing these letters yields the word "cell" (תא), a fundamental unit of all living organisms, symbolizing the micro within the macro. The human body comprises trillions of cells.

The word "cell," concealed within the word "letter," echoes the idea that just as cells are the fundamental building blocks of living organisms, letters are the building blocks of human communication and thought. A profound understanding of letters can unveil deep knowledge and insights, illustrating the interconnectedness of various aspects of the world and human experience, both macro and micro.

As previously mentioned, the Hebrew language is an encoded language where the interplay of lights (the letters) imparts insight into the secrets inherent in specific words. This concept will become clearer as you continue reading.

The Uniqueness of the Hebrew Letters

The uniqueness of the Hebrew letters is expressed in several ways. The first is their structure. Hebrew letters are constructed like a funnel, resembling the shape of a pyramid. This structure helps us understand how the spiritual divine forces operate in the world and the human soul, how thoughts are formed in our minds, and how we can attract spiritual and material abundance into our lives.

Diagram 3: The Pyramid of Letters

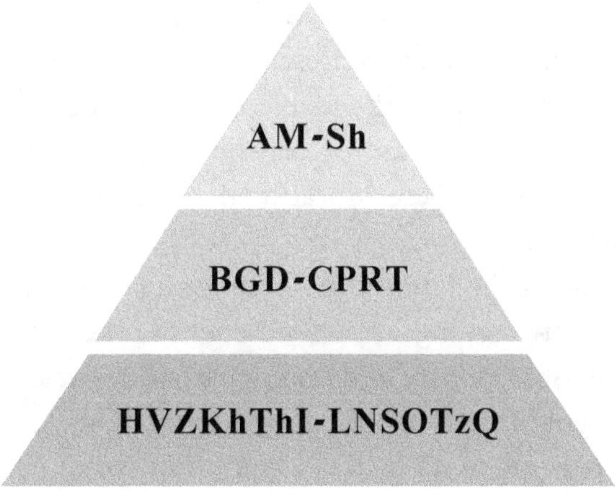

Three Spiritual Divine Forces – AMSh

The first category of letters, positioned at the top of the pyramid, represents the *Three Spiritual Divine Forces* that constitute, sustain and drive the universe forward. These profound divine forces present both in the world and within the human soul are represented by the letters Alef, Mem, and Shin, also known as AMSh (אמש).

These three letters signify the cosmic law that states that every phenomenon comprises three forces: active, passive, and neutral; positive, negative, and neutral. These three forces, present in everything within the universe and existence, are expressed in all structures and processes.

Seven Mind Forces – BGD-CPRT

The second category of letters, positioned at the center of the pyramid, represents the *Seven Mind Forces* that shape human reality. These mind forces, which drive human action or resistance, activate the law of "cause and effect" and "like attracts like." These seven mind forces are represented by the letters Bet, Gimel, Dalet, Caf, Peh, Resh, and Tav, also known as BGD-CPRT (בגד-כפרת) letters.

The BGD-CPRT letters represent the cosmic principle, which asserts that everything in the universe—every atom, object, and living creature—is in a state of constant motion and rotation at a specific frequency. These vibrational frequencies influence and provoke reactions.

Understanding the vibrational frequencies of these seven letters aids us in comprehending how mind energy functions, influencing the generation of responses and outcomes in our lives. Additionally, they offer insight into the formation of our thoughts and emotions—their style, pattern, and quality—and how they tend to create harmony or disharmony within us.

Twelve Physical Forces – HVZKhThI-LNSOTzQ

The third category of letters, situated at the base of the pyramid, represents the *Twelve Physical Forces* that assist humans in actualizing themselves in the physical plane. These forces are represented by the letters Heh, Vav, Zayin, Khet, Thet, Yod, Lamed, Nun, Samech, Ahyin, Tzadi and Qof. These twelve letters are referenced in *Sefer Yetzirah* as HVZKhThI-LNSOTzQ letters.

These twelve letters function in humans in a way that is similar to the operation of **meridians**[7] in the body. Since we attract into our lives only that which resonates with our vibrational frequency, aligning our frequency with the things we desire is essential to attract abundance. The vibrational frequencies of these twelve letters and their wisdom assist us in achieving this alignment.

The Letters in Genesis Narratives

Another effective way to understand the symbolic meaning of each letter is to examine its first appearance in the Bible. The letter's connection to its position in Genesis stories teaches us about the qualities it embodies and the messages it conveys. I will elaborate further on this in the upcoming chapter on the letters themselves.

Light and Shadow Symbolism in Hebrew Letters

The symbolic meaning of the letters can be understood through the concepts of light and shadow. For example, each letter represents the amount of light or shadow it contains. There are letters where light surrounds their shadow, like the letter Alef, where its contour lines are open from all directions, and there are letters where the shadow surrounds their inner light, like the letter Samech, where its contour lines are closed from all directions.

Diagram 4: Letters Alef and Samech

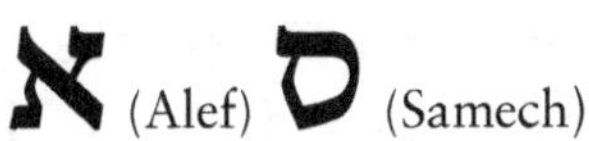

7　The term "meridians" refers to twelve different energy pathways dispersed throughout the physical body, each intricately linked to various organs. Meridians are channels or pathways through which the body's vital energy, known as "chi," flows. These meridians are associated with specific organs and are fundamental to practices such as acupuncture and acupressure, which aim to balance and enhance the flow of energy for improved health.

Furthermore, as the contour lines of the letter are smaller, the surrounding white light is more abundant in it, such as the letter Yod (י). Rabbi Moshe Chaim Luzzatto, a Kabbalist and researcher of Kabbalistic teachings, discusses this topic in his book *Derech Chochmat HaEmet LaRamchal*.

Diagram 5: Letter Yod

י

The simplest way to understand this concept is by likening light to spiritual awareness and shadow to lack of awareness. Following the previous example, while the letter Alef is enveloped from all directions in spiritual awareness, the letter Samech is enveloped from all directions in lack of awareness. Furthermore, the openness of the letter's structure, such as with Alef or Yod, facilitates an easier influx of divine light, allowing these letters to be filled with greater quantities of light.

The Way Each Letter Receives its Power

One important way to understand the uniqueness of the Hebrew letters is by familiarizing ourselves with how each letter receives its energetic power. To acquaint ourselves with these powers, we need to recognize three main characteristics of the letters: their graphic form, their gematrical value, and their pronunciation.

Through the letters of our name, which receive their light and power from these three channels, the divine light frequencies penetrate the world and the human soul, giving form to the physical reality we perceive through our senses. These divine frequencies of light flow through our body, mind, and spirit, creating both inner and outer manifestations of events and reactions, leading to a chain of cause and effect. It is important to understand that our external environment is merely a reflection of what occurs within our soul or internal environment.

Our reactions to situations are often influenced by our mind and tend to be mostly unconscious, thus creating in our life's reality the cycle of "dharma and karma"—the full circle of cause-and-effect relationships discussed in Hindu philosophy.

The principle of karma posits that each human action determines future experiences. According to this principle, a person's intentions, actions, and deeds affect their future in a cause-and-effect relationship. The concept of dharma refers to the principles of justice, morality, and ethics that govern a person's behavior and actions. Dharma represents the path of righteousness and duty that a person is expected to fulfill in their lifetime. In Hinduism, these two concepts emphasize the importance of ethical and moral conduct, affirming that an individual's thoughts and actions directly determine their present and future lives.

First Channel:
Letters Graphical Form and Structure

The graphical form of each letter provides insights into the degree of light it contains and the level of openness or closeness inherent within it.

To better understand the graphical form of each letter, we will divide the twenty-two letters into four groups based on a common denominator. This division will allow us to reflect on the degree of light these groups of letters contain and their inherent openness or closeness toward opinions, ideas, people, situations, and life changes. In this categorization, along with the twenty-two letters, I will also include the five final or ending letters known in Hebrew as CMNP'Tz (כמנפצ) letters.

Diagram 6: Hebrew Letters With a Common Denominator

Group A Completely Open		Group B Completely Closed from All Sides		Group C Both Open and Closed from Two Sides		Group D Closed from Three Sides	
ALEF	א	SAMECH	ס	GIMEL	ג	BET	ב
		FINAL MEM	ם	DALET	ד	KHET	ח
				HEH	ה	THET	ט
				VAV	ו	CAF	כ
				ZAYIN	ז	LAMED	ל
				YOD	י	MEM	מ
				AHYIN	ע	NUN	נ
				TZADI	צ	PEH	פ
				RESH	ר	QOF	ק
				SHIN	ש	TAV	ת
				FINAL NUN	ן	FINAL PEH	ף
				FINAL CAF	ך		
				FINAL TZADI	ץ		

The Level of Openness of the Letter's

The level of a letter's openness signifies its capacity to absorb large amounts of spiritual light. The more closed the graphical form of a letter is, the less spiritual light can penetrate its pattern. An open letter endows a person with the ability to flow with life in a light-hearted manner, to receive life events from a place of trust and faith, and to be open toward people, changes, and situations of uncertainty.

According to the Kabbalistic teachings, an open letter channels greater abundance and blessings to a person, whereas a closed letter makes it difficult for a person to open up to changes, new processes, and situations of uncertainty. This can hinder the ability to flow with life easily. It tends to draw a person toward closure, difficulty in making changes, difficulty in releasing and letting go, and challenges in compassion, forgiveness and forgetting. A closed letter tends to limit divine abundance, but at the same time, it grants preservation and protection.

A balanced name contains a combination of open and closed letters. The keyword here is balance. While open letters provide a person with abundance, blessings, and the ability to transcend the limitations of the earthly realm and to flow with life easily, closed letters offer grounding, preservation, and protection.

Group A: Completely Open Letter

Among the twenty-two letters of the Hebrew alphabet, plus the five final letters, there is only one completely open letter, and that is the letter Alef. This letter stands firmly on the ground (on the line) on two legs and embodies the measure of kindness and compassion.

A completely open letter like Alef symbolizes the ability to be open-minded toward different opinions and perspectives, including those that differ from one's own beliefs and stances. This represents not only openness and the capacity to embrace a variety of opinions

Diagram 7: Letter Alef

but also the ability to engage and connect with people, as well as to create friendships.

An open letter endows an individual with qualities such as openness, lightness, flow, movement, joy, adventurous spirit, trust, faith, and hope. It imbues the individual with optimistic energy, allowing them to see the half-full glass in every situation and matter. An open letter is like an open vessel, not bound by limitation.

Group B: Completely Closed Letters

Among the twenty-two letters of the Hebrew alphabet, plus the five final letters, there are only two letters that are completely closed, and those letters are Samech and the Final letter Mem. Information about the final letters appears in Chapter Six.

A completely closed letter indicates a tendency toward closure and resistance to opinions and perspectives that differ from one's own beliefs and positions. This manifests as a reluctance to embrace new experiences, difficulty in opening up to others, forming connections and friendships, and challenges in understanding others as well as allowing oneself to be understood.

Diagram 8: Letter Samech and Final Mem

A closed letter is akin to a closed vessel, limiting the entry of light. When the amount of light in the structural pattern of the letter is restricted, it adds a challenging aspect to the issue of openness. A closed letter draws a person toward closeness, self-centeredness, egocentricity, rigidity, and emotional, mental, and behavioral fixation. It also inclines a person toward judgmental attitudes, opinionatedness, and attachment to beliefs, ideas, opinions, and stances. Closed letters indicate a tendency to hold and store energy, manifesting in an inherent difficulty in releasing and letting go, being compassionate and forgiving.

The purpose of a closed letter is to draw a person inward to processes of introspection and deep self-reflection so they can become aware of the necessary processes required for their growth and development.

In a situation where a person's name is mostly composed of closed letters, it can indicate a personality inclined toward stubbornness, opinionatedness, judgmental attitudes, rigidity, anxiety, and frequent use of defense mechanisms. In such cases, it becomes difficult for the person to trust and have faith, to open up to uncertainty and new processes, to make significant changes, to flow with life events, and to move through life's path with ease and optimism.

Group C: Open and Closed Letters from Two Directions

Among the twenty-two letters of the Hebrew alphabet, plus the five final letters, thirteen letters have partly open shapes. These letters are Gimel, Dalet, Heh, Vav, Zayin, Yod, Ahyin, Tzadi, Resh, Shin, and final letters - Nun, Caf and Tzadi.

Open and closed letters, in both directions, contain within them tendencies toward both openness and closure, depending on the context. They indicate a partial openness or closure to positions, opinions, ideas, people, and situations, with a tendency to exhibit both behaviors, influenced by the proximity of other letters in the person's name.

Diagram 9: Letters Open from Two Directions

ג ד ה ה ו ז י ע צ ר ש ו ר ץ

For example, if a letter from this group is positioned between two closed letters or letters that are closed from three directions in a person's name, the tendency of that letter would lean toward closure. Conversely, if the letter is placed between open letters, its tendency leans toward openness.

For instance, the name **Pip**. The name consists of two letters, Peh, that are closed from three directions, and one letter, Yod, that is open and closed from two directions. This name comprises three letters, two of which represent a tendency toward closeness; therefore, this name indicates a raw tendency toward closure.

On the other hand, the name **Ala** consists of two open letters and a middle letter closed from three directions. Therefore, the tendency of the middle letter Lamed would lean toward openness.

Group D: Closed Letters from Three Directions

Among the twenty-two letters of the Hebrew alphabet, plus the five final letters, eleven letters are closed from three directions. These letters are Bet, Khet, Thet, Caf, Lamed, Mem, Nun, Peh, Qof, Tav and final letter Peh.

Letters that are closed from three directions indicate a tendency toward closed-mindedness, rigidity, self-centeredness, and an inhibiting of free-flowing energetic movement. They inherently make it difficult for a person to open up to new opinions, ideas, people and situations. These letters contain energy that tends to limit and constrict a person's consciousness, making it hard for them to see the whole picture and leading them to believe that the side they see and grasp is the only right and just one.

Diagram 10: Letters Closed From Three Directions

ף ת ק פ נ מ ל כ ט ח ב

Individuals with these closed letters in their name typically struggle to recognize their tendencies toward closure and rigidity. They find it challenging to acknowledge the necessity of change and often struggle to implement it.

Closed letters from three directions tend to draw a person into separate consciousness—the inclination to see the existing differences in everything and not what unifies them. In such situations, a person will struggle to contain the contradictions arising from the complex reality and simultaneously embrace the good and the bad, the pleasure and the pain. These letters tend to create a judgmental and biased perspective in a person, leading to challenging experiences. It invites them to explore and confront the very things the judge.

These letters intend to draw one's attention to several significant aspects. First, it underscores that every cause begins with a judgmental viewpoint and results in an experiential outcome. Second, it highlights the inherent tendency of those who possess these letters to form adhesions and attachments to people, circumstances, viewpoints, and stances. The third point focuses on the prevalent use of psychological manipulations by these individuals. Such manipulations function akin to defense mechanisms, creating barriers that conceal the absolute truth from the person. Situations where one robotically and habitually lives life on auto-pilot, asleep while walking. Finally, it serves as a reminder of the imperative need for change and transformation.

Second Channel:
The Gematrical Value of the Letters

The gematrical value assigned to each Hebrew letter provides us with an understanding of the unique alphanumeric value of each letter and its quality.

Gematria is an ancient cryptographic method for deciphering hidden codes within Hebrew letters text. The method converts the letters into alphanumeric codes, generating encrypted information based on various gematrical values inherent in each letter, as well as in the different combinations that these letters create. This technique assigns numerical values to letters, words, phrases, and texts and converts them into mathematical numbers to unveil the encoded and concealed information within. This technique takes into consideration the proximity of letters to each other and their positional order within a name or word.

Think of it like a puzzle. Each Hebrew word has its numerical value, and these numbers can reveal hidden meanings or connections between different words and phrases. It's not just the numbers themselves that matter, but also how the letters are arranged. For instance, the position of a letter in a word can change its significance in this numerical puzzle. Historically, scholars have used gematria to explore deeper meanings in ancient texts, finding connections that are not immediately obvious. It is a bit like looking for secret messages in a coded language, where single- and double-digit numbers offer a different way to understand words and ideas.

As I mentioned earlier, each Hebrew letter has a gematrical value—full, short, simple, complex—which helps us understand its secret within its three-dimensional sequence: where it comes from, what it contains (its secret), and what its purpose is, as well as its qualitative, valuable, and quantitative aspects.

There are various methods for calculating gematria, with nearly fifteen different and significant calculations. Among the more well-known ones is full gematria (גימטריה מלאה), in which the calculation of the letters is based on their full numerical value within the cycle of digits from one to nine hundred. This method takes into account units, tens, and hundreds without summing up the final result they produce. Conversely, short gematria (גימטריה קצרה) involves calculating the letters within the cycle of the digits one to nine. In short, gematria zeros are excluded from the numerical values of the letters, allowing for an understanding of the basic value of each letter.

According to these two methods, the twenty-two letters of the Hebrew alphabet, along with the five final letters—making a total of twenty-seven—are divided into three groups based on their numerical values. The first group represents the sequence of ones, the second group the sequence of tens, and the third group the sequence of hundreds in the following order.

Understanding the significance of zero is crucial when working with full gematria. Zero is a profoundly powerful number intimately connected with the frequencies of divine creation and linked to **Ein Sof**[8]. It symbolizes the eternal life force, embodying concepts of unity, interconnectedness, and the boundless possibilities open to humanity

Diagram 11: Hebrew Letters and Their Gematrical Values

Value	Hebrew Letter	Value	Hebrew Letter	Value	Hebrew Letter
1	ALEF	10	YOD	100	QOF
2	BET	20	CAF	200	RESH
3	GIMEL	30	LAMED	300	SHIN
4	DALET	40	MEM	400	TAV
5	HEH	50	NUN	500	FINAL CAF
6	VAV	60	SAMECH	600	FINAL MEM
7	ZAYIN	70	AHYIN	700	FINAL NUN
8	KHET	80	PEH	800	FINAL PEH
9	THET	90	TZADI	900	FINAL TZADI

---

[8] Ein Sof is a term used to describe the concept of "Endless Light" or the "Divine Essence." It represents the original, primordial existence of God prior to any self-manifestation in the production of spiritual realms. This divine essence existed before giving shape to the world, before producing any form. Ein Sof is characterized as a radiant infinite light that is beyond physical form and unlike anything else in existence. This concept highlights the limitless and incomprehensible nature of the divine essence, which precedes all creation.

This number reflects the infinite and eternal cyclical nature of the universe, representing both the void and the potential from which all creation emerges. Zero also encapsulates notions of emptiness or nothingness, concepts often associated with non-attachment, the relinquishing of ego and material desires, as well as signifying both beginnings and endings.

The key characteristic of the number zero lies in its ability to amplify the vibrational frequency of any number it accompanies. It endows the accompanying number with limitless potential, influencing it in both its constructive and inhibiting aspects. When zero is paired with any number, it multiplies the quality and energy of that number, propelling it toward the purest expression, realization, and manifestation of its intrinsic value and quality. This amplification occurs tenfold when zero is in the tens digit and a hundredfold when in the hundreds digit. Zero's key role is to facilitate a state of stillness and tranquility, attainable through practices like meditation, enabling a profound connection with the inner self or higher consciousness.

The energy of the number zero is refined, pure, and powerful. It guides individuals back to their inner center of tranquility and stillness, leading them toward their authentic selves and enabling the fulfillment of their soul's potential. The number zero acts as a value-pressure gauge. It compels individuals to transcend their ego and the layers they have accumulated over their lifetimes, urging them to step out of their inner bubble beyond their inner narratives and dramas. This detachment from the illusory self allows for a release from past constraints and opens pathways for new beginnings.

The number zero also prompts a person to pause and reflect. It invites introspection on one's journey thus far— assessing achievements, growth, insights, and transformations. It encourages consideration of future aspirations and the evolution of one's identity and purpose.

As illustrated in Diagram 11, starting from the letter Yod onward, there is a significant shift. The letters undergo a first-degree transition from single-digit to ten-digit units. From Yod to Tzadi, the letters incorporate an internal barometer, nudging individuals toward experiences aimed at awakening their higher heart wisdom. Beginning with the letter Qof onward, a second-degree transition occurs, moving from ten-digit to the hundred-digit units, further intensifying the pressure gauge within these letters.

It is important to note that for a complete and accurate interpretation of the name and to ascertain its alignment with a person's fortune, success, and mental and physical well-being, it is necessary to employ all the methods of gematria, or at least twelve of them.

Third Channel:
The Sound and Pronunciation of the Letter

The third channel through which each Hebrew letter receives its energetic power is through its sound. The phonetics of the letters helps us understand how vibrations and unique sounds are created through the power of speech.

Sound is a physical phenomenon that occurs when an object of any kind vibrates and creates sound waves that pass through a medium, such as air, water, or a solid substance. When sound waves reach our ears, they are interpreted by our brain as the phenomenon we perceive as sound. In order to better understand the concept of sound, I would like to address two terms related to sound, the first of which is vibration, and the second is frequency.

The term vibration refers to the back-and-forth motion of an object around a fixed point. Vibration can be described in terms of frequency, the number of cycles per second. The term frequency relates to the rate at which vibration occurs. For example, a higher frequency produces a higher vibration rate, while a lower frequency indicates a lower vibration rate. Frequency can either be audible or inaudible.

Sound is a specific type of vibration that our ears can perceive, but not all vibrations generate sounds that we can hear. For instance, if an earthquake occurs in a certain location, we can feel the vibrations caused by the movement of tectonic plates on the ground, but we might not necessarily hear the sound that these vibrations create.

Sound exerts a powerful influence on our consciousness, impacting us positively or negatively. It affects our emotional state, physical health, mental well-being, and even our attentiveness, memory, learning, and cognitive functioning. By interacting with our brain waves, sound influences our consciousness through physiological, neurological, and psychological pathways.

For example, certain sounds can induce relaxation, manifesting physically as reduced heart rate, lower blood pressure, and relaxed muscles. They also influence the mood, engaging the limbic system, the brain region responsible for emotional responses, and can alter brain wave patterns, eliciting specific states of consciousness.

Each organ in our physical body possesses a unique sound. Thus, our body is able to identify various sounds and vibrations and respond to them. Every physical organ vibrates and understands the language of the universe, which is the sounds. When a particular organ is imbalanced, it creates dissonance or disharmony in the body. By employing suitable sounds, we can restore balance and promote healing. *Sefer Yetzirah* provides us with this understanding by associating specific letters with distinct body organs. I am delving deeper into this subject in my upcoming books.

Sound's influence extends beyond the individual to the universe and our environment. Certain natural sounds, like bird songs or flowing water, positively affect our planet and ecological systems. Conversely, disruptive noises like traffic can harm humans, animals, and the ecological balance, leading to behavioral changes or, in extreme cases, death. By understanding the impact of sound and its vibrations, we can use this knowledge to enhance our physical and mental health, as well as the well-being of the world around us.

Manner of Pronunciation

The name and pronunciation of each letter provide us with additional clues and insights about the qualities it embodies and its inherent ability to facilitate movement.

Speech sounds are categorized into two groups: consonants and vowels. Consonants are characterized by a blocked or halted airflow during pronunciation, whereas vowels allow for a free, unobstructed flow of air.

The twenty-two letters of the Hebrew alphabet are divided into four vowel letters, also known as AHVY (אהוי) and eighteen consonant letters.

Vocalized Spelling and Unvocalized Spelling

Another important aspect of the Hebrew language relates to its spelling. Hebrew accommodates both vocalized spelling, also known as "partial spelling" (כתיב מנוקד / כתיב חסר), and unvocalized spelling, also referred to as "full spelling" (כתיב ללא ניקוד/ כתיב מלא).

The Hebrew language encompasses not just letters but also includes punctuation marks, known as vocalization signs. These signs are added to letters during the writing process, positioned either within the letters or around them, above or below. Punctuation marks serve the purpose of indicating the essential pronunciation of the letter—the sound it generates when spoken and its phonetic characteristics—the way it is pronounced. For those less familiar with the language, these vocalization signs play a vital role in ensuring accurate pronunciation and understanding of the word's phonetics.

Vocalized spelling is characterized by marked or dotted writing, where punctuation markings indicate all vowels, and the spelling of the word corresponds precisely to its marked punctuation.

On the other hand, unvocalized spelling is a form of spelling that omits punctuation markings. It relies on "mater lectionis" to guide the reader in correctly pronouncing the written words. In unvocalized spelling, the vocalization signs are replaced by vowel letters. Vocalization signs are always optional in Hebrew; they can be used fully, partially, or not at all. They are usually added to prevent ambiguity in reading the word correctly.

For example, the Hebrew letter Resh can be written as Resh (ריש) or Rash (רש), and the letter Gimel can be written as Gimel (גימל) or Gamal and Gmal (גמל). In partial spelling, a specific word can have multiple meanings. An example is the word "sefer" (ספר), meaning "book," which can be written, pronounced, and interpreted in many ways: book (סֵפֶר), tell (סַפֵּר), spoken (סֻפַּר), told (סִפֵּר), count (סָפַר), barber (סַפָּר), border (סְפָר), shortened his hair (סִפֵּר).

The Vowel Letters: The Power of Movement and Propulsion

In the Hebrew alphabet, which consists of twenty-two letters, four are designated as vowel letters: AHVY (אהוי). These vowel letters are unique in that they represent movement and motion and are, therefore, also called "movement letters."

The diagram below presents the vowel letters and their corresponding English letters. Detailed explanations regarding these correspondences are found in the chapter dedicated to letters, with each letter discussed separately.

Diagram 12: Hebrew Vowel Letters

Hebrew Vowel Letter	Hebrew Letters Name
א	ALEF
ה	HEH
ו	VAV
י	YOD

In the context of a person's name, the presence of these vowel letters is significant. Their energy empowers the individual to progress, propel themselves forward, and remain in motion. This influence aids in breaking free from the confines of their usual self, transcending habitual patterns that shape their personality. It also facilitates detachment from challenging situations or relationships, enabling creative and lighter handling of daily complexities.

The role of vowel letters is profound. They metaphorically provide a person with wings, or more precisely, the wind beneath those wings. They function in the name similar to a propeller, transforming heavy energetic movements into the ability to rise above the density and move through the air and land with ease.

The vowel letters signify the internal essence and the core of our being. They offer a glimpse into the most genuine and hidden desires of our hearts, providing insights into what genuinely motivates and fulfills us at a deeper level. These desires, when aligned with one's soul's path, generate an intrinsic sense of fulfillment and a powerful driving force. Conversely, when one is not aligned with their soul's path, these desires manifest as a longing and yearning for something yet unattained.

Diagram 13: Person in Motion

The vowel letters serve as a window into a person's deepest motivations and aspirations, illuminating what truly brings them joy and fulfillment. They reveal the underlying intentions that guide one's actions and influence life choices. Essentially, they disclose the ultimate goals and purposes that an individual's soul seeks to fulfill.

In our lives, we are often consumed by earthly pursuits and the need to secure our material existence. This preoccupation can cause us to neglect the deeper desires of our hearts. These intrinsic desires, which often tend to be dormant, occasionally emerge and touch the spiritual aspect within us. This aspect, known in esoteric teachings of the Kabbalah as the "point in the heart" (הנקודה שבלב), serves as a reminder of our deeper truth. The vowel letters (אהוי) connect us to this essential part of ourselves, representing our unaltered truth, unaffected by external influences like family, children, partners, friends, or society.

A name is considered balanced when it strikes a harmony between its consonant and vowel letters. Typically, a balanced name has an equal count of consonants and vowels. However, in three-letter names, like Dan, Ann, and Ron, a single vowel letter can create this balance.

Imbalances in names can occur in various ways. One instance involves a deficit of vowel letters, such as the Hebrew names Bat-Sheva (בת-שבע) and Gilad (גלעד), or English names like Clark (קלרק) and Flynn (פלין). Alternatively, an imbalance can arise from a surplus of consonants, as seen in names like Baruch (ברוך), Levana (לבנה), Griffin (גריפין), Konstantin (קונסטנטין), Glynn (גלין) and Maxwell (מקסוול).

Such imbalances can indicate several things. It might suggest rigidity, a sense of heaviness, and difficulty adapting to change. It could also point to challenges in leaving comfort zones, embracing new situations and processes, or shedding personal narratives. Additionally, it might reflect a struggle with physical, mental, or emotional mobility and difficulty in functioning efficiently in stressful situations and finding quick solutions.

Imbalance in a name can also occur in the opposite situation, where the individual's name contains an excess of vowel letters over consonants, like Ariela (אריאלה), Eliana (אליאנה), Iya (איה), Elaiah (אליה), Isaac (אייזיק), Aurora (אאורורה) and Eilyn (איילין).

An excess of vowel letters in a name can indicate several things. It might signify heightened spirituality (conscious or unconscious), restlessness, a need for much movement, and a challenge in grounding oneself and being fully present in the here-and-now moment. A dynamic that can lead to confusion, occasional emotional instability, and difficulty in solidifying personal identity.

Additionally, an excess of vowel letters in a name, compared to consonants, tends to create many aspirations in a person, often lofty and not necessarily grounded in reality. This imbalance can also lead to a situation where the individual is unsure of what they want from themselves and others, resulting in a state of ambivalence. In such cases, it is advisable to add at least one consonant to the name. Doing so can help ground the individual, provide them with anchors, and connect them to the practical and pragmatic aspects of life.

Consonant Letters: The Power of Grounding and Stopping Movement

Among the twenty-two letters of the Hebrew alphabet, eighteen are consonants. While vowel letters grant a person wings, consonant letters provide them anchors. Vowel letters embody a state of openness to change and mobility, whereas consonant letters embrace constancy and stability—a state of rest and rootedness that offers comfort and certainty.

The diagram presents the consonant letters and their corresponding English letters. Detailed explanations regarding these correspondences are found in the chapter dedicated to letters, with each letter discussed separately.

From the perspective of articulatory phonetics, consonants represent basic speech sounds characterized by a complete or partial closure of the vocal tract, resulting in a complete or partial blockage of airflow. Essentially, consonants disrupt the natural flow of speech and energy movement. In a constructive sense, they provide grounding, steadfastness, stability, and a strong connection to the earthly realm.

However, in their inhibiting aspect, they can immobilize a person by anchoring them in a static position for a prolonged period, leading to a fixation on certain traits or circumstances. This fixation can cause stagnation and hinder their ability to evolve or make necessary mental and physical transformations.

Diagram 14: Hebrew Consonant Letters

Hebrew Consonant Letter	Hebrew Letters Name
ב	BET
ג	GIMEL
ד	DALET
ז	ZAYIN
ח	KHET
ט	THET
כ	CAF
ל	LAMED
מ	MEM
נ	NUN
ס	SAMECH
ע	AHYIN
פ	PEH
צ	TZADI
ק	QOF
ר	RESH
ש	SHIN
ת	TAV

While vowel letters indicate the hidden content from everyone's eyes, consonant letters signify the content that is openly presented to society—the content a person feels comfortable showcasing to others. They symbolize a person's external image or the "personal business card" they present to others; therefore, these letters symbolize a person's personality.

The term "personality" originates from the Latin word "persona," which initially signified the mask worn by actors to portray characters on stage. Today, it refers to the inherent character traits a person exhibits beyond any metaphorical mask. Thus, consonant letters can be likened to a narrow entrance hall leading to a grand palace, symbolizing a person's true nature. These letters can also be called "censorship letters" due to their use in controlling the flow of specific information.

Diagram 15: A Person Standing in Place

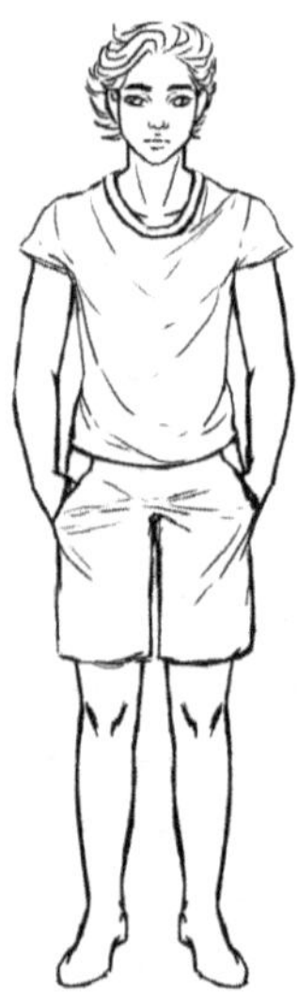

The cumulative value of the consonants in a name provides insight into the traits that the individual willingly chooses to reveal while suppressing others. This acts as a defense mechanism that protects the person. For instance, the persona we project allows specific individuals to approach us while simultaneously keeping others at a distance by creating a barrier with them. It functions as a protective filter designed to shield us from potential external threats.

Now that you understand the essence and uniqueness of Hebrew letters, in the next chapter, we will delve deeper into their influence and contribution to our full birth name (first, middle, last).

CHAPTER 3

Our Name as a Key to Self-Knowledge

*"You find that a man is known by three names: the name
by which his father and mother call him, the name by which
other men call him, and the one he earns for himself; the most
important name is the one he earns for himself."*

Sages in Midrash Tanhuma, Vayakhel, Siman1

The name of a person, like any word, is composed of letters. Each letter contains unique energetic forces, and their combination forms a dynamic energic dance within the person.

Spiritual theories suggest that a person's soul chooses their name before descending into the earthly realm, referred to as the earthly playground. According to the writings of Rabbi Yitzchak Luria, the Holy Ari, a renowned Kabbalist from Safed (Tzfat) in the sixteenth century, as recorded by his student Rabbi Chaim Vital, it is mentioned that when parents name their newborn, a prophetic spirit is infused into them. This spirit, akin to unconscious inspiration, implies that the name chosen for the newborn is actually the one selected by the incarnated soul, reflecting their essence.

It is important to emphasize that in our earthly journey through life, across various incarnations, we choose different names. However, the letters that represent our soul's essence tend to accompany us throughout this journey. This concept will become clearer as you continue reading.

The significance of personal names has been acknowledged in various ancient cultures throughout human history. In a masterpiece written by King Solomon in his old age, it is stated:

"A good name is better than good oil." (Ecclesiastes, Chapter 7, Verse 1) This statement emphasizes the significant importance of a person's name. In other cultures, including those of Egypt and India, it was customary to profoundly connect a person to their name. The prevailing belief was that concealing a person's full name protected them from harmful forces, such as curses.

Therefore, these ancient cultures believed in the concept of a revealed name and a hidden name. For example, in ancient Egypt, people held two names: the big name and the small name. The big name, also known as the main, good, and true name, was usually kept hidden and known only to the individual and a select few close to them, while the small name was used in everyday life. Even today, it is commonly believed that having a second name benefits a person and safeguards them from harm.

According to the Sages, during the ceremony of returning the physical equipment, or in other words, death, we are asked: Did we fulfill our spiritual mission and our soul's potential? They state that a person who did not fulfill themselves in their earthly life is someone who has forgotten the essence of their name and failed to connect to their role in this world.

It is important to note that when analyzing a person's name, the first consideration should be their birth name, which reveals, among other things, their soul's potential and the general purpose and direction of their life. For a more comprehensive and accurate analysis that expands the understanding of how individuals express their soul energy in the present, several additional factors should be considered.

First, any names added during their lifetime, such as a new surname or an additional middle name. Second, the shortened name they use, if applicable (e.g., Nathan instead of Nathaniel). Third, their nickname, if they have one (e.g., Nate). Fourth, the name by which they identify themselves on different platforms of social media. And lastly, the name that seals their signature on official documents.

The energy of one's birth name never disappears and continues to accompany them throughout their lifetime. The birth name helps the individual understand their basic psychological structure, the life lessons they are meant to acquire in this current incarnation, the personal rectifications they must undertake, and, at times, even the generational rectifications they seek. Changing a name without considering all these factors can impede the energy associated with the new name.

One of the best ways to understand this issue is to liken the birth name to the foundations upon which a house stands. We can renovate and change the house, but the underlying foundation remains the same. This is also one of the reasons why it is not advisable to rush into changing a name before fully understanding its profound meaning and ensuring that the personal lesson represented by the birth name is fully learned.

Another important point to understand is the issue of birthplace and name changes following marriage. A person's birth name is often tied to their birthplace, specifically, the country in which they were born. Sometimes, when a person changes their country of residence, their name may be well-suited for the new location, thereby enhancing their luck and progress in life. However, there are times when the name may not be a good fit, leading to challenges in that place over an extended period. This situation can be likened to being "full gas in neutral," potentially hindering their development and success in life.

Changing a surname following marriage is still a prevalent issue in many countries worldwide. Driven by societal and traditional norms, many women tend to change their last names upon marriage, thereby inviting new energies into their lives. Sometimes, the influence of the new name can yield positive effects and support them, while in other instances, it might not align, potentially causing obstacles and challenges and even leading to situations of energetic incompatibility between the individual and their spouse.

Full Birth Name:
Surname and Given Name

The full birth name, composed of the given name, middle name (if any), and surname, is not just an identification label. It reflects the potential by which a person is recognized and signifies the abilities and skills they possess for self-fulfillment in this earthly realm. Moreover, the full name mirrors the social identity of the individual, giving them a sense of belonging within a community. It also symbolizes the moral mission of the person's reincarnated soul and the spiritual and practical role they are meant to fulfill in their earthly journey.

The birth name of a person signifies the inherent soul energy with which they come into the world. It reveals their natural behavior and true identity, as well as their overall life purpose. The birth name discloses the type of person we aspire to become in our earthly journey and provides guidance on how we can best express the different aspects of ourselves.

Given Name

Our given name holds a significant influence on our lives, destiny, and fortune. It acts as our personal identification label, akin to a barcode, and encompasses the many aspects of our identity.

Firstly, our first name is a representation of our self-identity, embodying the unique energy of the ego that distinguishes us. Secondly, it reflects the level of inherent spiritual awareness we possess as we embark on our earthly journey. Thirdly, it symbolizes the personal life lessons we are meant to learn in our current life incarnation, which enable us to fulfill our spiritual and practical roles as agreed upon in our "soul contract" in the most effective and benevolent way. The fourth aspect relates to our heart's deepest desires, encapsulating our highest truth. Lastly, it mirrors the external persona we confidently display to the world, essentially crafting our personality.

Our name functions as a slogan, capturing the central idea displayed on our flag. It personalizes us, signifying the word most intimate to us, the one we hear most frequently in our daily lives, and toward which we develop a strong sense of identification.

The Hebrew word "name" (שם) is derived from the word "soul" (נ-שמ-ה). This highlights the deep connection between a person's name and their soul. According to Kabbalistic teachings, a person not in tune with their name may struggle to fulfill their soul's purpose. A soul that has not actualized itself is one that has not fully connected with its name and its spiritual role during its lifetime. This concept underlines why Kabbalah places great importance on a person's first name and the letters composing it.

Soul's Root

The significance of one's given name derives from its connection to the root of the soul. The soul's root, which emanates from the first name, reveals the uniqueness of an individual's soul and its spiritual role throughout various incarnations.

According to the Kabbalah, every soul comes into the world with a message, with essence, and with a gift to bestow upon humanity. Beyond our destiny in life, each of us also has a collective destiny, and every soul descends to the earthly realm in order to learn a personal lesson and teach something or impart a gift to others.

The term "soul's root" refers to the origin from which the soul emerges. The root of the soul stems from both the individual's given name at birth and the mother's given name at birth. This is why the Kabbalah attributes great importance to both the individual's given name and the mother's name. In Judaism, when blessing a person, it is customary to mention the name of the mother alongside the name of the person being blessed. A detailed explanation of how we identify a person's soul root is elaborated in Chapter Nine.

Surname

According to Judaism, a family name does not carry any spiritual significance. The Jewish people, as a tribal nation, adopted family names during times of exile and dispersion from the Land of Israel. These chosen surnames indicated affiliation with a community and were derived from lineage, social status, or profession. Similarly, in other cultures, surnames are often attributed based on place of birth, occupation, social status, or the father's name.

The family name reflects acquired energy, which is accumulated by ancestors throughout their lives in the process of education, culture, and socialization, passing from generation to generation. This energy is distinct from the spiritual energy conveyed by a personal name.

A family name does have an earthly and energetic significance. It contains a specific energy and vibrational frequency shaped by the experiences and characteristics of those who carried it before, indicating generational energy and generational karma linked to it.

Generational karma is a concept, in spiritual and philosophical contexts, that implies that our ancestor's actions and deeds can impact our lives and those of future generations. It represents an energy that carries either a positive or negative influence, transmitted from generation to generation within the family framework. This energy affects a person's beliefs, attitudes, emotions, and behavior in relation to their family name. In simpler terms, the family name carries karmic energy, which can entail privileges or obligations that a person voluntarily assumes. This energy tends to influence various aspects of their life, such as physical and mental health, emotional well-being, financial stability, and even the dynamics of their relationships.

For example, if a family member, like a parent or grandparent, experienced trauma, financial difficulties, emotional suffering, or physical or mental illness, and this experience has created a sense of fear or anxiety associated with the family name, that energy of fear is passed down to their descendants. This can make them more sensitive to issues in which the trauma occurred or was created. Conversely, if family members have engaged in positive and altruistic actions in their past lives, it blesses the family name with positive karma. This positive karma benefits the individual and can manifest as good health, financial stability, harmonious relationships, and various forms of emotional well-being.

The family name provides us with information not only about lineage and family history in terms of origin, status, and occupation but also encompasses a specific energy and vibration that connects an individual to their family's history and its generational energy.

For example, consider a family name that possesses a strong and powerful energy. Such a name may provide an individual with energy that can help them succeed in their personal and professional life and propel them forward. Conversely, it might pose obstacles or hinder their personal and spiritual development.

While the first name reflects the ego's energy closest to the individual, serving as the "umbilical cord" through which a person connects to life, the family name reflects the generational energy that the person's soul has chosen to adopt. This energy influences the person's consciousness and exerts its influence in a secondary manner. The family name reveals the vehicle in which the individual travels and the additional energy that accompanies them on their earthly journey.

In other words, the first name is like the tree, and the family name is like the garden bed around it. The garden bed can either be supportive, enriching the tree with nourishing compost and providing the conditions for the tree's roots to grow, or it can be limiting, tight, tall, and overly constricting, sometimes even thwarting its development. I will elaborate on this further in the next chapter.

It is important to ensure that a person's family name aligns with their first name and their life path. We learn about a person's life path from their date of birth. A family name that neither supports the private name nor aligns with the individual's life path, as determined by their date of birth, can significantly hinder their personal and spiritual development. It may also impede their luck, create difficulties, and introduce obstacles that hinder the realization of their personal potential and fulfillment of their soul's path.

CHAPTER 4

The Division of the Letters
According to *Sefer Yetzirah*

The twenty-two Hebrew letters represent the journey of the soul as it traverses in the earthly realm, a journey that begins with the letter Alef and ends with the letter Tav. Throughout this journey, the soul passes through twenty-two pathways that lead to self-mastery, the spiritual progress in the cycle of life. Each letter contains within it a specific level of consciousness that enables a person to understand themselves and the world around them, to learn the spiritual soul lessons for which they descended into the current incarnation, and to rectify what requires correction.

In order to achieve initiation and **self-mastery**[9], we must develop a high and deep self-awareness. We need to learn to recognize the workings of our soul to be familiar with our world of thoughts, feelings, impulses, and emotions so that we can properly use these soul's forces. In every thought, even the smallest, lies the potential to create love and compassion or to sow fear, destruction, and devastation.

The journey to self-awareness, like any journey, begins with a single step. Let's start this journey together.

---

[9] Self-mastery signifies a state in which a person has learned to control the lower aspects of their psyche and connect with the divine spark within them. Self-mastery involves high self-awareness, reflection, and self-discipline, along with awareness of internal mental, emotional, and physical processes and consciously directs them to make intentional choices in life.

The Letter Groups

In order to provide us with an understanding of how the twenty-two Hebrew alphabet letters shape our reality, the author of *Sefer Yetzirah* divided the letters into three main groups, each with a common denominator.

The first category of letters refers to the letters AMSH ((אמש – Alef, Mem, and Shin, three letters representing the fundamental forces that govern the fabric of existence. These three letters possess a high level of spiritual and creative power relating to topics such as prophecy, ideas, vision, and leadership. From these three letters emerge the four fundamental elements of creation: air, fire, water, and earth.

The second category of letters refers to the letters BGD-CPRT (בגד-כפרת) – Bet, Gimel, Dalet, Caf, Peh, Resh and Tav. These seven letters signify the seven cosmic creative energies in the Universe and Existence, representing the creative power of the mind through which mental and emotional patterns are formed in our universal space.

The third category of letters refers to the letters HVZKhThI-LNSOTzQ (הוזחטי-לנסעצק) – Heh, Vav, Zayin, Khet, Thet, Yod, Lamed, Nun, Samech, Ahyin, Tzadi, and Qof. These twelve letters, known in Kabbalistic teachings as "the twelve elementals" or "the simple ones," signify the practical and applied power existing within humans, functioning as twelve channels through which a person can draw divine abundance into the material realm.

Chart 16: The Wheel of Letters

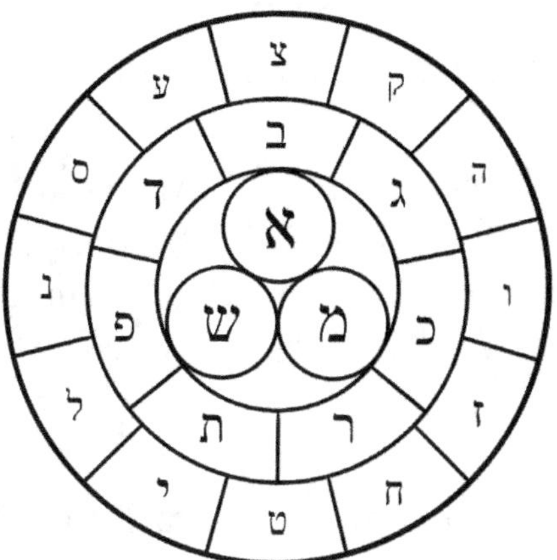

Self-mastery denotes a state in which a person has learned to control the lower aspects of their psyche and connect to the divine spark within them. Self-mastery involves high self-awareness, reflection, and self-discipline, alongside conscious awareness of internal processes—mental, emotional, and physical— and consciously directs them toward purposeful choices in life.

AMSh Letters:
The Fundamental Forces
Governing the Universe and Existence

The letters Alef, Mem, and Shin represent the language of the world and the fundamental forces of nature that operate in the world and within the human soul. These forces are manifested through the four fundamental building blocks of nature and celestial planetary forces.

AMSh Letters – The Three Generational Planets

One of the best ways to understand the power and strength of these three letters is by linking them to the three generation planets: Uranus, Neptune, and Pluto.

These planets are the slowest in our solar system due to their considerable distance from the sun. They move slowly and exert their influence over entire generations rather than just on individuals. They reveal patterns that shape people's lives and perceptions, symbolizing the shared character traits of individuals within the same generational age group. This includes their attitudes toward values, society, and life itself.

These celestial bodies play a vital role in human development, establishing a connection to our collective consciousness and wielding a significant influence on our awareness. This stands in stark contrast to the personal planets: Sun, Moon, Mercury, Venus, and Mars, which move with greater swiftness and exert immediate and more individualistic effects on individuals. Their vibrational frequencies draw many people, not just individuals, into experiencing profound transformative processes. These planets correspond to the high and low frequencies of the three human soul faculties: thought, feelings, and reactions.

The letter Alef, linked to the planet Uranus, symbolizes the high and low aspects of human thought, signifying the impulse to break free from tradition and establish new ways of existence.

The letter Mem, associated with the planet Neptune, symbolizes the high and low aspects of human feelings and represents the domain of the subconscious and the yearning for connection with something greater.

The letter Shin, linked to the planet Pluto, symbolizes the high and low aspects of physical expression, representing processes of growth and decay, as well as death and rebirth.

AMSh Letters – The Four Elements

The letters Alef, Mem, and Shin represent the four fundamental elements of nature that operate in the world and within the human soul: air, fire, water, and earth, with the element of earth being derived from water. As illustrated in the diagram below, each of the twenty-two Hebrew alphabet letters is associated with a particular element.

The diagram below displays the Hebrew letters, their associated elements, and the equivalent English letters. Detailed explanations of the correspondences between the Hebrew and English letters can be found in the chapter dedicated to letters, where each letter is discussed individually.

Diagram 17: Hebrew Letters and Their Corresponding Elements

Element	Hebrew Letter	Hebrew Letters Name
FIRE	ד	DALET
	ה	HEH
	ט	THET
	כ	CAF
	ס	SAMECH
	ש	SHIN
AIR	א	ALEF
	ג	GIMEL
	ז	ZAYIN
	ל	LAMED
	צ	TZADI
	ר	RESH
WATER	ח	KHET
	מ	MEM
	נ	NUN
	ק	QOF
	ת	TAV
EARTH	ב	BET
	ו	VAV
	י	YOD
	ע	AHYIN
	פ	PEH

One of the initial things to consider in analyzing a person's name is understanding their basic nature and inborn temperament, which are shaped by the fundamental elements composing their birth name.

Understanding the four elements and how they operate in the world and within the human psyche is important because all transformative processes in living matter result from various combinations of these elements or one element opposing another. For instance, the absence of a specific element in a person's birth name may suggest a weakness or the absence of a particular quality in their daily functioning. Conversely, when a specific element is excessively present in a name, it may indicate a dominant temperament.

To illustrate this concept, let us take the name **Lori** as an example. The name consists of two letters (L, R) associated with the air element and two letters (O, I) associated with the earth element. In this example, the name represents high intellectual capacity (air element), accompanied by practical ability (earth element). This combination suggests that a person with this name tends to approach life from an intellectual and practical standpoint. However, it is important to note that this name lacks the water element and fire element. This absence may suggest difficulty in establishing a deep connection with the world of their feelings and emotions.

The importance of understanding the elements and the way they function in the human psyche has been emphasized throughout history by philosophers, scientists, mathematicians, and physicians. Notable figures who have discussed this concept include Empedocles, Plato, Hippocrates, Pythagoras, and Aristotle. Additionally, various Kabbalistic interpreters such as Saadia Gaon, Judah Halevi, Moses Ben Maimon (Maimonides), Moses Cordovero, and others have delved into this theory. References to the theory of elements can also be found in astrology, Judaism, and psychology.

An impressive illustration of how these fundamental elements manifest in the human psyche is evident in the personality theory of psychoanalyst Carl Gustav Jung. Jung associates the four elements with four psychological functions that form the core of an individual's experience of the world: intuition, thinking, feeling, and sensation.

The Fire Element

The group of letters associated with the fire element consists of six letters: Dalet, Heh, Thet, Caf, Samech, and Shin. Fire can be hot and dry, steady or changing. The keywords that characterize the fire element are will and creative passion. It endows a person with vitality, enthusiasm, intuition, courage, inspiration, ambition, assertiveness, a drive for achievement, sexuality, intellectualism, and action based on intuition or inner drive.

The Air Element

The group of letters associated with the air element also consists of six letters: Alef, Gimel, Zayin, Lamed, Tzadi, and Resh. Air can be warm, moist, fast, and light. The keywords that characterize the Air element are intellectual understanding and connection between things. The Air element grants a person mental intelligence, intellect, reason, thought, comprehension, perception, awareness, and lightness. Air illuminates the soul, clarifies thinking, and sharpens reasoning.

The Water Element

The group of letters associated with the water element consists of five letters: Khet, Mem, Nun, Qof, and Tav. Water can be cold, warm, slow, deep, or shallow. It gravitates downward and represents depths and the realm of emotions. Water is associated with connection and experience. It provides emotional intelligence, sensitivity, inner strength, and flow. It enables a person to experience emotions in a deeply experiential way. While this can be intense and challenging at times, it also offers transformative abilities and the capacity to purify and cleanse one's inner waters.

In instances where a person's name lacks watery letters, there may be challenges in connecting emotionally with life, people, and processes. This deficit can lead to feelings of suffocation and difficulty purifying one's inner self, which can result in health issues. This is suggested by the name formed by these five watery letters: KhNQ-MT (חנק-מת), which together form the word choke-dead. You can find further information regarding these letters in the chapter dedicated to them.

The Earth Element

The group of letters associated with the earth element also consists of five letters: Bet, Vav, Yod, Ahyin, and Peh. The earth element, characterized by its cold, dry, strong, and slow nature, is the heaviest, most compact, and lowest of the elements. Key attributes of this element include existence and practical implementation. It endows individuals with physical (kinetic) and practical intelligence, grounding, stability, endurance, high tolerance, realism, structure, practicality, and the desire to preserve what exists.

BGD-CPRT Letters
The Creative Forces in the Universe and Existence

In the realm of quantum physics, it is posited that the universe and existence originated from a singular divine thought. This thought is seen as a manifestation of the divine's desire to explore itself, its energy, and the diverse facets of its divine power. Similarly, the Kabbalah theory suggests that the human mind can shape tangible realities and emanate them upon the divine creation. This powerful potential force is concealed within the vibrational frequencies represented by the letters BGD-CPRT.

The letters BGD-CPRT (בגד-כפרת) symbolize the seven creative, life-giving forces and the seven powers of the human mind. They have a unique ability to generate mental and emotional patterns within our existential space. These patterns are transmitted into space through electromagnetic pulses, giving rise to distinct realities. The underlying principle guiding this creative process is that we ultimately become what we consistently think and feel.

Our thoughts, akin to seeds, possess their own existence. What we sow in the realm of our thoughts is what we inevitably reap. The power of thought manifests simultaneously in two realms—within our minds and in our emotional bodies—prompting corresponding reactions. Therefore, to create enlightened creations, it is imperative to master the use of both thought and emotion. While thoughts are the language of the mind, emotions are the language of the body. Our mindset and the quality of our present experiences are shaped by the synergy between our thoughts and feelings.

The letters BGD-CPRT represent the seven mind consciousnesses embedded in the personal and collective consciousness of human beings. These consciousnesses perpetuate themselves through the vibration, frequency, and resonance inherent in each letter, forming the architecture of an individual's ego and personality. Given their significant influence, it is crucial to understand how to effectively engage with these letters when they appear in a person's name.

The journey toward enlightenment begins with basic understandings. Firstly, the patterns of the mind do not inherently belong to us, and they do not derive from our spirit. Secondly, these mind patterns are communicated to our consciousness through electromagnetic pulses. Thirdly, identification with the mind leads to attachments, creating a metaphorical "inner prison" and entanglement in the maze of our minds. These mind patterns, akin to passing clouds in the sky, can be observed with equanimity to prevent identification and attachment.

Mind Patterns (Mental and Emotional Patterns)

*"You are wherever your thoughts are;
make sure your thoughts are where you want to be."*

Rabbi Nachman of Breslev

Our world is composed of energy, structural patterns, numbers, frequencies, and sounds. One of the key factors that hold our energetic field in its current form is our personal and collective consciousness. Therefore, one of the first things we should do is to learn about the creative power hidden within these seven letters so that we can choose freely and consciously to whom and for what purpose we give our power.

Every thought, feeling, and emotion possesses energy, form, and a unique vibrational frequency that we emit into our environment. When we focus on a specific thought or emotion and give it our heartfelt concentration, we infuse it with energy, thereby increasing its vibrational frequency. As the frequency of a thought or emotion becomes stronger, its magnetic power also intensifies. Thus, we attract toward us people, events, thoughts, emotions, and experiences that resonate at a similar frequency level.

The thoughts we maintain over time evolve into beliefs. For example, if a person believes they are a victim of life's circumstances, they will attract into their life energies that resonate with this belief.

Every thought and emotion possesses a dual nature. Thoughts can be loving or negative, and emotions can be calm and balanced or intense and turbulent. There is a bidirectional relationship between thoughts and emotions: thoughts can influence emotions, and emotions can influence thoughts. The letters BGD-CPRT invite individuals to identify the underlying beliefs that tend to operate within them subconsciously and release the beliefs that no longer serve their highest good.

Scientist Dr. Bruce Lipton, in his book The Biology of Belief, describes how our cells function scientifically. He indicates that what controls the cell is our mind or our perception. In other words, what controls the fifty trillion cells in our body are our mindset, thoughts, and beliefs. So, when we change our mindset, we are actually changing our biology. The mindset is a primary factor contributing to diseases in the world today. What a person thinks or believes is what they create within their biology. Therefore, our perception can essentially rewrite our genetic code.

The Duality of the Mind

The seven BGD-CPRT letters contain duplicity within them. Each letter in this group can be written in two different forms: one with a dot inside the letter and one without a dot (ב"ב, ג"ג, ד"ה, כ"כ, פ"פ, ר"ה, ת"ת). Additionally, these letters can be pronounced with two distinct sounds: a soft sound or a hard sound. This duplicity offers insights into how soft and hard vibration frequencies are generated in our cosmic space.

For instance, the letter Bet can be written with a dot inside (בּ), resulting in a hard sound and pronounced as B. Alternatively, it can be written without the dot (ב), producing a soft sound and pronounced as V. Another example is the letter Peh (פ) that can be written with a dot inside, resulting in a hard sound and pronounced as P. Alternatively, it can be written without the dot (פ), producing a soft sound and pronounced as F. Therefore, these seven letters behave in two distinct forms, producing two different sounds and behaving in two opposing manners.

These letters contain within them both something and its antithesis, such as optimism and pessimism, joy and sadness, light and darkness, female and male. This duplicity tends to create duality in the human mind.

The duality that these seven letters represent is the one that misleads and distracts individuals away from their soul's path by making them believe that one aspect of life is better than the other. This duality fosters a viewpoint that categorizes everything with a positive or negative connotation, affixing labels of good and bad.

The purpose of these seven creative letters is to teach humans to understand the essence of things from both sides, refraining from labeling either side as good or bad. One of the simplest ways to grasp this concept is by considering a coin: every coin possesses two sides. A coin does not have a good or bad side; it is a singular coin with two distinct faces.

A lack of awareness in understanding the duality represented by these letters can foster internal conflict, leading to clashes between opposing desires, such as between inner and outer wills, personal and social desires, and the perception of good and evil. These conflicting psychological forces tend to create **cognitive dissonance**[10], confusion, and mental contradiction within an individual.

Hard and Soft Sounds

In this group of letters, the presence or absence of a dot inside a letter signifies the pronunciation of the sound associated with it. When a dot is present inside the letter, it indicates the accentuated or hard sound, which is often likened to a masculine frequency (yang). Conversely, when there is no dot inside the letter, it signifies the soft sound, which is often associated with a feminine frequency (yin). As a general rule, in Hebrew, when a letter from this group appears at the beginning of a name or a word, it consistently receives the accentuated sound.

Examples of this can be seen in hard-sound Hebrew words such as: "פְּקָק" (traffic jam), "פְּגִיעָה" (injury), "פְּרִיצה" (burglary) and "פְּצָצָה" (bomb), and soft sound Hebrew words such as: "רפיון" (laxity), "חבר" (friend) and "רפואה" (medicine). These examples illustrate the clear distinction between hard and soft sounds in this group of letters.

---

[10] Cognitive dissonance is the internal disharmony and discomfort that a person feels when their behavior does not align with their beliefs, values, and positions. It occurs when a person holds contradictory beliefs simultaneously when they are exposed to information that contradicts their existing beliefs, values, and positions or when they act in opposition to them.

These letters possess the ability to either amplify or diminish vibrational frequencies. An accentuated letter is one whose potency, whether on a mental or emotional plane, is intensified, both in its constructive and inhibitory aspects. On the one hand, when the power of the letter is heightened, it can manifest a specific reality more quickly. However, on the other hand, there is also a risk of creating something from a position of elevated ego and pride. Conversely, when a letter lacks accentuation, it can create things at a more gradual pace but from a place of acceptance and giving that counters ego and pride.

We are sentient beings capable of profound thought. Our thoughts can be optimistic and joyful or disturbing, confusing, and horrifying. They can be creative and fruitful or fixated and terrifying. At times, they can repeat themselves obsessively and oppressively, being intrusive and invasive, thereby instilling fear and dread in a person and even causing them to lose touch with reality and be disconnected from the here and now.

Throughout human history, our consciousness has experienced challenging experiences that have filled our awareness with fear and a sense of separateness. These experiences have fostered patterns of confusion, doubt, anxiety, and competitiveness, often overshadowing our innate tendency toward **altruism**[11]. For these creative letters to manifest their positive essence and draw us back to altruism and unity consciousness, we must develop an awareness of their power and purpose within us. This heightened awareness enables us to direct our abundant energy toward positive and enlightened purposes.

---

[11] Altruism, a fundamental human trait, goes beyond mere kindness and selflessness. It embodies the concept of empathy, the ability to put oneself in another's shoes, and the willingness to act in ways that promote the well-being of others, even when it may require personal sacrifices. It serves as a cornerstone of interconnected societies, fostering cooperation and solidarity among individuals and communities. Altruism not only contributes to the greater good of society but also strengthens the bonds that tie us together as we extend a helping hand to one another, often echoing the sentiment that we are, indeed, our brothers' and sisters' keepers.

HVZKhThI-LNSOTzQ Letters:
The Practical and Applied Forces

The third category of letters, referred to as HVZKhThI-LNSOTzQ (הוזחטי-לנסעצק), comprises twelve letters. These letters are endowed with the power for practical implementation, enabling the transformation of ideas into reality. Serving as twelve channels, they allow humans to direct divine abundance into the physical realm, thereby enabling them to actualize their potential.

These twelve letters are associated with the twelve zodiac signs and Hebrew months. This connection provides deeper insight into the characteristics of each zodiac sign and the stages through which a person's reincarnated soul progresses through its earthly journey, a journey known in Kabbalah as "the rectification of the soul."

A human being possesses a spirit and soul. The soul encapsulates the entirety of an individual's experiences, personality, and uniqueness, which form their inner world. The soul encompasses various aspects of human essence, including thinking, perception, memory, feelings, and unconscious impulses. Furthermore, the soul encompasses elements of conditioning that tend to subjugate the person and activate them in a hypnotic, unconscious, and subconscious manner.

To enhance our understanding, we can envision the soul as an actor on a stage, with the spirit being the master, the proprietor, and the divine spark residing within us. The spirit represents our higher self and embodies the "I AM" consciousness. It is the aspect within us that writes the script of our earthly journey.

Now, having grasped how to identify the three primary forces—spiritual, mental, and practical—that shape the reality of our lives through our names, we can delve into another significant aspect that constitutes the essence of our work in our present life.

CHAPTER 5

The Watery Letters

One of the most significant categories to understand is the group of five water-related letters: KhNQ-MT (חנק-מת), which together form the phrase "suffocating-dead." These five letters, rich in emotional and expressive significance, address the emotional realm within us, encompassing feelings, emotions, instincts, the unconscious, and the subconscious. They represent the various ways our inner water functions and navigates us.

Emotion is one of the most important aspects to understand, as it serves as the bridge to higher consciousness. This concept is symbolized in the Hebrew language, where the word for "emotion" (regesh) becomes (gesher), meaning "bridge" when reversed (גשר- רגש). Connecting with our emotions, understanding and identifying their operation mode, and regulating and expressing them in a balanced, precise manner are key to mental well-being and success in life.

Since our primary work in earthly life focuses on emotional work and spiritual development, I would like to deepen your understanding of water's power in the world and the human soul.

The Power of Water

Life cannot exist without water. Water is the most vital component of our existence. Every life form in our world contains water. Life on Earth began with water. *"Then God said, "Let the waters teem with swarms of living creatures..." (Genesis, Chapter 1, Verse 20)*
Our lives begin as aquatic beings, originating from the fluid of semen. Our fetal stages occur in the womb, an area filled with amniotic fluid that provides us with tranquility and protection. The Hebrew word womb (רחם) is contained within the word mercy (רחמים), presenting water as the sea of mercy (רחמ-ים). Upon our emergence from the womb, the first nourishment we consume is milk, whether it is mother's milk or another liquid milk whose main component is water. Throughout the rest of our lives, water sustains and quenches our physical and spiritual thirst.

Water possesses many important and varied properties, crucial both globally and within the human soul. As a chemical compound, it underpins all life forms, serving as a nourishing, hydrating, and revitalizing force in the world. This remarkable substance is found everywhere: in the sky, on the earth, and in the air we breathe. It covers numerous surfaces in the world and within us and is the primary component of our cells. Water can constitute up to ninety percent of a living being's weight and over seventy percent of human body fluids, including about eighty-five percent of our brain cell content.

Water has the ability to penetrate, fill, dissolve, and float. It can heat up and freeze, embodying the three states of matter: liquid (water), solid (ice), and gas (vapor). Transparent and colorless, water is capable of reflecting or absorbing colors. It possesses a distinct sound and rhythm, which can vary from quiet and calm to loud and turbulent. Water is a substance with a vibrational frequency endowed with the power of absorption and dissolution. This enables it to absorb various minerals, coalesce and mix with them, and even alter its composition.

Through these remarkable qualities of water, we are given the opportunity to feel people and situations. Every facet of our experience finds its genesis in water. Without water, we would struggle to feel, experience, and remember.

Water also acts as a carrier for various chemical substances. It is flexible and agile, embodying the essential characteristics we need as humans. It enables us to feel and experience things, helping us to uncover the mysteries of the universe, creation, and our deepest selves. Water can exhibit high or low vibrational frequencies; they can be clear and pure or murky and turbid. It can quench the thirsty soul or stir up emotional storms and turmoil. At its core, water embodies the principles of creation and formation.

Advanced research on water, exemplified by the work of immunologist Jacques Benveniste and water researcher Dr. Masaru Emoto, reveals that water possesses a molecular memory. It has the remarkable ability to restore and recreate any substance it once contained. This applies to the water within the human body as well. The water molecules present in the human head and body remember the thoughts and emotions the person ever experiences and retain them in their **base body**[12]. These molecules are able to aid in the restoration of these thoughts and emotions, retrieving the 'data' from their various life incarnations.

---

[12] The term "base body" in esoteric contexts refers to the energetic body that accompanies an individual through their various reincarnations. It is referred to as the base body because the physical body relies on it. This concept is often associated with the idea that our soul evolves and learns through multiple lifetimes. It suggests that the base body carries with it the accumulated wisdom, experiences, and karmic imprints from each incarnation. It acts as the soul's vessel through various lifetimes, deeply connected to the individual's karmic path.

KhNQ-MT (חנק-מת) Letters: The Inner Child

The water element is intimately connected to the realm of emotions, representing the significant, expansive, and plentiful aspects within us. These aspects often do not receive the appropriate attention and acknowledgment they deserve. It is in this rich inner realm that our "inner child" resides, embodying our most authentic self with a genuine voice. This voice, however, is often repressed and sometimes even forgotten. The term inner child therapeutically refers to the childlike part within us—the sensitive and emotional aspect that is spontaneous and creative.

We enter the world as joyful, happy infants, brimming with energy and enthusiasm, untainted by worry and fear. However, as we go through life, influenced by education, socialization, and societal norms, we learn that the external world is not always safe. To survive emotionally, this sensitive and feeling part retreats into a metaphorical closet, concealing itself and shutting the door.

Despite being locked away, our inner child yearns to be loved, cherished, heard, seen, accepted and understood. Encountering this inner child, trapped within our adult personality, is a crucial aspect of our personal and spiritual growth. It silently waits to emerge, to be acknowledged and heard.

In each one of us resides a wounded child. Encounters with the physical world often generate vulnerability and sometimes even rejection. As a result, this part becomes suppressed within us, causing our natural spontaneity, inner joy, zest for life, and creativity to diminish gradually.

If our inner child is not acknowledged or nurtured over time, our emotional and physical well-being can suffer significantly. This leads to a sense of inner emptiness and a feeling that something fundamental is missing in our lives. This is what the five KhNQ-MT (חנק-מת) letters speak of. They refer to the living and breathing part within us that lies beneath our conscious awareness, within our emotional body. This part is responsible for our moments of joy or sadness, elation or despondency, creativity or vulnerability, love or anxiety and fear of getting hurt.

Ignoring our inner child can trigger anxiety and, in some cases, even physical illness. It forces us to slow down, stop, rest, be quiet, and enter a state of mind that allows this inner aspect to surface and be heard. Remaining disconnected from our inner child and continuing to neglect it eventually leads to emotional detachment. This detachment breeds a sense of separation, making it challenging to experience genuine intimacy in our relationships, both with ourselves and with others.

Diagram 18: The Inner Child

KhNQ-MT (חנק-מת) Letters: Human Emotions

KhNQ-MT (חנק-מת) letters indicate the various ways in which internal water, representing emotions, functions within a person and navigates them. Emotions have many facets, including love, joy, enthusiasm, empathy, cheerfulness, fear, anger, insult, sorrow, shame, disgust, and frustration. Emotions can be deep or shallow and dense, happy or painful, bringing either excitement, happiness, ease, and upliftment or cause reactions like alarm, worry, embarrassment, paralysis, and negative states such as depression and anxiety.

An illustration of the profound influence of human emotions on our lives and the way they tend to shape our reality can be found in the biblical story of Cain and Abel, particularly in the conversation between Cain and the Lord Jehovah. In this narrative, God counsels Cain on the importance of emotional regulation. This ancient biblical tale provides historical insight into the consequences of failing to manage emotions, highlighting the spiritual responsibility bestowed upon us: free choice.

In the book of Genesis, Jehovah's words to Cain emphasize this principle: *"Then the Lord said to Cain, 'Why are you angry? And why is your face gloomy? If you do well, will your face not be cheerful? And if you do not do well, sin is lurking at the door; and its desire is for you, but you must master it."* (Genesis, Chapter 4, Verses 6-7)

Human emotions hold immense power. In ancient times, understanding and mastering emotions were key lessons for those in the priesthood. Emotions generate physical responses within our bodies, triggering sensations, both pleasant and unpleasant, as well as physiological and behavioral reactions, such as changes in heart rate, speech tone, and body language. These responses often operate automatically and unconsciously, leading to various patterns of action and thought, such as joy or sadness.

The KhNQ-MT letters connect us to our emotional world and to the inner child that permanently resides within us, irrespective of our chronological age. These letters provide insight into the emotional challenges we are meant to face in our current lives.

The first step in self-development and spiritual growth begins with a deep understanding of our emotional world in all its shades and nuances. This includes meeting our inner child, which represents our authentic inner voice and seeks to emerge, be seen, and heard, even in our adult personality.

Now, with the understanding of how to identify the four faculties through which a person experiences their inner and outer world—the spiritual, mental, emotional, and practical powers—we can move toward comprehending a person's fundamental patterns, their level of compassion or judgment, their aspirations, and their emotional stability. To achieve this, I will further categorize the twenty-two letters.

Diagram 19: Emotional Dysregulation

CHAPTER 6

Additional Divisions of the Letters

To enhance our comprehension of how letters impact us and guide us toward self-awareness, we will explore additional aspects of the Hebrew letters.

One of the primary classifications refers to the group: soul, rectification, and outcome letters. This categorization helps us to understand the fundamental pattern of the person.

It is important to note that this book focuses primarily on Hebrew letters, which are considered the original foundation of human language. To the best of my knowledge, the English alphabet and other languages that utilize the Latin alphabet do not have similar categorization of letters into groups, like open and closed, nor do they assign specific attributes such as compassion or judgment to each letter. Furthermore, there is no established correlation between the letters and elements, planets, zodiac signs, months, and other categories specified in this book. The practice of associating the letters with these categories stems from the ancient Hebrew alphabet. In standard linguistic languages, such as English, there are no such divisions of the letters.

Soul, Rectification, and Outcome Letters

Diagram 20: Soul, Rectification, and Outcome Letters

Category	Hebrew Letter Name	Hebrew Letter
Soul Letters	ALEF	א
	BET	ב
	GIMEL	ג
	DALET	ד
	HEH	ה
	VAV	ו
Rectification Letters	ZAYIN	ז
	KHET	ח
	THET	ט
	YOD	י
	CAF	כ
	LAMED	ל
	MEM	מ
Outcome Letters	NUN	נ
	SAMECH	ס
	AHYIN	ע
	PEH	פ
	TZADI	צ
	QOF	ק
	RESH	ר
	SHIN	ש
	TAV	ת
	FINAL CAF	ך
	FINAL MEM	ם
	FINAL NUN	ן
	FINAL PEH	ף
	FINAL TZADI	ץ

Soul Letters

Soul letters represent the spiritual truths that every person must acquire from early childhood prior to engaging in any interactive, experiential experiences. They indicate the developmental journey that the evolving soul undergoes during a given life incarnation, illustrating six different ways a human being experiences oneself and the world, along with six paths to authentic self-development.

These paths involve embracing new experiences, taking risks, trusting intuition, and embracing the unknown. They also include refining personal skills, accumulation of self-knowledge, gaining deep self-understanding, and realizing personal desires through authentic self-creation and fair cooperation. Another aspect is exploring the inner wisdom and mysteries of the subconscious and unconscious mind and connecting with the inner voice, often termed the inner child.

Furthermore, taking personal responsibility for one's life, decisions, and actions is crucial. This involves creating structure and organization in daily routines through self-discipline and self-leadership. Emphasizing personal well-being, self-nourishment, supporting others, and embracing creativity by exploring and expressing creative potential through art, ideas, or innovation is also key. This path includes discovering unique creative potential, connecting with life's abundant opportunities, and fostering gratitude and fulfillment. Lastly, it encompasses exploring and investigating personal beliefs, spiritual truths, and adherence to high moral principles.

Soul letters represent the developmental journey the evolving soul goes through in this lifetime. Understanding and connecting with the wisdom of these letters can help individuals explore and answer essential questions about their identity and their unique way of integrating into the world. Questions such as "Who am I?" "How do I uniquely fit into the world?" and "What distinct personal strengths and resources do I have to support my life journey?"

These six letters embody patterns that are deeply embedded in both individual and collective human consciousness. These patterns include instinctual behavioral tendencies and latent energies that reside within human consciousness and are passed down from generation to generation, transcending boundaries of religion, culture, and nationality.

Rectification Letters

The rectification letters, also known as "Karma Letters," are profoundly significant as they reveal conditioned behavioral patterns influencing human actions subconsciously. These letters provide insight into how individuals instinctively face the challenges of their earthly journey, their approach to life and their attitude toward people.

This group of letters highlights personal, interpersonal, and societal challenges. When courageously faced, these challenges act as catalysts for self-awareness, leading to a conscious understanding of one's motivations and behaviors. The approach to these challenges can either uplift an individual to a state of unity consciousness or cause a regression to a state of separation consciousness.

Within these letters, the principle of "everything is foreseen" and "permission is given" (הכל צפוי והרשות נתונה) is embedded. This grants humans the freedom to choose between embracing and manifesting their divine, godly nature or rejecting it. Therefore, rectification letters are crucial for profound transformation and self-realization toward a higher state of consciousness.

The seven rectification letters, also termed karma letters, embody the casual energy shaping Karma, which seeks rectification. Karma represents cosmic justice and is expressed through these letters, linked to an individual's actions in current or past lives. If a person's name contains a letter from this group, they bear the responsibility of improving their interactions with people and overall life approach.

Each of these seven letters is tied to specific rectification tasks that a person's soul undertakes. In Kabbalistic terms, rectification refers to correcting one's attitude rather than the individual themselves. According to **Baal HaSulam**[13], a person does not need to correct themselves but rather their attitude and approach toward themselves, their Creator, and others, and their self-centered desires to receive for themselves alone.

According to the Kabbalistic teachings, self-centered desire operates as a poison. The Hebrew acronym for "receive for oneself" is "<u>R</u>atzon <u>A</u>zmi <u>L</u>ekabel" (רָצוֹן עַצמִי לַקבל), forming the word "poison" (RAL=רעל). Baal HaSulam points out that problems and distortions in the world arise from individuals' tendencies to correct others instead of their attitudes and their self-serving desires.

In the *Gate of Reincarnations* (שער הגלגולים), Rabbi Isaac Luria, the renowned Kabbalist, expounds on the repercussions of our actions and words toward others. He explains that harming others with words or actions wraps our souls in "shells," known in the esoteric teachings as "coverings." These shells create barriers between our souls and the divine spark. The deeper one immerses in self-centered desires and lack of respect, appreciation, consideration, and compassion, the thicker these coverings become, obscuring the divine reality within. This eventually leads to a disconnection from the source of light and the soul's purpose.

Kabbalistic teachings state that if a person has harmed another body, finances, or soul in this or past life, they must undertake "tikkun" (תיקון), a process of rectification. This spiritual journey facilitates soul rectification and restores harmony with the divine essence, paving the way for genuine enlightenment.

---

[13] Baal HaSulam is the nickname of Rabbi Yehuda Leib HaLevi Ashlag, who was one of the interpreters of Kabbalah and contributed to its dissemination.

In every human interaction, whether pleasant or painful, a process of rectification is at play. Recognizing this and cultivating gratitude toward those causing us distress or suffering is vital. These individuals, as disguised companions of our souls, guide us to recognize and rectify past errors. They prompt us to focus on the present and the changes needed for growth and redemption.

Consequential Letters

Consequential letters symbolize the consequences of specific karmic actions preserved in an individual's soul memory. The intense energy these letters carry tends to activate a person subconsciously in a way that attracts challenging life experiences into their lives. Since each individual is accountable for their actions, it is imperative to understand and address the karmic lessons these letters signify, striving toward rectification and growth.

Each consequential letter provides insights into the lessons that a reincarnated soul has elected to learn in their current life. Every letter in this group signifies a distinct lesson. When individuals comprehend and amend their approach to life and interactions with others, the energy of these letters transforms into a "master key," enabling them to unlock many doors.

The primary objective of the consequential letters is to foster a heightened self-awareness in individuals about their soul lessons. The experiences these letters bring forth are tied to spiritual lessons that remain unlearned and unaddressed. They serve as a wake-up call and a call to action, encouraging individuals to awaken, self-reflect, achieve inner balance, and pursue the enlightened trajectory of their soul's destiny. These experiences invite individuals to engage in empowering educational processes, where they release any impediments to the fulfillment of their soul's purpose. More details on this subject will be presented in a forthcoming chapter dedicated to letters.

Many people fear change, but it is essential to understand its inevitability and constancy in life. Nature itself is a testament to ongoing, often unnoticed change. Human life mirrors this pattern of continuous transformation.

Consider human development. From the obscurity of a watery womb where we exist as aquatic beings, we abruptly transition into air-breathing creatures at birth. This remarkable transformation is a reminder that change is an intrinsic part of life.

Welcoming change is the first step toward progress and evolution. Recognizing that change enables us to advance, evolve, influence our environment, and initiate positive shifts in our lives opens us to its transformative power. Embracing change offers opportunities to explore, experience new facets of life, and deepen our understanding of ourselves and the world. As we engage with change, our lives become richer and more expansive.

The next step involves implementing small, manageable, and gradual changes. These incremental steps provide a sense of control over the process. By adopting this approach, we can establish new habits and routines, allowing change to seamlessly integrate into our lives, enhancing our well-being and growth.

Compassion, Mercy, and Judgment Letters

The following classification of the twenty-two letters into five distinct groups provides insight into the extent of compassion or judgment an individual may possess.

This grouping is based on shared characteristics, dividing the letters into those symbolizing compassion, mercy, judgment, a blend of judgment and mercy, and absolute judgment. Each group offers insights into the distinct essence and fundamental virtue the letters signify, along with the moral principle and a specific perspective through which individuals perceive life, situations, and people.

Diagram 21: Degree of Kindness, Mercy and Judgment Measure in Letters

Kindness and Compassion Letters		Mercy Letters		Judgment letters		Combination of Mercy and Judgment Letters		Absolute Judgment Letters	
ALEF	א	ZAYIN	ז	DALET	ד	BET	ב	PEH	פ
GIMEL	ג	KHET	ח	VAV	ו	CAF	כ	TZADI	צ
HEH	ה	THET	ט			SAMECH	ס	QOF	ק
		YOD	י			AHYIN	ע	RESH	ר
		LAMED	ל					SHIN	ש
		MEM	מ					TAV	ת
		NUN	נ					FINAL CAF	ך
								FINAL MEM	ם
								FINAL NUN	ן
								FINAL PEH	ף
								FINAL TZADI	ץ

A "measure" in this context refers to a moral, conductive, and judicial principle that embodies the manifestation of divine power in the world through various forms. Within Judaism, the notion of measures is closely linked to key moral principles derived from ethical and judicial teachings of The Torah. One such principle is "gmul" (reward), which explores the harmonious connection relationship between a person's actions and the consequent rewards for those actions, outlining the nature of these rewards based on individual conduct.

In Christianity, the concept of measure refers to moral principles grounded in the notion of purpose, deeply influenced by Aristotle's moral philosophy. Aristotle, a significant figure in Western philosophy and a student of Plato posited that every individual has a specific purpose and goal in life.

It is imperative for individuals to discover and understand their purpose, fostering self-awareness in their quest. This understanding involves a deep reflection on one's actions, discerning whether they are motivated by virtues such as humility and generosity or by vices like pride and greed.

Group A – Letters of Kindness and Compassion

The letters of kindness and compassion embody virtues such as grace, compassion, mercy, generosity, and a magnanimous spirit. These virtues manifest in an individual's will to give and grant others their abundance, wisdom, resources, or time. This form of giving is unconditional, stemming from the innate qualities within a person's soul, driven by a genuine desire to benefit others without expecting anything in return.

Characterized by traits such as pleasantness, kindness, gentleness, generosity, empathy, and a warm and inviting nature, these letters also promote charitable acts, care, consideration, and a willingness to forgive and pardon others. They are graced with unwavering optimism, always seeing the half-full cup in every situation and everything around them. These letters embody four of the seven virtues discussed in the ethical teachings of the philosopher Aristotle: self-confidence (both in oneself and the divine within), hope (the expectation of good), magnanimity, and charity.

Individuals whose names contain letters from this group often show a natural inclination toward initiating acts of giving and assistance, even without a direct request. This inherent altruistic behavior extends beyond mere obligations, encompassing an understanding of challenging circumstances and a propensity to judge others favorably, thereby granting them opportunities. Such a measure of kindness is essential for fostering a harmonious world.

Group B – Letters of Mercy

The letters of mercy contain the measure of mercy, representing a person's willingness to empathize with others and ease their burdens. This measure helps individuals to develop the virtue of equilibrium, which is a crucial component of a conscious and fulfilling life. It enables individuals to maintain equilibrium and composure amidst life-challenging trials, consciously observing and examining circumstances without undue attachment. Vipassana meditation places great emphasis on nurturing equilibrium as a central aspect of its practice.

The letters of mercy signify the principle of cause and effect. This principle proclaims that the energy you impart to others echoes back to you from the vast universe. In other words, what you give to those around you is what you will receive from the universe in return.

The measure of mercy provides individuals with an opportunity for rectification, allowing them time to amend their deeds. According to the Kabbalistic teachings, those whose names bear these letters are entrusted with the mission of nurturing their inherent qualities and developing their inner light, thereby positively influencing those around them.

In their obstructive aspect, the letters of mercy tend to lead a person toward arrogance and a sense of superiority, fostering a condescending attitude toward those perceived as weaker. This mindset challenges personal and spiritual growth, attracting similar energies into their lives in the form of experiential trials. Moreover, it often prompts actions driven by self-interest, where situations are viewed through a profit and loss lens. This perspective encourages calculating personal gain, seeking the easiest path without exerting effort, and prioritizing personal benefits above all.

The intended purpose of these letters is to cultivate essential traits within individuals, such as justice and spiritual insight. These traits enable fair judgments in matters of personal interests and rights while respecting the rights of others. In this context, it is important to understand two crucial points: firstly, the antithesis of equilibrium is indifference, and secondly, unrefined mercy can provoke self-pity in a person, fostering a victim mentality. Recognizing these lessons is valuable, and those bearing these letters must endeavor to master them throughout their life journey.

Group C – Letters of Judgment

The measure of judgment is complex, as it encompasses a high level of judgment, critical scrutiny, limitation on giving and generosity, and a reduction in the qualities of compassion and mercy. The letters of judgment are said to contain "drops of bitterness" because they carry frequencies that tend to disrupt a person's inner harmony. This disruption potentially leads to psychological imbalances by tilting the scales toward negativity.

This measure is characterized by feelings of jealousy, strictness, harshness, and inflexibility. It emits vibrational frequencies that tend to restrict and limit the expression of kindness and compassion, while fostering a strong desire to receive for oneself.

The measure of judgment coaxes individuals to focus on the empty half of the cup and to perceive evil in others. This perspective causes them to approach situations without considering mitigating circumstances, thus hindering their ability to see both sides of an issue. Consequently, it becomes challenging for individuals influenced by this measure to empathize, understand, forgive, and extend compassion or pardon to others.

According to Sages, adopting a demeanor aligned with the measure of judgment leads a person to encounter life's trials and tribulations, following the principle of "measure for measure." Interestingly, in Hebrew, the word "machala" (מחלה), meaning disease when its letters are reversed, spells "chemla" (חמלה) meaning "compassion." This suggests that hardships, obstacles, and illness can stem from a lack of compassion toward oneself and others.

According to the writings of the holy Ari'zal (Ha'ari Hakadosh), the measure of judgment involves a stance where individuals refrain from offering help or generosity to others unless it aligns with their convenience and serves their interests. As it said, "the permission is granted" (הרשות נתונה) to those whose names carry these letters to decide how to manifest their inner light, whether through acts of giving or through restraint and limitation.

The letters of judgment have two primary objectives. Firstly, they aim to limit the measure of kindness to establish and shape boundaries. This means to judge a specific situation based on absolute justice rather than the societal or personal justice of an individual. The divine conduct is built upon both the measure of boundless kindness, characterized by unrestricted giving, and the measure of judgment, characterized by restraint and the acknowledgment that gifts are not entirely free. The sovereign path lies in maintaining an equilibrium between the dimensions of kindness and judgment.

Secondly, they aim to develop essential qualities within an individual, such as courage, patience, and prudence. These attributes provide psychological fortitude, empowering one to confront fears and uncertainties effectively. The virtue of prudence, in particular, fosters sound judgment and grants individual the ability to exercise control over their words and actions.

Group D – Combination of Judgment and Mercy Letters

This group of letters contains a unique fusion of judgment and mercy. These letters exhibit a dynamic nature, akin to a pendulum swinging between judgment and mercy. Yet, their prevailing inclination is toward judgment due to their graphical structure being enclosed from three directions.

This energetic composition tends to incline individuals toward self-centeredness and difficulty in opening up to others and embracing different perspectives. Consequently, it restricts their capacity for understanding others, showing empathy and compassion, forgiving, releasing grudges, and moving past old grievances. Furthermore, this disposition presents challenges in accepting personal responsibility, often leading to a focus on the negative aspects or the empty half of the cup.

Group E – Absolute Judgment Letters

The final set is characterized by six letters that embody the measure of absolute judgment. This measure is marked by qualities such as jealousy, strictness, harshness, and rigidity. It emits vibrational frequencies that often restrict and limit generous giving while heightening judgment and a desire to receive solely for oneself.

The measure of absolute judgment tends to dull human senses and impose issues such as inflexibility, pessimism, sadness, harsh and stringent judgment, destructive criticism, suspicion, excessive worry, a constant feeling of lack, and an unconscious expectation of the worst scenario. It inclines individuals to see the glass half empty, making it difficult to see both sides of the coin, and consequently hinders understanding of others, empathizing with them, forgiving and pardoning them.

This measure leads individuals to behave harshly toward others, adhering to the principle of "measure for measure"—"an eye for an eye, and a tooth for a tooth"—seeking exact retribution for perceived wrongs. Essentially, this measure operates as a prosecutor, opposing and accepting things as they are without considering any mitigating factors. It follows the law strictly, with all its severity, based on what a person deserves as a consequence of their actions.

An eye for an eye and a tooth for a tooth is an ancient patriarchal moral principle mentioned in The Torah in the book of Exodus. A principle that states that God treats humans in the same way they treat Him, therefore justifying punishment that mirrors the offenses committed as a form of divine justice. I contend that this principle is more patriarchal than divine, aiming to instill fear and intimidation.

The energy of absolute judgment receives greater emphasis in letters that their graphical form is closed from three directions. In these letters, this energy tends to evoke feelings of closure, self-centeredness, irritability, anger, arrogance, envy, and unwillingness to take personal responsibility. These vibrational frequencies can easily disrupt the internal balance, leading to inner disharmony—a lack of synchronization and harmony between different aspects of the soul.

This energy receives even greater emphasis in consequential letters that their graphical form is closed from three directions, manifesting as a tendency to point a blaming finger. This blame often serves as a psychological defense mechanism known as projection, where the accusing individual projects their feelings of guilt onto others, holding them responsible for the current situation and consciously or unconsciously expecting the other side to express remorse, change their ways, and act in a manner that will make the accuser feel good. Thus, the one who projects do not need to make an effort to change their ways.

The act of pointing a blaming finger carries within it violent and aggressive energy, whether directed toward oneself or others. This violence can manifest internally through thoughts, intentions, emotions, or self-talk or externally through actions that may harm oneself or those around them. Violent energy can take many forms, including manipulation, finger-pointing, jealousy, obsession, coercion, restriction, humiliation, dictating a personal tone, domineering behavior, demanding explanations, or making threats.

It is crucial to understand that violence and victimhood are energies that go hand in hand. Victimhood represents a psychological state in which an individual perceives themselves as wronged or harmed. Such a victim mentality obstructs the person from assuming personal responsibility, creating psychological barriers that hinder growth and development. This mindset also leads to a state where the individual feels entitled to seek attention and retribution from others due to their perceived status as a victim. However, the ability to take personal responsibility is a fundamental aspect of maturation and is essential for bringing about positive change in oneself and one's circumstances.

This group of letters serves as an invitation for introspection, urging individuals to identify internal sources of violence toward themselves or others, whether in their thoughts, intentions, emotions, or actions. The high degree of judgment contained within these letters acts like an energetic vacuum, attracting into a person's life experiences that reflect internal judgments, in line with the cosmic principle of like attracts like.

The primary goal of this measure is to lead individuals to realize that they are the creators of their own lives through their thoughts, emotions, actions, and speech. By acknowledging this, individuals can consciously and responsibly shape their reality.

The Letters of Aspiration: ThLQ'Tz (טלקצ)

Another categorization I wish to discuss is the division of letters into upper and lower letters. Among the twenty-two letters of the Hebrew alphabet, there are four letters that rise above the writing line and one letter that descends below the writing line.

Diagram 22: Letters Ascending Above the Line

The letters ascending above the writing line in handwriting are Thet, Lamed, and Tzadi. Out of these upper letters, the letter Lamed is unique, as it also rises above the line in both print and handwriting.

In essence, these upper letters symbolize aspirations toward higher concepts, principles, or ideals. For instance, the letter Thet represents the desire for unique and creative self-expression, the letter Lamed strives for a spiritual ideal—to high moral principles and divine justice, and the letter Tzadi yearns for spiritual elevation and transcendence.

However, in states of emotional imbalance, these elevated vibrations may lead individuals with these letters in their names toward fantasies and grandiose and unrealistic dreams, along with a feeling of superiority over others.

Diagram 23: A Letter Descending Below the Line

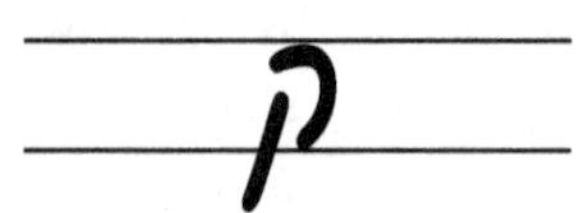

Descending letters extend downward below the writing line, symbolizing the inclination toward the matters of the earthly realm. Among the twenty-two letters of the alphabet, only the letter Qof descends below the line, both in handwriting and in print. The letter Qof belongs to the water element letters, and as such, it draws a person downward toward the world of emotions and the subconscious.

According to the Kabbalistic teachings, in the inhibiting aspect, these letters tend to evoke a sense of alienation and difficulty in accepting differences. This pertains to differences found in others as well as within themselves.

The Letters of Redemption:
CMNP'Tz (כמנפץ) - Final Letters

In addition to the twenty-two primary letters of the Hebrew alphabet, there are five unique letters that are written differently when appearing at the end of a word or a name, both in print and in handwriting. These five letters are Caf, Mem, Nun, Peh, and Tzadi, known in Kabbalistic terms as the letters of redemption.

**Diagram 24: The Letters of Redemption
and Their Gematrical Values**

Hebrew Letter	Hebrew Letter Name	Gematrical Value
ך	FINAL CAF	500
ם	FINAL MEM	600
ן	FINAL NUN	700
ף	FINAL PEH	800
ץ	FINAL TZADI	900

When these letters appear at the beginning or middle of a name or a word, their graphical form is typically bent, whereas, at the end, they tend to be straight.

Additionally, these letters not only change their graphical form but also their numerical value. The final letters extend the numerical sequence from the last letter, Tav, which has a numerical value of four hundred. Consequently, the numerical values of these final letters are as follows: Caf equals five hundred, Mem equals six hundred, Nun equals seven hundred, Peh equals eight hundred, and Tzadi equals nine hundred.

These letters carry significant meanings and exhibit distinct tendencies. Understanding their meanings and energetic power is important when considering names for children that include these letters. The term "final" letters denotes their role in guiding individuals toward completion, complementing the developmental processes embodied by the initial twenty-two letters.

The primary purpose of the final letters is to aid individuals in releasing fixed and rigid conditions, freeing themselves from the bondage of the illusionary ego and anything that hinders their highest good, thereby enabling them to embark on their spiritual path.

Moreover, people whose first names contain final letters carry a profound commitment to doing things for the common good. Therefore, it is highly recommended that they actively engage in spiritual development; otherwise, these letters may lead them into stagnation, impeding their progress without their awareness.

Each of the five final letters embodies the measure of complete judgment. When they appear in a person's first name, they often present challenges, while in the last name, they offer support.

The final letters are powerful, possess a transformative quality, and have a significant impact on a person. They tend to amplify the traits associated with the letter, in either a constructive or inhibiting aspect, pushing a person to extremes.

The purpose of the final letters is to endow the experiences of a person's life journey with a distinctive flavor, enabling them to truly sense the quality of their choices and gain experiential wisdom. In their constructive aspect, these letters strengthen individuals and provide the opportunity to purify themselves from the karma accumulated over their life incarnations. Moreover, they assist in shedding the limiting "shells" (impurities, negativity) that enveloped them in their current incarnation.

People whose names include one of these final letters are presented with a remarkable opportunity to effect significant changes in their lives. Through profound inner processes, they can attain redemption, which is why these letters are referred to as the letters of redemption in the esoteric teachings of Kabbalah.

The term redemption in the Bible signifies liberation and salvation from bondage and exile, so in order to understand what redemption is, we must first understand what exile is.

Kabbalistic teachings suggest that when individuals fail to break free from their personal limitations, restrictions, and comfort zones, their souls remain imprisoned in a private state of exile. Escaping this exile requires transcending narrow-mindedness and confronting the dark and fixed aspects within oneself. This transformative journey leads to self-redemption—a profound connection with the divine source within.

An example of this process is found in the ancient biblical command given to Abraham: *"Now the Lord said to Abram, 'Go from your country, and from your relatives, and from your father's house, to the land which I will show you."* (*Genesis*, Chapter 12, Verse 1)

In this verse, God commands Abraham, the father of many nations, to rise and journey forward. It illustrates that redemption involves movement, progress, and breaking free from stagnation. It encourages stepping outside our comfort zone through voluntary choices, leading to self-discovery and embracing spiritual growth. Interestingly, the final letter Caf appears seven times in this short verse in Hebrew, further emphasizing this concept.

The final letters possess high spiritual vibrational frequencies and may not be suitable for everyone. In ancient times, these letters were given to prophets, priests and seers like Abraham and Aaron, who had the capacity to handle the energetic forces and spiritual missions they carried. In the current era of spiritual awakening, most individuals with these letters may not possess the fully developed spiritual awareness and application necessary to manage these powerful forces. As a result, the high vibrational frequencies and essence of these letters can present challenges for those who bear them.

When an individual's name ends with a final letter, overlooking their spiritual mission may result in challenging life experiences.

When selecting a name that ends with a final letter, it is advisable to choose a name that is ideally associated with a wise and righteous individual known for a life free of undue suffering and hardships. It is important to note that the final letters in a person's surname are endowed with a significant power of implementation.

The Degree of Mental and Emotional Stability

Another important division of the letters is based on their graphical shape: those with a stable base or sturdy legs and those standing on one leg or swaying on a narrow and unstable base. This categorization offers insights into the inherent stability of each letter, aiding in recognizing human inclinations toward grounding, balance, and daily stability.

Diagram 25: Energetic Stability of The Letter

The Degree of Energetic Stability	Hebrew Letter Name	Hebrew Letter Shape
Letters with Stable Base	BET	ב
	CAF	כ
	NUN	נ
	PEH	פ
	TZADI	צ
	FINAL MEM	ם
Letters with Stable Legs	ALEF	א
	GIMEL	ג
	HEH	ה
	KHET	ח
	MEM	מ
	TAV	ת
Letters with Unstable Base	DALET	ד
	VAV	ו
	ZAYIN	ז
	THET	ט
	YOD	י
	LAMED	ל
	SAMECH	ס
	AHYIN	ע
	QOF	ק
	RESH	ר
	SHIN	ש
	FINAL CAF	ך
	FINAL NUM	ן
	FINAL PEH	ף
	FINAL TZADI	ץ

When analyzing an individual's name, a key aspect is to examine the level of mental stability indicated by the letters in their name.

**Diagram 26: Letter That Stands on a Wide Base,
Two Legs, and One Leg**

ד   ג   ב

Graphically, the twenty-two Hebrew letters and the five final letters can be divided into three main groups: those standing on a stable base, providing grounding; those on two legs, offering balance; and those on one leg or a narrow base, exhibiting instability. For more information on this topic, please refer to the chapter titled "The Letters."

Before concluding this significant chapter, I wish to highlight another important point. Throughout my writing, I frequently use the term "raw energy" to underscore the idea that "everything is expected, and permission is granted" to a person.

Let us take, for example, the letters of judgment Dalet and Vav. These letters, in their raw essence, carry energies of self-centered focus, a desire to receive for oneself, judgmental attitudes, and conditional giving. When a person's name contains one or more of these letters, and they develop an awareness of these inherent psychological traits, they are given the opportunity to transform them through free choice, thereby altering their approach to life and people.

Having understood the fundamental essence of the Hebrew letters, we can now delve deeper. In the next chapter, you will explore your uniqueness, strengths, and weaknesses, among other aspects.

CHAPTER 7

The Hebrew Letters

"Not Christian or Jew or Muslim, not Hindu, Buddhist, Sufi, or Zen.

Not any religion or cultural system. I am not from the East or the West, not out of the ocean or up from the ground, not natural or ethereal, not composed of elements at all.

I do not exist, am not an entity in this world or the next, did not descend from Adam and Eve or any origin story.

My place is the placeless, a trace of the traceless. Neither body nor soul.

I belong to the beloved, have seen the two worlds as one and that one call to and know, first, last, outer, inner, only that breath-breathing human being."

Jalal ad-Din Rumi

אבגדההוזחטיכלמנסעפצפקרשת

*"The path is known to everyone, but few are
the ones who choose to follow it."*

Jalal al-Din Rumi

Uniqueness and Purpose

The letter Alef (אָלֶף), being the first letter of the Hebrew alphabet holds immense significance. It is widely regarded as a blessed letter that unlocks the gateway to one's fortune. Alef embodies the vital life force energy present in all things, known by different names in various ancient languages and cultures. In Judaism, this energy represents the "force of life." In the Genesis stories, it is referred to as "the spirit of God." Christianity calls it "the holy breath," while in Hinduism and Buddhism, it is known as the **prana energy**[14]. In Chinese culture, this energy is referred to as "chi."

This life force, symbolized by the letter Alef, represents everything in the universe and existence. It permeates all aspects, enabling our physical bodies to exist and sustaining existence itself. More vital than air, its absence would cause our energetic body to die out, followed by our physical body. This energy departs the physical body upon death. It is the same energy mentioned in the Genesis creation narrative: *"and breathed into his nostrils the breath of life" (Genesis, Chapter 2, Verse 7)*

---

[14] Prana energy, in Hindu philosophy, is the vital life force or cosmic energy that permeates the universe and sustains all living beings. A primordial energy that flows through the body, governing physical and mental well-being.

According to Hindu philosophy, as derived from the **Upanishads**[15], human consciousness develops through the energetic flow of Prana, distributed throughout our body. This life force encompasses energies from the sun, moon, and water and is present in the air we breathe. Unfortunately, many people are unaware of how to breathe correctly, and as a result, they fail to absorb this energy fully. As long as this remains the case, the development of humanity's divine consciousness will be hindered.

The purpose of this high spiritual letter is to remind us that the Pranic breath directly connects a person to their soul. Kabbalistic teachings assert that every aspect of the universe contains the spiritual life energy symbolized by Alef. Without this force, life as we know it would cease, rendering existence an impossibility.

The energy of the letter Alef is tranquil, representing a state of being—the ability to be present in the moment, from a place of stillness, without reference to past or future. It expresses awareness of wholeness and unity and the essence of divine potential in the human soul. Alef indicates the energy embracing two opposite divine forces, held together in complete harmony. Connecting to Alef's vibrational frequencies allows one to break the cycle of karma.

The letter Alef includes all spiritual forces present in other letters within it, analogous to a white ray of light encompassing all colors. It radiates its spiritual light onto other letters.

The letter Alef is the first letter that opens the essence of The Torah's commandments, including the Ten Moral Commandments: "*I am the Lord Thy God*" (אנכי יהוה אלהיך). It is also the first letter in the name of the first human being, Adam (אדם), signifying the divine essence inherent in humans. Moreover, the Hebrew word for God, "Elohim" (אלוהים), begins with the letter Alef, further reinforcing its spiritual significance.

---

[15]   The Upanishads are the oldest scriptures of Hinduism. These scriptures deal with meditation and philosophy, as well as a variety of stories about the creation of the world, the war of the gods, the flood, etc.

The Letter in Creation Stories

The letter Alef makes its first appearance in the biblical Genesis stories within the opening phrase, *"In the beginning, God created the heavens and the earth"* (*Genesis*, Chapter 1, Verses1-2). In Hebrew, both "God" (אֱלֹהִים) and "the" (אֵת) begin with the letter Alef. Alef appears in this verse within the word God (Elohim), a term representing the supreme being who created the world and governs it. Immediately after, Alef also appears in the word "the."

The Hebrew word for "the" (אֵת) consists of two letters: Alef and Tav. Alef, as the alphabet's first letter, represents the beginning of processes, while Tav, the last letter, symbolizes the completion of processes. This pairing highlights the wholeness that Alef encompasses. The word "the," opening the creation stories, suggests that divinity encompasses everything, from the beginning to the end, integrating both cause and effect.

Interestingly, inverting the order of the Hebrew letters for the word "the" (את) yields "cell" (תא), the smallest unit of all living organisms. Proper cellular function is vital to our physical existence. Thus, to maintain our bodily health, it is crucial to prioritize correct breathing, as emphasized in ancient Eastern teachings, including the Pranayama breathing technique and conscious breathing.

Pronunciation of the Letter

The letter Alef is pronounced as "A-lef" and can be represented in English as A, E, or AH, influenced by its position in a word or name. For example, when Alef appears as the last letter in a name, it may be paired with the letter Heh. Thus, the name Amrita, in English, would typically be written as Amritah.

The name, pronunciation, and meaning of the letter Alef offer profound insights into its essence and the potent energy it embodies. Interpretations of its name and pronunciation can be viewed from several perspectives. One perspective focuses on "wonder" (פלא), a word derived by reversing the letter's name (אלף). This word conveys the notion of magic, miracles, and divine occurrences.

Another interpretation arises from the letter's pronunciation, leading to two meanings. The first is "commander" (אַלּוּף), a term representing the notion of a governor, ruler, sovereign, or someone of high rank. The second interpretation is "taming" (אִילוּף), which pertains to the act of educating, guiding, and training individuals or animals to perform specific tasks. These interpretations suggest that the letter Alef possesses an extraordinary energetic force that transcends the natural realm.

Letter's Graphic Shape

Among the twenty-two letters of the Hebrew alphabet, the letter Alef is unique in that its graphical shape is open in all directions, symbolizing its ability to embrace any possibilities. It is open upward toward the wisdom of the spiritual realm and downward toward the matters of the earthly realm, embodying an understanding of both higher and lower realms.

The letter's shape is also open on its right and left sides, toward the wisdom encapsulated by the preceding letter, Tav, and the succeeding letter, Bet. As such, Alef contains a high level of spiritual energy. Its level of openness plays a significant role in aiding humanity to embrace unified consciousness.

The letter Alef possesses a distinct graphical form, featuring a body with two legs firmly planted on the ground, providing balance and stability, and two arms extended upward and outward. These arms resemble antennas or extensions, reaching toward the upper realms, toward infinity, as if seeking to receive and spread divine light emanating from "ein" (אין), meaning "nothing" to "ani" (אני), meaning "I am." The Hebrew word "ein" (nothing) represents the infinite celestial divine light. Alef's shape symbolizes an inherent willingness toward receptiveness and giving.

The open configuration of Alef signifies a lack of limitations. Nothing restricts the spread of its light, which radiates freely, unimpeded by earthly matters, societal norms, rules, or human constraints. This level of openness grants a person the ability to think outside the box and observe life with equanimity. It encourages viewing life with tranquility, openness, and a neutral perspective, thereby creating a more meaningful present.

Diagram 27: Weathervane

The form of Alef resembles a wind vane, which pushes and directs the wind. Just as the wind vane guides the wind, Alef similarly drives the spirituality within a person. Additionally, Alef's shape is reminiscent of the open posture in a dance, akin to the **Sufi Dance**[16], where individuals surrender to the spinning motion, twirling slowly and experiencing a profound balance and unity between thoughts, emotions, body and soul.

---

[16]　The Sufi Dance, also known as the whirling Darvish dance, is a routine in which the dancer spins in an attempt to reach a sense of elation through which they can connect with God.

Diagram 28: Sufi Dance

Letter's Gematrical Value

The gematrical value of the letter Alef' is one, a value associated with unity, originality, primacy, independence, and fundamental guiding principles. The number one embodies a sense of commencement, signifying the birth of new ideas and opportunities, as well as the initiation of fresh perspectives. It represents the vital force that propels individuals forward, empowering them to take the lead and overcome obstacles on their path toward complete self-realization.

The number one, being the first of the single-digit numbers arising from zero, signifies the all-encompassing nature of infinity. It heralds the start of a new system and a clean slate. One is a conceptual, theoretical, logical, and intellectual number, denoting qualities of unity, wholeness, and independence.

Furthermore, the gematrical value of the Hebrew word Alef (אלף) itself is 111. This value obtained by adding the numerical values of its constituent letters (1+30+80=111) highlights its preeminent status as first and foremost in all matters and aspects of life. This value underscores Alef's foundational significance, emphasizing its role as the genesis of new beginnings and the bedrock upon which all other ideas and concepts can be built.

The Planet Associated with the Alef

Kabbalistic teachings link the letter Alef to the planet Uranus, known in Hebrew as Oron (אורון). This association provides insights into the qualities embodied by Alef.

Uranus, classified as a generational planet in Western astrology, is one of the largest planets in our solar system. It is associated with attributes such as nobility, progress, modernization, and growth. Uranus is connected to the individual's higher self (the "I AM"), the development of personal and collective consciousness, and prophetic abilities. It represents the spark that ignites advanced inventions, groundbreaking discoveries, flashes of genius, inspiration, and enlightenment, symbolizing the infinite potential of the human spirit.

Uranus represents a state of mind that enables individuals to transcend narrow viewpoints and connect with a higher, more elevated perspective. It symbolizes humanity's capacity to expand their perception beyond the usual limits and to achieve a more comprehensive understanding of both the world and the self.

Uranus also symbolizes the human capacity for holistic observation, the ability to see the interconnectedness among all aspects of life, including mental, social, economic, and spiritual domains. By integrating these facets into a unified whole, individuals can attain a more enlightened state of being, encompassing a broader range of human experiences.

The vibrational frequencies of Uranus are characterized by keywords such as independence, innovation, uniqueness, rebellion, breakthrough, and progress. These energies significantly impact an individual's awareness, challenging established norms, social structures, and attachments to beliefs, opinions, values, frameworks, and people. The frequencies of Uranus urge individuals to break free from attachments, routines, and conventions, shatter old boundaries, and replace them with new ones that offer greater opportunities for soul growth and expansion.

For many generations, humanity has been conditioned to live in a state of victimhood and separation, led to believe that they are "victims of circumstances" without real power, controlled by their genes, biology and external forces.

However, this paradigm is undergoing a significant shift. Today, we find ourselves in a historical period where it is recognized that our lives are controlled by our consciousness, our perceptions, our reactions to life and people, and, most importantly, our willingness to open up to developmental processes. We possess the power to shift our mindset and lives. The letter Alef embodies this spirit of openness and willingness, essential for this transformative journey toward a more conscious and empowered life.

In astrology, Uranus is acknowledged as the catalyst for the Great Awakening, earning the nickname "The Great Awakener" due to its ability to invoke significant shifts in consciousness. Uranus is at the forefront of new technological developments and the energy that liberates humans from mental enslavement. Its vibrational frequencies offer a refreshing and unique perspective, encouraging people to view life differently and create a new order in the world and their lives. The influence of Uranus urges individuals to break free from limiting beliefs and embrace a new paradigm, paving the way for personal and collective evolution.

The Groups the Letter Alef is Associated With

Air Element Letter

The element associated with the letter Alef is air—a light and quick element that facilitates energetic connections. It symbolizes the energy that provides individuals with breathing space and, with it, the opportunity to re-examine things. The letter Alef represents the highest expression of the air element, signifying its purest and most refined form, also known as Prana Energy.

Alef is an airy, mobile, light, and swift letter, with the power to illuminate the soul, brighten consciousness, and clarify logic. This letter endows individuals with spiritual and mental intelligence, original thinking, curiosity and imagination. It is characterized by effective communication through speech, writing, persuasion, and social engagement.

Soul Letter

The letter Alef belongs to the group of soul letters. It encourages individuals to embrace their life journey as perpetual, free-spirited students. This approach allows them to fully feel and experience life as it unfolds, flowing with whatever life brings.

As a soul letter, Alef represents spiritual truths essential to one's life journey. These truths involve a deep understanding of oneself and the pursuit of absolute truth. To gain this profound knowledge, individuals must remain open to new experiences, continually learning and exploring both themselves and their surroundings. This process involves uncovering the hidden wisdom within the letters of the alphabet.

The Measure of Grace and Compassion

The letter Alef embodies the measure of ultimate grace and compassion. This measure includes traits such as grace, compassion, generosity, and magnanimity. The letter instills in a person faith, optimism, hope, kindness, consideration, understanding, charity, empathy, and caring. It grants them the ability for unconditional giving, the capacity to see the positive in every situation, the glass-half-full mindset, and the willingness to forgive, pardon, let go, and become free from situations and people that do not serve their highest good, thereby achieving personal freedom.

A Letter of Movement

The letter Alef possesses a dynamic nature, embodying motion, drive, mobility, flexibility, lightness, and flow. These qualities enable individuals associated with this letter to progress, step out of their comfort zones, disconnect from situations that are binding and fixating, and embark on new paths. Alef's qualities support individuals in coping better, growing personally, and navigating life's complexities in a more light-hearted and creative way.

Spiritual Letter

Alef belongs to the group of AMSh (אמש) letters, a group of three letters endowed with nobility, wisdom, insight, spiritual power, vision, and the purpose of creating a new reality. Its inherent spiritual qualities enable individuals to embody faith, mobility, lightness, fluidity, and the ability to break free from the constraints that hinder their uniqueness and freedom and start anew when needed.

The power of faith and creative movement that Alef embodies can be found in the biblical figure Abraham. Abraham, with his unwavering faith in God, embarked on a journey of self-discovery and started his journey in life anew, from scratch.

Strengths

The strengths associated with the letter Alef include acceptance, trust, faith, courage, dedication to ideals, empathy, kindness, compassion, hope, optimism, enthusiasm, independence, uniqueness, progress, creativity, curiosity, willingness, openness, adaptability to uncertainty, adventurousness, holism, desire for new experiences, and an intuitive ability to discern right actions in any given moment.

Weaknesses

The weaknesses associated with the letter Alef include difficulty staying grounded, innocence, naivety, hastiness, distraction, dispersion in many directions, and difficulty setting boundaries. Individuals with the letter Alef in their name who have experienced a crisis during childhood may find it challenging to be fully present in the moment and struggle to stay grounded in this earthly realm. The hindering aspects of the letter Alef manifest as restlessness, unawareness of people's motives and behaviors, and a tendency to take uncalculated risks.

Due to the potent energetic forces contained within the letter Alef, in a state of energetic imbalance, its vibrational frequencies may lead to a dysregulated nervous system. Consequently, the individual may experience symptoms such as restlessness and a mental distraction.

Furthermore, the inherent rebelliousness and the desire to remain true to oneself, while invaluable qualities, may result in an undeveloped personality, appearing as a rebellious and disobedient character. This may manifest in behaviors such as disobedience, provocation, and an ongoing struggle with authority figures.

אבגדהוזחטיכלמנסעפצקרשת

"God turns you from one feeling to another and teaches by means of opposites so that you will have two wings to fly, not one. If thelight is in your heart, you will find your way home."

Jalal al-Din Rumi

Uniqueness and Purpose

The letter Bet (בֵּית) is the second letter in the Hebrew alphabet and is the letter that opens the Bible and the Genesis narratives about the creation of the world and humankind. This letter, with its dynamic and energetic force, creates a distinct and differentiated reality, encompassing both a creator and the creation—a creational space with a dual nature that contains within it an oxymoron.

The vibrational frequencies of the letter Bet connect individuals to a dualistic consciousness, an awareness that perceives the world and everything in it as consisting of two different and opposite categories, such as good and evil, right and wrong.

The letter Bet symbolizes the "house," the creational framework in which the soul undergoes lessons through time and space, imparting an understanding of the law of cause and effect.

The letter's purpose is to connect the person to their inner house, to their inner sanctum—a unified divine space that exists within. Through this connection, individuals can fully comprehend the essential nature of duality inherent in all creation. This understanding will help the individual to unite all contradictions within themselves and thus transcend above the dualistic vibrational frequencies and attain a state of unity.

The Letter in Creation Stories

The first time we encounter the letter Bet in the biblical stories is in the opening verse of *Genesis*, in the words "beginning" and "created." *"In the beginning, God created the heavens and the earth."* (*Genesis*, Chapter 1, Verse 1)

This verse provides us with a philosophical and theological perspective on the initiation of the world's creation. It portrays a process where a clear distinction emerges between the upper world, symbolizing eternal spirituality, and the lower world, representing temporary physicality. In this creation, a new divine reality is forged, encapsulating both the concepts of unity consciousness and the dichotomy of dualistic consciousness.

The words "In the beginning" (בראשית ברא) symbolize a process of separation from unified divine light and an entry into a home—a space where created beings undergo various developmental processes. This space serves as a playground for these beings, allowing them to explore different facets of their "self", and experience various earthly adventures that facilitate their learning and evolution.

Pronunciation

The letter Bet is pronounced as "Bet" and can be represented in English as B or V, depending on its position in a word or name and its hard or soft pronunciation.

The pronunciation of the letter Bet hints at its essence and the secret it conceals within. The letter's name is "House" (Bait), which also represents its interpretation. The Hebrew word for "house" embodies both spiritual and earthly meanings.

In the spiritual context, the meaning of the word house is structure and tabernacle, a sacred space where the divine spirit dwells. This house exists both inside and outside of us. A house is not just a physical location but an inner quality. It is a quiet inner space that embodies a state of being and acceptance, concepts that the letter Alef speaks of.

In an earthly context, the house refers to a defined and enclosed external structure - the physical and earthly house. A house is a frame, a structure, and a residence where we spend much of our human lives. We live, work, and spend significant time in structures, and even our thinking tends to be structured. Therefore, the house (בית) serves as the transition point from inside to outside and the viewpoint from which we observe the world. This sacred structure and space are known in the Hebrew language by names such as "House of Creation" (Beit Habryiah), "House of God" (Beit El), "Tabernacle" (Beit Hamishkan), "Temple" (Beit Hamikdash), or "House of Glory" (Beit Hacavod).

Diagram 29: The Letter as the Shape of a House

The first two letters of the Hebrew alphabet, Alef and Bet, represent the two primary planes on which we perceive, understand, and live our lives: the unitary and the dual planes. These letters thus draw our attention to the two primary levels of human awareness: unity and duality.

Graphic Shape

The graphical shape of the letter Bet resembles a defined structure, much like a house with a base, roof, separating walls between the outside and inside, and a single open side, akin to a welcoming entrance of a building. This shape symbolizes that the letter, like a house, represents a physical place where the soul can find rest, strengthen itself, establish roots, ground itself, and secure its position in the earthly realm before embarking on a journey into the earthly material world.

The role of a house is to protect, provide shelter, and a sense of belonging and to assist the life force in organizing itself. The words in the Hebrew language that include the letter Bet emphasize this theme. Words such as "house" (bait), "building" (benyan), "foundation" (basis), "security" (bitachon), "health" (briut), "blessing" (bracha), and more, all indicate structure, certainty, security, and the absence of danger.

The graphical shape of the letter Bet is closed off from three directions: upward, symbolizing its closure to the affairs of the spiritual world; downward, signifying its closure to the affairs of the earthly matters; and it turns it's back to the wisdom embodied in the preceding letter, Alef. The degree of closure that the letter Bet embodies reflects the soul's inclination to accumulate emotions, situations, and life events.

The letter's graphical form symbolizes the energy that constrains and limits consciousness. This energy tends to draw a person toward a separate consciousness and a tendency to see the differences in everything and everyone rather than the unifying aspects. This shape signifies a profound closure toward diverse ideas, opinions, people, and situations. Such a level of closure often leads to a narrow point of view, distorting a person's perception of themselves and the world around them.

Gematrical Value

The gematrical value of the letter Bet is two, a number often associated with the concept of duality. While duality is typically given a negative interpretation, it actually encompasses both opposing forces and represents the two sides of the same coin.

The negative interpretation of duality primarily arises from situations of inequality and an imbalanced perspective, where a narrow viewpoint focuses on one side while neglecting, preferring, or failing to acknowledge the other. This inequality creates tension and conflict, leading to division and strategies of divide and conquer.

The value of the letter Bet symbolizes the principle by which two opposing forces can coexist peacefully and harmoniously. It represents concepts such as light and vessel, body and spirit, night and day, light and darkness, male and female. This value embodies coexistence and qualities like responsiveness, receptivity, holding, partnership, and cooperation. It relates to concepts like 'me and you,' diplomacy, and maintaining a status quo.

Even the graphical form of this numerical value echoes the principle of coexistence. The shape of the number two resembles a person sitting on their knees, leaning forward with a bowed head. This posture may be interpreted as submission, weakness, or helplessness, but in reality, it symbolizes the ability to be receptive and accepting. These qualities allow something to take form. The ability to absorb and hold energy enables alignment with the other side, facilitating coexistence and life in unity.

The Planet Associated with Bet

"He made the letter Bet king and bound a crown to it and combined one with another, and with them, he formed Saturn in the Universe..." (*Sepher Yetzirah*, Chapter 4, Verse 5)

Sefer Yetzirah connects the letter Bet to the planet Saturn, thus providing us with a profound understanding of the qualities the letter contains and how its vibrational frequencies shape our human reality.

The planet Saturn is one of the two planets known in Western astrology as supporting planets. Saturn symbolizes the collective tendencies of humanity. Its role is to guide individuals through experiential lessons about **lessons in time**[17] and **the law of cause and effect.**[18] These experiences help individuals understand that they are the creators of their life reality.

Saturn, with its strict and disciplined nature, represents patriarchal thought patterns. Its vibrational frequencies influence matters of reward and punishment. The energy of Saturn guides individuals through challenging experiences and maturation processes within the framework of limitations, rules, and boundaries. The purpose of these trials is to foster a correct viewpoint, balanced ego, tenderness, and compassion. They aim to bring individuals to a state of clearer self-perception and understanding of the world,

---

[17] The term lessons in time refers to the profound spiritual experiences and wisdom gained by the soul as it journeys through various life periods across its incarnations. These lessons are pivotal for the soul's growth and evolution, encompassing trials, challenges, and opportunities encountered in each lifetime. They are seen as essential aspects that contribute significantly to the soul's developmental journey.

[18] The law of cause and effect is a foundational concept in various disciplines, including philosophy and science. It posits that every action or behavior has consequences, with these consequences being closely linked to the nature of the action itself. This principle highlights the idea that our choices and actions significantly shape our reality. Understanding these intricate relationships is crucial for making informed decisions and effectively navigating life's complexities.

realizing that external realities are, in essence, reflections of their inner soul.

The processes Saturn orchestrates are neither easy nor straightforward. Its vibrational frequencies compel individuals to let go of rigid thinking, limiting beliefs, and fixed patterns that often unconsciously govern their lives, urging them to abandon identities that do not serve their soul's path. Saturn presents challenges but also opportunities for growth and development. Through these experiences, individuals delve deep into their souls, confront hidden complexities, and recreate themselves from a place of free choice, becoming masters of their destiny.

Unpleasant experiences are an inseparable part of the learning process, sometimes essential for better organizing our lives and gaining self-confidence through deep self-knowledge. From initial rigidity, positive traits such as understanding, compassion, and patience may emerge, along with significant values like self-respect, respect for others, and a commitment to good deeds.

Known as the Lord of Karma, Saturn serves as a teacher and guide, directing individuals to take personal responsibility for their actions rather than attributing them to others or circumstances. Even if one tries to avoid life's lessons, the experiences will persist until one learns to develop qualities related to personal responsibility, discipline, diligence, perseverance, and adherence in pursuing their goals.

The Groups the Letter Bet is Associated With

Earth Element Letter

The element of the letter Bet is earth, a rooted, strong, and solid element characterized by physical strength, moderation, patience, survival ability, resilience, conventionality, and the preservation of what exists. Bet, being an earthly letter standing on a broad base, indicates a level of stability that helps a person maintain balance and inner equilibrium throughout their earthly journey.

Creational Mind Letter

The letter Bet is a creational mind letter, symbolizing the human mind and the energetic power capable of creating mental patterns and thought structures in our cosmic space. Characterized by its dualistic nature, it can create mental patterns with dualistic tendencies and grant these patterns that deal with both unity and separate consciousness, life force, and independent existence.

Understanding the letter Bet is crucial as its wisdom forms the cornerstone for developing the consciousness of unity. It invites individuals to examine the lens through which they view themselves and the surrounding world, scrutinize their intentions and motives, and understand their origin, whether they emanate from the frequency of unity and interconnectedness or duality and separateness.

Hard and Soft Sound

As a creative mind letter that can have a hard or soft phonetic emphasis, the letter Bet can vary the intensity of its vibrational frequency. A hard sound gives the letter a masculine (yang) and more intense tone, while a softer sound imparts a feminine (yin) and gentler tone. As a hard-sounding letter, it signifies difficulty in softening and being flexible when needed. Conversely, as a soft-sounding letter, it represents the ability to be flexible and dissolve the ego.

For instance, when the letter Bet appears as a hard-sounded (B) letter in the word "bitachon" (בִּטָּחוֹן), meaning "security," it possesses greater strength and presence, but there is also a higher risk of ego-driven action. Conversely, when the letter Bet appears in its soft form (V), as in the word "ahava" (אהבה), meaning "love," it weakens its vibrational frequency, thus diminishing the influence of the ego and allowing for greater capacity to give and receive love.

Soul Letter

The letter Bet is classified as one of the soul letters. As a soul letter, it represents the spiritual truths that an individual is meant to acquire during their life journey. These truths involve complete self-knowledge, an awareness that arises from integrating opposing aspects within the soul: the consciousness of unity and separateness, the spiritual and material aspects, the feminine and masculine principles, and the balance between them. To achieve this spiritual wisdom, individuals must be open to new experiences, continuously learn, explore themselves and their surroundings, and seek to uncover the hidden wisdom within the letters of the alphabet.

The Measure of Mercy and Judgment

Bet embodies both the measures of mercy and judgment. While its initial tendency leans toward judgment, its dual nature enables individuals to exercise discretion and choose between these two contrasting principles. The letter emphasizes the importance of cultivating a consciousness of unity within ourselves. Unity is the power that enables us to transcend earthly confines, rise above them, and master ourselves rather than being enslaved by the laws of separate consciousness. Unity consciousness is our point of origin and our ultimate destination.

Strengths

The letter Bet embodies qualities such as realism, grounding, constancy, structure, ambition, conservatism, purposefulness, seriousness, determination, consistency, practicality, perseverance, restraint, caution, discretion, durability, discipline, adherence to law and order, perception, a sense of proportion, patience, tolerance, frugality, devotion, orientation, and resourcefulness. It grants its bearers the ability to make slow, systematic, focused, thorough, and consistent progress toward their goals in a constructive manner.

Weaknesses

The weaknesses associated with the letter Bet include a consciousness of separateness, procrastination, conventionalism, skepticism, suspicion, narrow-mindedness, stinginess, strictness, self-interest, manipulation, judgmental tendencies, an excessive need for structure, order, and method, excessive stubbornness, utilitarianism, materialism, a desire to receive for oneself, rigidity, cynicism, pessimism, adhesions, attachments, and a tendency to remain stagnant and unyielding in the face of change, clinging to the existing.

אבּגּדההוזחטיכּלמנסעפצקרשת

"The Lord God planted a garden toward the east, in Eden;
and there He placed the man whom He had formed."

Genesis, Chapter 2, Verse 8

Uniqueness and Purpose

The letter Gimel (גִּימֶל), the third letter in the Hebrew alphabet, symbolizes the path of kindness and benevolence and represents the virtue that enriches individuals with longevity, spiritual abundance, and blessings.

Gimel is associated with hidden knowledge and heightened telepathic and intuitive capabilities. Its vibrational frequencies expand an individual's consciousness, connecting them to divine spiritual wisdom, intuition, and hidden realms— a space where endless possibilities of creation exist.

The letter's purpose is to expand individual consciousness, develop awareness of human feelings and verbal expression, and connect individuals to **metacognition**[19]. It underscores the idea that the human mind is limited. To properly understand ourselves and the world around us, we must first learn to connect with our feelings and the unconscious.

---

[19] Metacognition is a high-level perception that includes awareness of the thought processes and their content and the identification of the patterns underlying them.

The Letter in Creation Stories

The first independent encounter with the letter Gimel in the *Genesis* stories is in the word "gan" (גן), meaning "garden." This story emphasizes that divine creation takes place within the boundaries spoken by the letter Beit: *"The Lord God planted a garden toward the east, in Eden."* (*Genesis*, Chapter 2, Verse 8)

This reference to the garden represents a powerful metaphor for creation and nurturing life. The use of the letter "Gimel" in this context highlights the role of benevolence in creating a spiritually rich and fulfilling existence. The placement of the garden in the east symbolizes the dawn of a new beginning, representing the potential for growth and renewal.

The Hebrew word garden (gan) has various meanings, each carrying distinct and unique significance. The first is a **gene**[20] (gen-גן), pertaining to the fundamental physical and functional unit of heredity, comprised of protein and DNA. The second, "garden" (gan - גן), refers to fertile ground, representing the location from which Adam and Eve were banished in the biblical story. The third, "garden" (gan-גן), denotes a place where individuals experience growth and development, such as a kindergarten.

Diagram 30: Gene / DNA

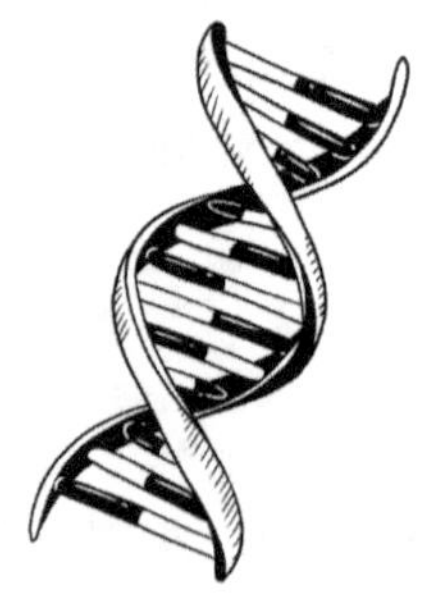

---

[20]   Gene is a segment of DNA that contains the instructions for building a specific protein or performing a particular function within an organism's cells.

The word garden (gan) has many idioms in Hebrew. For example, "gan eruyim" (גן אירועים), meaning "event garden," is a place where important life events such as **Bar/Bat Mitzvah**[21] ceremonies, weddings and circumcisions are celebrated. Another well-known idiom is "gan eden" (גן עדן), meaning "Heaven"— the place we go after death when we return our earthly equipment or physical form to the earth.

Pronunciation

The letter Gimel is pronounced as "Gi-mel" and can be represented in English as G or J, depending on its position in a word or name and its hard or soft pronunciation.

The pronunciation of the letter Gimel reveals its essence. It incorporates the root letters G, M, and L (גמל) found in the words "Gmul" (גמול) and "Gmila" (גמילה), which signify a number of meaningful interpretations.

The first interpretation of Gmul (גְּמוּל) conveys giving and assisting, emphasizing the idea of rewarding and aiding others. This underscores the importance of benevolence and helping those in need. The second interpretation revolves around the concept of exchange, where one offers something in return for another, highlighting the principles of reciprocity and mutual exchange within human relationships.

The third interpretation pertains to recompense for one's deeds and actions, closely connected to the theory of retribution, concerning the rewards or punishments received based on actions or inactions. This emphasizes the significance of personal agency and accountability, illustrating that one's choices have consequences.

---

[21] Bar Mitzvah and Bat Mitzvah is a significant rite of passage in Judaism, celebrated by Jewish boys and girls upon reaching the age of twelve or thirteen. This ceremony signifies the moment when a young individual transitions into adulthood, assuming personal responsibility for their actions and having the freedom to choose their own path in practicing Judaism.

The act of giving in Hebrew comprises three fundamental components: Gomel (גומל) – the giver; Nigmal (נגמל) – the receiver, and Gmul (גמול) – the thing that is given (the payoff) when all these three intentions are mentioned in the same root.

The words Gemel and Gmila also refer to the process of weaning, symbolizing breaking free from habits or addictions. They signify the stages an individual undergoes to break free from a specific habit or addiction. Upon completing this process, the individual is described as "gamul" (גָמוּל), meaning "weaned."

Kabbalistic scholars point out that the letter Gimel carries within its vibrational frequencies of a **soul burden**[22]. They indicate that those with this letter in their name may face a challenging earthly journey, encountering neglect, oppression, and wrongdoing in various aspects of their lives, be it within their families, social circles, or professional endeavors. The burden associated with the letter Gimel can be understood by the animal the letter is named after "gamal," meaning "camel."

Diagram 31: Camel

---

[22] Soul burden refers to the emotional, psychological, or spiritual weight or responsibility that a person carries. This burden can be related to personal experiences, emotions, or moral dilemmas that deeply affect one's inner self or conscience.

The camel, a desert animal known as the ship of the desert, assists its riders in safely crossing the scorching deserts. It is a relentless giver, requiring very little in return. The camel sustains itself and is highly adaptable to its environment. Despite the challenges of life in the desert, the camel is renowned for its resilience and endurance and for its ability to survive in harsh conditions with minimal resources.

The key attributes often associated with the camel are adjustment and regulation. It is the only mammal that can thermoregulate its body and adapt to extreme temperatures. Its long legs provide it with greater height, keeping its body above the scorching hot desert sands. This elevation allows for longer strides and swift movement, enabling the camel to reach higher speeds. The camel's back, adorned with one or two humps, serves as a reserve of fat, providing energy during journeys and enabling it to transport substantial loads with ease.

The letter Gimel is associated with priesthood and **hidden knowledge,**[23] accessible only to a select few, known as **gatekeepers**[24]. In the past, this knowledge was available solely to spiritual leaders, mystics, healers, shamans, fortune tellers, mediums, and spiritual channelers who possessed advanced intuition and telepathic abilities, enabling them to receive messages from higher realms. These gatekeepers could connect with various states of consciousness and transition seamlessly between them, relying on their advanced intuition and telepathic capabilities. Their exceptional gifts granted them access to hidden knowledge and facilitated communication with other realms—a privilege not easily attainable by the common populace.

---

[23]   Hidden knowledge refers to information or insights that are not widely known or readily accessible, often requiring special access, expertise, or discovery to uncover.

[24]   Gatekeepers are intermediaries believed to control access to spiritual realms or provide guidance and protection during spiritual experiences, often taking on various roles such as psychic guides or protectors of sacred spaces. These guides may assist in channeling spiritual information or offer wisdom, protection, healing and guidance to individuals on their spiritual journeys.

Throughout history, many priests, mystics, and healers have faced persecution enduring physical, emotional, and mental torture. Often accused of practicing witchcraft, they were subjected to trials and executed in horrifying ways. Their voices of truth, knowledge, and divine wisdom were frequently silenced and extinguished through stoning, burning, and hanging. This suppression not only curtailed their ability to express their voice and wisdom but also stifled their creative, spiritual, and divine abilities, leaving a profound and lasting impact.

This is one of the reasons why individuals with the letter Gimel in their name struggle to find their voice and express themselves confidently at the beginning of their life journey. The trauma inflicted upon these gatekeepers has left an enduring mark on their ability to stand up for themselves and verbally express their ideas with clarity and confidence.

The letter Gimel is a powerful creational letter that possesses boundless wisdom. It grants an understanding of how mental traumas and emotional scars passed down from one generation to the next through the "base body," leaving lasting imprints that shape both individual and collective consciousness. Gimel underscores the importance of nurturing and healing the inner creative child, within each of us, allowing for vocal and verbal expression to this inner creative aspect.

Graphic Shape

The letter Gimel exhibits a graphical shape that resembles an individual moving along a path, with a leg and a head extended forward, as if in motion. This representation is akin to the image of a person leaving his "home" (the letter Bet) and heading toward the "door" (the letter Dalet) to provide assistance and support to those in need. Gimel's graphical shape suggests that charitable acts are not merely passive occurrences but stem from an active willingness to emerge from one's own shell and comfort zone.

The graphical shape of the letter Gimel features two open sides and two closed sides, with both legs firmly planted on the ground. This unique shape suggests a degree of openness and closeness toward people and circumstances encountered in life, highlighting the capacity to maintain internal balance and adaptability when faced with life's challenges. In essence, the letter's shape embodies a harmonious flow between openness and closure, allowing for a dynamic and resilient approach to navigating life's complexities.

Diagram 32: Gimel's Graphic Shape

ג

Gematrical Value

The letter Gimel possesses a gematrical value of three, symbolizing the completeness of divine creative forces. This number embodies the concept of synthesis, where two distinct elements merge to create a new, unified whole. This value suggests that all dual and polar concepts (discussed in the letter Bet) are connected by a middle line, creating integration, balance, and harmony. It emphasizes that two opposing factors can unite to form a complete and integrated unity.

Gimel serves as a bridge between contradictory opposites, representing the essence of this concept. Examples include the middle ground between birth and death, which is life; the space between beginning and end, which is the middle; the present that lies between past and future; and the neutral force emerging from the interplay of positive and negative forces. That is the essence of the letter Gimel, to be a bridge between contradictory opposites.

The value attributed to Gimel is associated with positive and constructive qualities such as optimism, spontaneity, creativity, and flow. These traits are closely tied to the "inner child" and testify to an individual's inherent capacity to express emotions naturally and unrestrainedly, free from apprehension or fear.

For instance, children often exhibit unbridled joy through laughter or express anger by stomping their feet and raising their voices. The letter's value suggests that such natural abilities are innate in individuals with this letter in their names, but to express them genuinely, one must connect with their inner child and resolve any underlying issues, if present.

The numerical value of Gimel highlights significant areas of personal development that are essential for all individuals, particularly for those with this letter in their name. The first is self-image, which involves an individual's perception of themselves in relation to their environment. The second area is a connection, encompassing the ability to connect various aspects, such as emotions and physical sensations, and to express them coherently. The third and most crucial area is communication across multiple levels, including internal, external, personal, interpersonal, verbal, non-verbal, spiritual and telepathic. This includes the ability to communicate effectively both with oneself and with others.

Effective communication across diverse levels enables individuals to be attuned to their physical body's needs, like nutrition and rest and fosters a deep connection with their inner emotional and cognitive landscape. It also enables them to receive and convey messages from higher spiritual domains.

Gimel emphasizes the importance of communication as a critical tool for personal and professional growth. The letter hints that to develop and flourish fully, individuals must learn to communicate their thoughts, emotions, and ideas verbally, with clarity and compassion. Effective and compassionate communication facilitates meaningful connections, promotes mutual understanding, and helps establish a sense of community and belonging. It also allows individuals to address their own needs and advocate for themselves and others.

When the ability to communicate is blocked or impaired, individuals may experience negative consequences such as misunderstanding, trust issues, unfulfilled needs, conflicts, decreased self-esteem, frustration, helplessness, and social isolation.

The Planet Associated with Gimel

"He made the letter Gimel king and bound a crown to it and combined one with another, and with them, he formed Jupiter in the Universe..." (*Sefer Yetzirah*, Chapter 4, Verse 6)

Sefer Yetzirah associates the letter Gimel with the planet Jupiter, thus offering us a deeper understanding of the intrinsic attributes that Gimel embodies.

In Western Astrology, Jupiter is classified as one of the two supporting planets. It symbolizes humanity's collective inclinations and serves as a teacher guiding individuals toward the expansion of awareness, knowledge and consciousness.

Jupiter is considered a beneficial celestial body, believed to bring good fortune and abundance, both materially and spiritually. It is unique as the only planet that not only receives energy from the sun but also radiates its own energy. In Judaism, Jupiter is often linked to prophets and seers, earning the moniker "the planet of wisdom." The vibrational frequencies of this planet inspire qualities such as nobility, generosity, a desire for a meaningful life, the instinct to heal and protect others, and a quest for idealism, wisdom, justice, and ultimate truth.

Jupiter is associated with growth and expansion in all aspects of life. Its influence encourages individuals to learn, develop, progress, and evolve without considering limitations. It facilitates the expansion of personal and collective awareness, leading to insights, risk-taking, and the seizing of opportunities. The acquisition of knowledge and insight is the initial step toward the development of self-awareness in an individual.

The Groups the Letter Gimel is Associated With

Earth Element Letter

The letter Gimel is associated with the air element, symbolizing mental intelligence, analytical thinking, logical reasoning, and the ability to examine everything rationally. This element is expressed in Gimel through spiritual and intellectual abilities, allowing for intuitive perception and telepathic comprehension of the structures and configurations behind material patterns.

Soul Letter

As a soul letter, Gimel represents the spiritual truths acquired throughout an individual's life journey. These truths, linked to various stages of initiation, enable the rediscovery of spiritual essence and ancient wisdom embodied within them. Pertaining to spiritual wisdom, vocal expression, and verbal communication ability, this initiation process becomes possible as individuals learn to heal their emotional wounds and express their inner truth without fear or concern.

Creational Mind Letter

The letter Gimel is a creational mind letter endowed with the power to create dualistic patterns of thoughts in our cosmic space, such as joy and sadness, peace and war. It carries energetic coding imprinted in both personal and collective consciousness, with motifs related to the fear of expressing one's personal voice and inner truth.

Understanding the creational power of Gimel is crucial, as the wisdom it embodies serves as a fundamental building block for authentic spiritual development. The letter encourages individuals to examine their spiritual practices, recognize their vulnerabilities, and assess how effectively they express their voice and inner truth.

Hard and Soft Sound

As a creative mind letter that can have a hard or soft phonetic emphasis, the letter Gimel can vary the intensity of its vibrational frequency. A hard sound gives the letter a masculine (yang) and more intense tone, while a softer sound imparts a feminine (yin) and gentler tone. As a hard-sounding letter, it signifies difficulty in softening and being flexible when needed. Conversely, as a soft-sounding letter, it represents the ability to be flexible and dissolve the ego.

When the letter Gimel appears as a hard-sounded letter, for instance, in words such as "gvura" (גְּבוּרָה) meaning "bravery,"ga'ava" (גַּאֲוָה) meaning "pride," and "grira" (גְרִירָה) meaning "dragging," it possesses greater strength and presence, but there is also a higher risk of ego-driven action. Conversely, when the letter Gimel appears in its soft form, for example, in words such as "haginut" (הֲגִינוּת) meaning "decency," "hagana" (הֲגָנָה) meaning "defense" and "hagshama" (הַגְשָׁמָה) meaning "fulfillment," it weakens its vibration frequency, thus diminishing the influence of the ego, allowing for greater capacity for actions from a level of humility.

Measure of Grace and Compassion

The letter Gimel embodies the measure of grace, kindness and compassion, qualities related to generosity and magnanimity. This measure inspires individuals with faith, hope, and optimism, fostering a glass-half-full mentality in any circumstance.

The letter symbolizes caring, kindness, consideration, understanding, charity, and unconditional giving, reflecting a willingness to extend aid and support to others. Those whose names incorporate Gimel demonstrate a lawful character and exhibit a capacity for absolution, forgiveness, and the ability to let go.

Gimel's energy exudes delicacy and high empathic capacity, showing consideration for others. It struggles to refuse requests for assistance and tends to initiate acts of kindness and generosity independently.

Its Achilles' heel is the difficulty in setting healthy boundaries and refraining from unconditional giving. The powerful combination of compassion and containment found in this letter, along with a caring nature and the desire to give, may lead to situations of injustice, iniquity and intentional wrongdoing toward individuals with this letter in their names. These are some of the lessons that the bearers of the letter are destined to encounter and learn from in their earthly life journey.

Strengths

The letter Gimel embodies qualities such as realism, intuition, wisdom, telepathy, inner vision, mediumship, a broad and philosophical worldview, holistic understanding, spiritual perception, curiosity, a desire for knowledge and understanding, optimism, faith, compassion, generosity, charity, benevolence, sensitivity, adaptability, discernment of body language and subtle non-verbal communication, cooperation, and problem-solving abilities.

The letter is also associated with an attitude of gratitude, providing its bearers with the ability to experience happiness and fulfillment; as the ancient proverb states, *"Blessed is the man who is happy on his part."* Gimel rewards those who follow the path of honesty and giving.

Weaknesses

The weaknesses associated with the letter Gimel include nervousness, indifference, impulsiveness, taking things out of context, pride, detachment, stagnation and fixation. In a state of mental imbalance, its vibrational frequencies may lead to restlessness, mental dispersion, paralysis of willpower, decision-making difficulties, withdrawal or seclusion, self-cancellation or reduction, concealment, becoming lost in thoughts, and developing anxieties and fears.

Gimel is not a simple letter. It embodies wisdom, kindness, compassion, and generous giving alongside emotional vulnerability and difficulty in emotional and verbal expression. It may be challenging for those not receptive to the profound healing processes it represents.

The letter signifies individuals who value personal space, freedom, and movement. They often find it challenging to navigate situations involving forceful, militant, and aggressive energies. Its energy is not suited for conflict and intrigue. Therefore, those with the letter Gimel in their name must prioritize developing effective verbal communication skills to express the murmurs of their hearts and the wisdom of their souls.

Additionally, they must learn to establish healthy boundaries for themselves and others, avoiding self-cancellation or reduction. These are essential lessons for individuals with this letter as they embark on their life journey.

א ב ג ד ה ו ז ח ט י כ ל מ נ ס ע פ צ ק ר ש ת

*"Anything which is more than our necessity is Poison.
It may be Power, Wealth, Hunger, Ego, Greed, Laziness,
Love, Ambition, Hate or anything. If you have much, give
of your wealth; If you have little, give of your Heart."*

Jalal ad-Din Rumi

Uniqueness and Purpose

The letter Dalet (דָּלֶת), the fourth letter in the Hebrew alphabet, serves as a symbolic gateway, marking the transition from one state of consciousness to another. It embodies the manifestation of the divine masculine force, representing both the inherent power of bravery within the human soul and the capacity for distribution. The letter Dalet's purpose is to awaken a person's awareness of their intentions and motives, connecting them to their authentic inner strength.

The Letter in Creation Stories

The first independent appearance of the letter Dalet in the Genesis stories is in the word "deshe" (דשא), meaning "grass" or "vegetation": *"Then God said, 'Let the earth sprout vegetation, plants yielding seed, and fruit trees on the earth bearing fruit according to their kind with seed in them"; and it was so."* (Genesis, Chapter 1, Verse 11) The letter is found in the word that represents the material formation of our mother planet, a state in which the earth becomes material and is adorned with grass and plants.

A close reading of this verse reveals a botanical categorization of vegetation, breaking it down into three parts: the first is represented by the word "grass" (דשא), referring to seedless plants (which reproduce by spores such as fungi, moss, and ferns); the second, by the phrase "grass that sows seed" (עֵשֶׂב מַזְרִיעַ זֶרַע), refers to plants that have seeds yet do not produce fruits; and the third, by the phrase "fruit trees that bear fruit of their kind" (עֵץ פְּרִי עֹשֶׂה פְּרִי לְמִינוֹ), to plants that have seeds and produce fruits.

This biblical verse raises important issues for understanding, which I elaborate on further in my writing. These issues relate to the division of vegetation between humans and animals, between the fruit of the tree and the fruit of the earth, the different ways biological reproduction occurs in our existential space, and how this space is adorned with different layers, or as the theory of Kabbalah calls them, "covers" (כיסויים), through the energy the letter Dalet speaks of.

Pronunciation

The letter Dalet is pronounced as "Da-let" and is represented in English as D.

The pronunciation of the letter Dalet hints at its essence and energetic force. Its pronunciation and name encompass several meanings. The first is "delet" (דֶלֶת), meaning "door," a term indicating a two-way passage through an opening in a building's wall, allowing movement from inside to outside and vice versa. A door can represent both an opening entrance and a barrier.

The second connotation emerges from the word "dlia" (דְלִיָּה), meaning to "draw out" or "pull out." This signifies the capacity to extract or elicit something, such as information. The third significance is intertwined with the word "dal" (דל), meaning "meager," a concept concealed within the letter's name, indicating poverty or deficiency.

The letter Dalet is the first in the Hebrew alphabet to embody the consciousness of lack. Among the twenty-two letters of the Hebrew alphabet, only two—Dalet and Resh—represent a state of absence. While the letter Dalet embodies emotional poverty, evoking in individuals an increased yearning for more attention, love, affection, and care, the letter Resh signifies material poverty, leading to an enhanced desire for material possessions and earthly pleasures, such as food and sex.

Diagram 33: Door

Graphic Shape

The graphical shape of the letter Dalet resembles an open door, allowing the energy of preceding letters to pass through and manifest in the physical realm. This manifestation results in the subsequent letter, Heh. In essence, Dalet establishes the boundaries of the framework introduced by the letter Bet, allowing for controlled materialization within these confines. This concept can be visualized as ocean water being poured into a bottle - a practical material vessel defined by boundaries that enable control over its content.

On a physical plane, the door functions as both an entry and an exit gate, while on a metaphysical plane, it acts as an energetic gateway or a galactic passage for dimensional transitions. A dimension represents not just a location but varying perspectives on reality. The wisdom embedded in the letter Dalet suggests that we exist in multiple dimensions simultaneously and have the capability to shift our consciousness from one dimension to another.

The graphical form of the letter Dalet features a partially open and partially closed structure, with a roof and a dividing wall. This configuration indicates its closure toward spiritual matters and the wisdom embodied in the preceding letter, Gimel, while it remains open to the material world and the energy of the subsequent letter, Heh

Dalet is distinguished as the first letter in the alphabet that stands on one leg in the row, symbolizing the ground. This stance reflects its inherent instability, volatility, and the challenge of maintaining internal equilibrium over time.

Gematrical Value

The gematrical value of the letter Dalet is four, symbolizing structure, institutions, and frameworks. This value is associated with qualities such as order, organization, precision, focus on details and goals, and a methodical, process-oriented approach. It reflects the universal cyclicity of formation observed in four types of creation (mineral, plant, animal, and human), the four fundamental elements (air, fire, water, and earth), the four seasons, the four winds, the four types of basic physical reactions, and the four lunar phases.

The gematrical value of Dalet relates to the square, a geometric figure with four equal sides representing the material, physical world. This underscores the concept that while the spiritual realm is boundless and can extend in myriad directions, the physical realm is confined, finite, and limited.

In biblical contexts, this gematrical value is evident in the four rivers flowing from the Garden of Eden: *"Now a river flowed out of Eden to water the garden; and from there it divided and became four rivers."* (*Genesis*, Chapter 2, Verse 10), and in the depiction of four sacred animals beside the throne in the vision of the prophet Ezekiel (Ezekiel, Chapter 1, Verses 4-9).

In Judaism, the gematrical value of four represents the four modules of the Kabbalistic teachings, known as **PaRDeS**[25] (פרדס). This encapsulates various levels at which the entire Torah can be learned and understood. In Kabbalah, the gematrical value of four signifies the four worlds: "Atzilut" (nobility), "Briah" (creation), "Yetzirah" (formation), and "Asyiah" (doing).

In biblical contexts, this gematrical value is evident in the four rivers flowing from the Garden of Eden: "*Now a river flowed out of Eden to water the garden; and from there it divided and became four rivers.*" (*Genesis*, Chapter 2, Verse 10), and in the depiction of four sacred animals beside the throne in the vision of the prophet Ezekiel (Ezekiel, Chapter 1, Verses 4-9).

In Judaism, the gematrical value of four represents the four modules of the Kabbalistic teachings, known as **PaRDeS** (פרדס). This encapsulates various levels at which the entire Torah can be learned and understood. In Kabbalah, the gematrical value of four signifies the four worlds: "Atzilut" (nobility), "Briah" (creation), "Yetzirah" (formation), and "Asyiah" (doing).

The Planet Associated with Dalet

"*He made the letter Dalet, king and bound a crown to it and combined one with another and with them, he formed Mars in the Universe...*" (*Sefer Yetzirah*, Chapter 4, Verse 7)

Sefer Yetzirah associates the letter Dalet with the planet Mars, thus offering profound insight into how the vibrational frequencies of Dalet shape our reality.

---

[25] PaRDeS is a method through which the entire Torah can be learned and understood. The It stands for four approaches: P (Pshat) – simple understanding, R (Remez) – hints, D (Drash) – fables and parables, and S (Sod) – Kabbalistic, mystical, and mysterious aspects of it.

In Western astrology, Mars is categorized as one of the personal planets, revealing individual characteristics, tendencies, needs, and desires. It symbolizes a person's approach to life and the way they acquire earthly life experiences. The vibrational frequencies of Mars often evoke competitive urges, such as the desire to take a stand, compete, attack, fight, and conquer.

While Mars is not directly associated with emotions, it is believed to stir various emotions. Its energies are characterized by breakthroughs and a forward movement toward the unknown.

Constructively, the energy of Mars encourages individuals to stand their ground with self-confidence and assertiveness, fostering a desire to deviate from social norms and break free from the shackles of home, parents, family, society, and culture in pursuit of personal independence. Conversely, its inhibitory aspect can lead to haste, aggression, and inconsideration, qualities that can be sources of tension and conflict.

Mars represents warm and warlike energy, with primitive, bold, aggressive, and instinctive drives, embodying energy that does not "stop at red." In various mythologies, Mars is associated with the God of War. The energies of Mars symbolize the urge to prove oneself, showcase worth, stand firm at any cost, and highlight the "I" through qualities such as bravery, strength, passion, enthusiasm, and daring. This is coupled with a desire to take steps toward the development of individuality, unique self-expression, and the satisfaction of personal passions and desires.

The influence of Mars inspires individuals with a pioneering spirit, independence, ambition, decisiveness, initiative, and spontaneity. The energy it instills is powerful in both its constructive and inhibitory aspects, an energy that needs to be channeled positively and constructively, especially toward spiritual matters. In a state of imbalance, these warm, daring and aggressive vibrational frequencies can evoke in individuals with this letter in their names a feeling of absence and restlessness.

In normal mental development, the vibrational frequencies of Mars pave the way for the development of individuality and personal uniqueness. They empower individuals to protect themselves and their interests by discarding anything that does not serve their goals.

To illustrate the energetic power of the letter Dalet, I would like to introduce you to a unique and multifaceted biblical figure known as King David, whose name twice contains the letter Dalet. As mentioned earlier, the purpose of biblical stories, like that of King David, is to offer insights into human psychology and the soulful qualities that support our spiritual ascension, as well as those that hinder it.

King David, the third king of the Kingdom of Israel, ascended to the throne after the death of King Saul. His reign lasted about four hundred years up until the destruction of the First Temple. In reading the story of David in the Bible, we encounter a character filled with contradictions.

On the one hand, David is depicted as a spiritual personality, devoted to the study of Torah and striving for holiness and transcendence, a person with a strong faith in God and a gifted poet. On the other hand, he is seen as a down-to-earth personality: simple, humble, passionate, a military man, and a statesman with vision, achieving both military and political goals during his tenure.

Known for his beauty, ruddy complexion, red hair, beautiful eyes, and good looks, David was not born into privilege. He rose from humble beginnings entirely on his own. David was a humble man and a shepherd, and from a very young age, he was rejected and ostracized by his family. His family not only did not accept him and provide security but also attempted to hinder his path to greatness.

Despite this rejection and ostracism, David rose to greatness through bravery, courage, resourcefulness, and his musical and lyrical talents. He was a poet, writer, and harp player, and according to Jewish tradition, he composed the *Book of Psalms*.

Humility is another quality attributed to King David, and it is one of the most important traits for those on the spiritual path.

According to the Bible, this quality contributed significantly to David's rise to kingship.

However, despite being the Bible's greatest warrior and possessing humility and great faith in God, David was not permitted to build the Temple due to his aggressive nature. His warlike side overshadowed everything else. The honor of building the Temple was passed to his son, King Solomon, a king who aspired for peace throughout his reign.

The Groups the Letter Dalet is Associated With

Fire Element Letter

The element associated with the letter Dalet is fire, symbolizing vitality, vivaciousness, vigilance, movement, vigor, and initiative. This burning and blistering flame, however, can also stimulate urges, compulsions, ego, pride, and a desire for adoration and recognition. At its core, fire thrives on drama and attention. When imbalanced, it may pose risks for both the individual and those around them. Fire can offer warmth, but it can also burn and destroy if it becomes unruly.

Soul Letter

As a soul letter, Dalet symbolizes spiritual truths one must acquire in life. These truths are related to initiation processes that enable individuals to recall the consciousness of unity, guiding them to lead their lives with pure intentions—whether expressed verbally or through actions. This initiation becomes achievable when a person masters the control of their combative, mental, and emotional impulses. It unfolds as the individual learns to regulate their inner temper, manage the fiery and combative emotional aspects within themselves, and cultivate authentic self-confidence.

Creational Mind Letter

The letter Dalet is a creational mind letter, carrying within its energetic coding motives linked to bravery and warfare. It has the power to create dualistic patterns of thoughts in our cosmic space, such as anger and peace, bravery and cowardice. As a creational mind letter, Dalet imprints motifs into personal and collective consciousness associated with force, intent, authority, and control. It invites individuals to develop awareness of their intentions and become more conscious of how they express their thoughts, feelings, needs, and desires.

Hard and Soft Sound

As a creative mind letter capable of both hard and soft phonetic emphasis, the letter Dalet can vary the intensity of its vibrational frequency. A hard sound gives the letter a masculine (yang) and more intense tone, while a softer sound imparts a feminine (yin) and gentler tone. As a hard-sounding letter, it signifies difficulty in softening and being flexible when needed. Conversely, as a soft-sounding letter, it represents the ability to be flexible and dissolve the ego.

When the letter Dalet is pronounced with a hard sound, for instance, in words such as "da'at" (wisdom), "dibur" (speech), "drama" (drama), and "din" (judgment), it exhibits greater strength and presence, but also a higher risk of actions driven by ego and self-interest.

Conversely, when the letter Dalet appears in its soft form, for example, in words like "adivut" (kindness), "gdula" (greatness), and "ideal" (with the same meaning as in English), its vibrational frequency is weakened, thus diminishing the influence of the ego and fostering a greater capacity for actions from a level of humility.

The Measure of Judgment

The letter Dalet embodies the measure of judgment, a measure that tends to lead individuals to harsh and rigid judgment and criticism. This involves affixing labels to people, situations or matters. As a letter of judgment, Dalet represents an approach where individuals may not consistently strive to support or contribute to others from the depths of their being. Instead, such efforts are typically exerted only when convenient and aligned with personal objectives.

Strengths

The strengths associated with the letter Dalet include courage, self-confidence, assertiveness, independence, vitality, energy, physical strength, authority, persuasion, enthusiasm, self-care, self-expression, initiative, activeness, a desire to explore and conquer the world, earthly wisdom, durability, swiftness, studiousness, stubbornness, the ability to stand their ground, focus, practicality, order, organization, strategy, and the skill in delegating authority.

Weaknesses

Conversely, weaknesses associated with the letter Dalet include self-interest, selfishness, a desire to receive as much as possible, authoritarianism, invasiveness, impetuousness, a controlling nature, rigidity, an inability to adjust and let go, argumentativeness, rejection of authority, evading responsibility, excessive stubbornness, abusing authority and personal leverage, impatience, intolerance, impulsiveness, obsessiveness, competitiveness, rudeness, aggressiveness, and belligerence.

When energetically imbalanced, individuals with the letter Dalet in their name may tend to be controlling, possessive, and domineering and force their desires on others, either directly or indirectly. They may exhibit dominance, intrusiveness, tyranny, aggression, militancy, and misuse of their articulation and verbal ability. This imbalance might also manifest tendencies toward slyness, gossip, and slander. The letter Dalet invites its bearers to cultivate an attitude of gratitude within themselves.

א ב ג ד ה ו ז ח ט י כ ל מ נ ס ע פ צ ק ר ש ת

*"This world is like a mountain. Your echo depends on you.
If you scream good things, the world will give it back. If you
scream bad things, the world will give it back. Even if someone
says badly about you, speak well about him. Change your heart
to change the world."*

Shams Tabrizi

Uniqueness and Purpose

The letter Heh (הֵה), the fifth letter of the Hebrew alphabet, carries deep symbolic and spiritual significance. This letter is associated with creation and revelation. It is considered a blessed letter, believed to unlock the door to one's good fortune and luck.

The letter Heh embodies the manifestation of the divine creative feminine force and represents the inherent power of achieving spiritual and earthly abundance. It is also associated with fertility and procreation, the concept of monarchy, and matriarchal sovereignty. Furthermore, it symbolizes the ability to transform ideas into practical deeds, manifesting them in reality.

Heh is a powerful letter. It is the first letter to embody the practical and applied power within humans. It functions as a channel through which a person can draw divine abundance into the material realm. Its vibrational frequencies awaken the desire for unique self-expression. The letter's purpose is to guide individuals toward creative and physical fertility and achievements in both earthly and spiritual aspects and to foster a connection to one's senses, self-love, and authentic self-expression.

The letter Heh appears in various names of God, such as "Yah" (יָה), "Eloha" (אֱלוֹהַ), "Elohim" (אֱלוֹהִים), and "Eheye" (אֶהְיֶה) meaning

"I will be," and "Eheye Asher Eheye" (אֶהְיֶה אשר אֶהְיֶה) meaning "I am what I am" and "I will be what I will be."

The letter also plays a significant role in the explicit name of God, such as "Yehovah" (יְהֹוָה) and "Havaya" (הֲוָיָה), meaning "Being." In these names, Heh appears twice. The first Heh represents the celestial divine female known as the "Shekinah," while the second Heh represents the earthly divine female, known as Mother Earth or Gaia.

The Letter in Creation Stories

The first occurrence of the letter Heh in the Bible is found in the opening verse of the creation stories in Genesis. It appears in words "ha'aretz" (הָאָרֶץ) meaning "earth," "ha'shamayim" (הַשָּׁמַיִם) meaning "heavens," and "ha'yta" (הייתה) meaning "was." This verse marks the initiation of the creation narrative. *"In the beginning God created the heavens and the earth. And the earth was a formless and desolate emptiness, and darkness was over the surface of the deep, and the Spirit of God was hovering over the surface of the waters."* (*Genesis*, Chapter 1, Verses 1-2)

This biblical verse introduces the creation stories without offering clear and defined indications of historical time, the central hero of the plot, the author of this literary masterpiece, the time of composition, or its intended purpose. Additionally, there is no reference to the situation that precedes the narrative. Nonetheless, the letter Heh appears in this verse as the "letter of knowledge," signifying something known and explicit, suggesting that the concepts of heaven and earth are not entirely novel.

In the Hebrew language, the letter Heh holds significant importance. It is regarded as the letter of knowledge, responsible for conveying information of importance that demands attention. When added to a specific word, Heh imparts emphasis and unique meaning. In this initial verse, the letter Heh serves as an informative letter for the words representing the upper world—

"ha'shamayim," meaning "heavens," and the lower world, "ha'aretz," meaning "earth."

That being said, the first independent appearance of the letter Heh in the creation stories, not as an informative letter, occurs in the word "ha'yta," meaning "was." This word, feminine in Hebrew, indicates presence and occurrence. It offers insight into the situation preceding the Genesis narrative, where the earth was composed of a mixture of formless materials and deep, dark waters, setting the stage for divine creation.

Pronunciation

The letter Heh is pronounced as "Heh" and can correspond to various English equivalents, such as A, E, H, AH, HA, or EH, depending on its position in a word or name. When Heh is the first letter, it may be represented as A, E, or H. However, when Heh is the last letter in a word or name, it can be paired with the letter Alef. For example, the name Angela ends with the letter A in English, but in Hebrew, its correct representation is rendered with Heh, as in Angelah. Similarly, Amritha is used instead of Amrita.

The pronunciation of the letter Heh closely resembles its name, incorporating a double repetition of the letter itself. Among the twenty-two letters of the Hebrew alphabet, only two have names formed by a double repetition of the letter: Heh (הה) and Vav (וו).

The letter Heh is a light, guttural sound, pronounced as a breath of air. To pronounce it correctly, one simply needs to open the mouth and allow the sound to emerge from the throat, our natural resonance center. The sound of the letter Heh functions as an echo, creating resonance and reverberation. These auditory effects exemplify the vibrational frequencies of Heh, both in the world and within humans.

Diagram 34: Echo

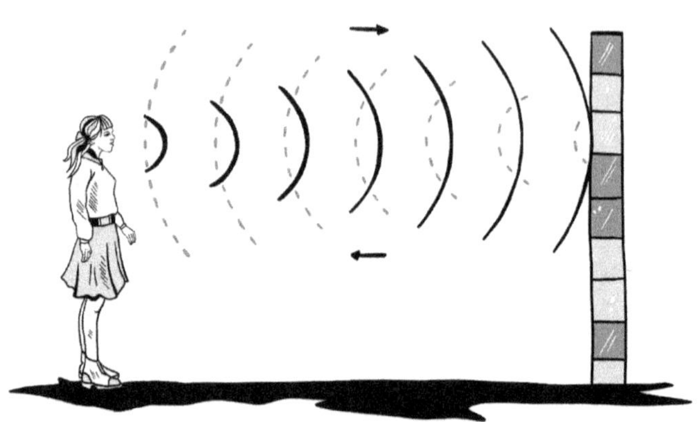

Graphic Shape

The graphic shape of the letter Heh offers a deeper understanding of its energetic essence. The shape of the letter comprises the letter Dalet (ד) coupled with an upside-down letter Yod (י) positioned at the center of Dalet, resembling a fetus in an upside-down posture within the womb. This configuration suggests that the letter Heh embodies the energies of both letters: the earthly (material) energy signified by Dalet, and the spiritual energy symbolized by Yod.

The shape of the letter Heh is composed of three lines, representing length, width, and depth, and evokes the image of an open space. These lines define the physical dimension, creating a space that facilitates earthly, energetic formation.

The echo effect generated by the pronunciation of Heh is also reflected in its graphic shape. The repetition of the letter's structure results in an elongated shape, akin to a corridor or a three-dimensional geometric figure, enabling movement through time and space.

Diagram 35: Hallway/Shape of the letter Heh

Additionally, the letter Heh possesses a unique form. It is written with two separate strokes rather than a single continuous line. Its shape, simultaneously open and closed, signifies that individuals associated with the letter are inclined to see both sides of the coin. They have the ability to perceive the whole as well as the separate and maintain a degree of openness toward various opinions, attitudes, people, and situations. The letter's firm stance on both legs along the line symbolizes its ability to maintain inner equilibrium amidst challenging life circumstances.

Gematrical Value

The gematrical value of the letter Heh is five, a number closely associated with humanity. Every human being is composed of five elements: air, fire, water, earth, and the divine spirit. Humans possess five earthly senses: sight, smell, hearing, taste, and touch. Additionally, each human hand has five fingers, and each foot has five toes. In many esoteric and mystical traditions, the human body is depicted as a five-pointed star, with its vertices representing the head, two arms, and two legs, as famously illustrated in Leonardo da Vinci's *Vitruvian Man.*

Diagram 36: The *Vitruvian Man*

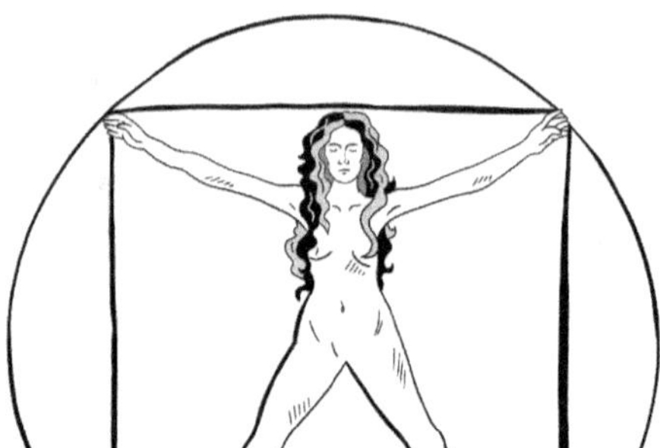

In Hebrew, the number five is associated with the number of organs used to produce sounds: the lips, teeth, tongue, palate and throat. It also correlates to the **five levels of the human soul: Nefesh, Ruach, Neshama, Haya and Yechida**[26]. Furthermore, the number five features prominently in each of the covenant tablets.

---

[26] "Five levels of the human soul" is a concept in Kabbalistic teachings that provides an understanding of the various levels of the human soul and its connection to the divine. **Nefesh:** The lowest aspect of the soul. It is linked to the physical body, representing basic life force, physical desires, and instincts. Nefesh finds expression in the blood, embodying our animalistic nature and concerns for survival and physical pleasures. **Ruach:** The level associated with intellect and energy in motion (dynamic life force). Ruach enables the expression of human qualities such as love, compassion, and rational thinking. It serves as a bridge between the lower level (Nefesh) and the higher spiritual aspects of the soul. **Neshama:** The divine and spiritual aspect of the soul. It is often regarded as the source of individuality and serves as a conduit for a person's connection to God. This level is associated with the highest intellectual and moral development. **Chaya:** A level transcending individuality, connecting with the collective and cosmic aspects of existence. It embodies the concept of life beyond the self and is often linked to the idea of eternal life. **Yechida:** The highest and most profound connection with God, akin to a blissful state. It is often described as the divine spark within each person and is an experience rarely encountered by most individuals.

Five is a dynamic and vibrant gematrical value, empowering individuals to engage in multiple activities simultaneously and handle various tasks successfully. It is associated with qualities such as communication, movement, curiosity, adaptability, wit, resourcefulness, and self-control. This value represents the individual's need for mobility, social interaction, diversity, and connection to nature. It also carries a somewhat rebellious aspect, challenging existing conventions and aspiring to change them by setting a personal example.

The Zodiac Sign Associated with Heh

Sefer Yetzirah links the letter Heh to the zodiac sign Aries, providing deeper insight into the inherent qualities of Heh. Aries, the first sign in the zodiac, is characterized by such keywords as desire, creation, initiative and breakthrough. It symbolizes the power of regeneration, marking a new beginning in the cycle of life and the reawakening of life forces from their winter dormancy.

Aries is known for its fast-paced lifestyle. Its vibrational frequencies and its rapid rhythm inspire the individual with a desire to embark on new endeavors: to initiate projects, move forward dynamically, create, compete, excel and conquer. Aries' energy is bold and vigorous, occasionally presenting challenges due to its intensity. This energy typifies individuals driven by a sense of mission, such as wrestlers, athletes, warriors, warlords, and leaders —all characterized by fiery determination.

The zodiac sign Aries symbolically represented by an animal from the sheep family. A young sheep is referred to as a lamb, and upon reaching adulthood, it becomes a sheep. This domesticated animal is considered the gentlest among livestock. In Judaism, the lamb is revered for its extreme mercy and submission, qualities believed to surpass those found in humans. This is exemplified in the biblical narrative of the Plague of the Firstborn in Egypt, where God instructed the Israelites to smear their doorposts with lamb's blood. This act underscores the belief that only the power of ultimate, complete, and pure submission can manifest miracles and wonders.

Diagram 37: Aries Zodiac Sign

The Groups the Letter Heh is Associated With

Fire Element Letter

The element of the letter Heh is fire. The fire associated with this letter is pleasant and gentle, akin to the warm characteristics of the spring season. It embodies an enthusiastic and optimistic energy, evoking qualities such as courage, vigor, vitality, vigilance, inspiration, creativity, growth, and progress in an individual.

The fire energy represented by Heh is dynamic and exhilarating, propelling individuals forward with joy and enthusiasm. It is driven by a sense of capability and a desire to create. This energy requires a broad spectrum of action space and avenues for self-expression. However, if this energy is not balanced within a person, it may lead to restlessness and a tendency to rush forward without a clear understanding of the reasons, defined direction, or specific goals.

Movement / Vowel Letter

The letter Heh is also characterized as a dynamic movement letter, endowing individuals with qualities such as movement, mobility, maneuverability, flexibility, lightness, and fluidity. These attributes empower individuals to advance, progress beyond their current state, detach from limiting situations and concerns, and embrace new beginnings. Such qualities enable individuals to adapt and assimilate, be flexible, and thus approach complex issues with a lighthearted and creative mindset.

Soul Letter

The letter Heh belongs to the group of soul letters. Its fundamental structure is associated with creativity, fertility, and procreation, as well as with the principle of matriarchy and the creative force that nourishes both the world and human beings.

The letter establishes a connection between the individual and their five basic earthly senses, enabling full engagement with the abundant divine creations through sight, hearing, touch, smell, and taste. These earthly senses allow individuals to hear the wind and the birds, to touch, smell and taste the fruits of Mother Earth. Such sensory experiences transform our earthly existence into a captivating journey, fostering a sense of unity with divine creation.

As a soul letter, Heh represents the spiritual truths one must acquire in life. These truths pertain to initiation processes associated with a worldview in which the individual perceives themselves as being one with nature, collaborating harmoniously with it, and having complete faith in its support. This soul letter encourages individuals to reflect on their connection to the female aspect within themselves, embracing intuition, sensuality, love, and complete self-acceptance.

The Measure of Grace and Compassion

The letter Heh belongs to the group of letters associated with grace and compassion, embodying qualities such as kindness, compassion, generosity, and magnanimity. The letter instills in individual traits like faith, hope, optimism, kindness, consideration, understanding, charity, empathy, mental strength, and a spirit of unconditional giving. Moreover, it cultivates the ability to see the glass as half full in every situation, fostering a mindset that embraces pardoning, forgiving, forgetting, releasing, and freedom from challenging circumstances.

Formative Letter

Beyond its informative function, the letter Heh plays several pivotal roles in the Hebrew language. Firstly, it is used to form questions when placed before a noun or verb, introducing an element of doubt. For example: "ha'ydat?" translates to "Did you know?" as opposed to "ydat," which means "You know." Similarly, "ha'asit?" means "Have you done?" instead of the simple "asit," which means "You done."

Secondly, the letter Heh adds a feminine quality when added to the end of words or names. For instance, "ahavah" (love), "chemlah" (compassion), "havanah" (understanding), "haarachah" (appreciation), "hachalah" (containment), "hachzakah" (holding), "holadah" (birthing), "haanakah" (giving), and "kabbalah" (acceptance).

Lastly, when the letter is placed at the end of a noun, it transforms the word from masculine to feminine. For example, "yeled – yaldah" (boy – girl), "ahuv – ahuvah" (beloved), and "ish – isha" (man – woman).

The Power of Procreation and Fertility

The empowering significance of the letter Heh is vividly illustrated in the biblical narrative of Sarah and Abraham, as recorded in Genesis, Chapter 17, Verses 15-16. Sarah, originally named Sarai, was the first matriarch of the Jewish nation and the wife of Abraham, originally named Abram. Sarai remained barren until the age of ninety. Through divine intervention from God, her name changed from Sarai to Sarah, and Abram's name changed to Abraham. The addition of the letter Heh to their names bestowed upon them the ability to bear children.

Strengths

The strengths associated with the letter Heh include qualities such as willpower, vitality, optimism, cheerfulness, vigilance, independence, self-confidence, courage, vigor, motivation, initiative, curiosity, adventurousness, resourcefulness, expressiveness, directness, assertiveness, tenaciousness, determination, proactiveness, self-control, flexibility, openness to new experiences, authoritativeness, dedication, goal-oriented mindset, achievement, success, high self-discipline in goal achievement, leadership, and management ability.

Weaknesses

Conversely, weaknesses associated with the letter Heh include restlessness, hastiness, impulsiveness, inner tension, impatience, and a tendency to suffer from inner noise, potentially leading to a rushed impression, short temper, hot temper, anger, carelessness, bluntness, rashness, reactivity, verbal outbursts, aggressiveness, and even violent behavior.

These traits create an active and dynamic individual with a short fuse. When such individuals are fixated on a goal, they often display relentless persistence and refuse to give up until the objective is achieved as quickly as possible.

This fiery and rapid energy can sometimes be difficult to channel toward a focused goal, potentially leading to a state where the internal fire quickly extinguishes due to constant exertion. To navigate these tendencies, individuals with these traits are advised to select one goal at a time and dedicate their energy solely to it. A recommended practice for managing these tendencies is to engage in grounding exercises multiple times a day.

אבגדההוזחטיככלמנסעפצצקרשת

"Do not judge others in order not to be judged. Remember that what you see in others exists within you."

Letter Vav

Uniqueness and Purpose

The letter Vav (וָו) is the sixth letter in the Hebrew alphabet. It embodies the manifestation of the divine creative masculine force and the power of reproduction. The letter Vav is associated with the concept of kingship and patriarchal authority, as well as the ability to transform ideas into practical deeds, manifesting them in reality.

The letter Vav is a powerful letter, bestowing individuals with high communicative abilities, creative verbal expression, and the art of speech. These qualities can turn a person into a master of speech. The communicative ability associated with the letter Vav signifies external communication, encompassing interpersonal, group, organizational, and cultural communication. The purpose of Vav is to connect a person to divine spiritual and earthly wisdom, as well as to spiritual and earthly moral values.

The Letter in Creation Stories

The first appearance of the letter Vav in the creation stories is as a letter of connection in the word *"and,"* as exemplified in the verse: *"In the beginning God created the heavens and the earth. And the earth was a formless and desolate emptiness, and darkness was over the surface of the deep, and the Spirit of God was hovering over the surface of the waters."* (*Genesis*, Chapter 1, Verses 1-2)

The letter Vav has multiple roles. It serves as a letter of contrast, inversion, connection, and separation. It contains the power to unite or divide between factors and people. Vav can connect opposites, words, phrases, proper nouns, subjects, and themes, or separate them. It is capable of transforming verb tenses, moving from the future to the past as a letter of inversion. Its power is evident from the early verses of the *Genesis* narrative in the Bible.

Pronunciation

The letter Vav is pronounced as "Vav" and can be represented in English as V, W, O, or U, depending on its position in a word or a name.

The pronunciation of Vav is similar to its name, which means "hook," "connection," or a means through which one connects to something else.

Among the twenty-two letters of the Hebrew alphabet, only two letters have their pronunciation and letters creating their name: the letter Heh (הֵה) and the letter Vav (וָו). These two letters signify the way in which divine feminine and masculine energy duplicates itself and expands in time and space. While the letter Heh symbolizes the duplication of divine feminine energy, the letter Vav represents the duplication of divine masculine energy. Through the vibrational frequencies of the letter Heh, life is created, whereas through the vibrational frequencies of the letter Vav, organization and order emerge in life.

Graphic Shape

The graphical shape of the letter Vav is a straight, long, continuous, and linear line, resembling an upright rod with narrow dimensions.

This letter occupies little horizontal space, allowing it to approach adjacent letters, such as Heh and Zayin.

The graphical shape of Vav bears a resemblance to the phallic form. In its constructive aspect, this symbolizes fertility, strength, and power, while in its inhibiting aspect, it represents repression, aggression, dominance, and the exertion of power over others.

Diagram 38: Letter Vav Shape/Pipe

Diagram 39: Walking Stick

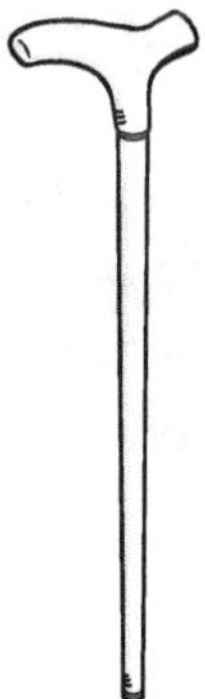

As illustrated in the sketch, the letter Vav features a curved protrusion, giving it the appearance of a hanger, hook, or hanging loop. Its shape, akin to a rod or stake, serves as a connection to something, like a structure, that connects to the ground. This design allows it to take deep roots in the ground, assimilate, and establish itself in the soil or earth.

Diagram 40: Connection of a Structure to the Ground

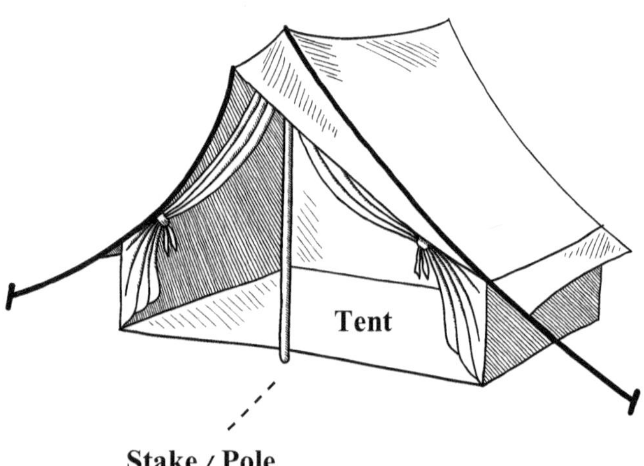

The letter Vav is an open letter in both directions, indicating partial openness toward opinions, positions, people, and situations. Its shape suggests that those associated with the letter possess the ability to grasp both the whole and the separate, and to see both sides of an issue. The letter stands on one leg on the ground, symbolizing a lack of stability and proneness to relatively rapidly lose its internal imbalance, unlike letters with two legs.

Gematrical Value

The gematrical value of the letter Vav is six. This value represents the aspiration for internal and external balance and harmony. It signifies a desire for belonging and affiliation to someone or something. Additionally, this value reflects the adaptive ability that enables a person to easily integrate into earthly life, adapt to society, embrace new situations and quickly gain acceptance within a peer group. It also indicates a tendency toward conservatism and conformity.

The keywords associated with this value are adaptation and assimilation, qualities that allow a person to align themselves and their behavior with existing social and cultural values, codes, and norms. These qualities aid individuals in social interactions, their ability to accurately read social cues, and provide them with tools to identify social situations and understand the intentions and expectations of those around them.

However, when the inclination for assimilation meets conservatism and conformity, it presents a more complex challenge. The unconscious internalization of behavioral values and codes that are not aligned with one's inner essence can distance a person from their core personal and authentic values. This may lead to persistent and unconscious cognitive dissonance, causing ongoing inner unrest.

Psychologically, the value of the letter Vav signifies the superego in a person's personality. This aspect of personality tends to develop tendencies such as self-criticism, criticism of others, self-judgment, judgment of others, social judgment, and feelings of guilt and blame. These tendencies manifest in an inhibiting aspect, often symbolized by a pointed finger of accusation.

The Zodiac Sign Associated with Vav

Sefer Yetzirah links the letter Vav to the zodiac sign of Taurus, thus providing insights into its prominent characteristics. Taurus, the first earth sign in the zodiac, is characterized by keywords such as maintaining perspectives, holding positions, and preserving the existing.

Taurus follows Aries in the zodiac, which is marked by a vigorous and fast-paced entry into life. In contrast, Taurus slows down this pace, making life's rhythm slower and less mobile. It instills in individuals the desire to anchor themselves and establish roots—to find a place, settle in it permanently, and preserve the material aspect they have achieved with all their strength.

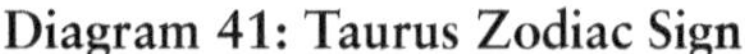

Diagram 41: Taurus Zodiac Sign

The symbol of the Taurus zodiac sign is the bull, a domesticated animal from the cattle family. The term "bull" typically denotes a castrated male used for work. In Judaism, this animal is associated with traits such as enjoyment, a desire for earthly pleasures, and an excessive preoccupation with indulgence in sensual delights.

In a constructive aspect, the attraction toward such traits can serve as a lever for spiritual growth. However, if taken to an extreme, they can lead to hedonism, a lack of purpose, and a relentless pursuit of physical pleasures and materialistic enjoyment.

The energy of the Taurus zodiac sign characterizes individuals who never rush and prefer to take their time. They do not like changes and are comfortable with a regular daily routine where each day resembles the previous one.

However, when the inclination toward conservatism meets routine and attachment to the familiar, it tends to create in individuals associated with this letter issues such as attachment, development of commitments, and challenges in letting go of things like situations, people, beliefs, opinions, values, conditions, and habits.

An additional keyword characterizing the Taurus zodiac sign is the "comfort zone." Individuals of this sign typically prefer to stay within a familiar range that provides them with material pleasure and economic security. To achieve these goals, they tend to be diligent workers, investing significant effort in pursuits that offer existential security, pleasure, and comfort.

The Groups the Letter Vav is Associated With

Earth Element Letter

The element of the letter Vav is earth, representing solid and material energy. It provides a foundation that connects a person to the ground, offering physical strength and endurance. Vav is a warm and pleasant earth letter, awakening in individuals the desire to be rooted and establish a solid foundation. It imparts qualities such as grounding, patience, resilience, high endurance, caution, survival skills, frugality, conservatism, practicality, and preservation of the existing.

This earth letter characterizes people who rely on structure and a sense of belonging. In a state of imbalance, the attachment to the familiar and the preservation of the existing, coupled with the fear of release and letting go, can lead individuals associated with this letter to become reliant on familiar frameworks and materiality—a state where they persist in one place for an extended period, reluctant to change their established ways of living and material circumstances.

Movement / Vowel Letter

The letter Vav is a movement letter, granting individuals qualities such as mobility and motion. These qualities empower individuals to move forward, progress beyond their current circumstances, detach from limiting situations and concerns, and embark on new beginnings. They enable individuals to adjust, assimilate, and tackle complex issues with a creative mindset.

Soul Letter

The letter Vav is the final letter in the group of soul letters. Its fundamental structure is associated with earthly wisdom, moral principles, and verbal communication. The developmental path it points individuals toward involves the cultivation of moral and ethical principles, authentic personal beliefs and values, alongside compassionate verbal communication. These abilities transform the earthly experience of a person into a unifying experience and a sense of unity.

As a soul letter, Vav symbolizes spiritual truths one must acquire in life. These truths are related to initiation processes associated with the examination of spiritual heritage and practices. This soul letter prompts individuals to deeply examine the beliefs and values by which they conduct their daily lives and to assess the extent to which these internalized beliefs and values, often acquired in childhood, align with their personal and authentic beliefs and values.

The letter Vav serves as the cornerstone for the development of an authentic personality and non-violent communication. It invites individuals associated with this letter to examine their communicative style —the way they tend to communicate with their surroundings.

The Measure of Judgment

The letter Vav embodies the measure of judgment. A measure draws individuals toward harsh and critical judgment, along with a propensity to label everything and everyone. As a letter of judgment, Vav suggests a person's tendency not to make an effort to help or give to others unless it is convenient and serves their personal goals. The vibrational frequencies of the letter tend to draw individuals to act based on self-interest and to engage in actions aimed at achieving personal gain. The letter 'Vav' invites individuals associated with it to develop an attitude of gratitude within themselves.

Strengths

The strengths associated with the letter Vav include qualities such as groundedness, realism, practicality, ease, restraint, patience, tolerance, sense of order and timing, aesthetic sense, loyalty to commitments, consistency, purposefulness, caution, bureaucracy, ability to adhere to routine, sensory enjoyment, self-control, goal orientation, conservatism, stubbornness, perseverance, concern for personal well-being, and involvement in earthly matters.

The various combinations within the letter create a strong character type with a long fuse. This type is someone who is attached to the familiar and known, values stability, and likes to be involved in everything.

Weaknesses

The weaknesses associated with the letter Vav are multifaceted, including traits like perfectionism, conventionality, and passivity. This letter also influences an adherence to routine or, contrastingly, a tendency toward rebellion, which is affected by the neighboring letters in a name. Recognizing and implementing the need for change can be challenging for those influenced by Vav, as can tendencies toward materialism, a strong desire to acquire, jealousy, arrogance, and narrow-mindedness. Additionally, individuals may exhibit excessive caution and conservatism, stubbornness, righteousness, anger, rigidity, demandingness, irritability, impatience, aggressiveness, suspiciousness, and greed.

Vav's inhibiting aspect is further expressed in traits such as difficulty in letting go of people, situations, beliefs, opinions, and behaviors. There is a marked tendency to insist on one's own beliefs and methods, along with the desire to have things done their way. These characteristics often lead individuals associated with this letter into a state where they expect or demand others to accept their principles, firmly believing that their way is the right and just way. Consequently, such individuals may become entrenched in their beliefs over long periods. These inhibiting issues are prone to developing into fixation, obsessiveness, and compulsiveness.

א ב ג ד ה ה ו ז ח ט י כ ל מ נ ס ע פ צ ק ר ש ת

*"Once the seed of faith takes root, it cannot be
blown away, even by the strongest wind."*

Jalal ad-Din Rumi

Uniqueness and Purpose

The letter Zayin (זַיִן), the seventh letter in the Hebrew alphabet, embodies an earthly presence with spiritual potential. Its essence centers around connection and communication. Zayin symbolizes the power of consciousness that fosters cognition, knowledge, and free will in a person. The letter's purpose is to guide individuals toward self-awareness and the recognition of their autonomy, aiming to develop within them an understanding of the principle that what they sow is what they reap.

The Letter in Creation Stories

The first appearance of the letter Zayin in the creation stories occurs in the word "zera" (זרע), meaning "seed": *"Then God said, 'Let the earth sprout vegetation, plants yielding seed, and fruit trees on the earth bearing fruit according to their kind with seed in them'; and it was so."* (*Genesis*, Chapter 1, Verse 11)

In this brief verse, the letter Zayin appears three times in the words: *"seed"* (zera), *"sowing"* (mazria), and *"his seed"* (zer'o). These three words represent the seed found in plants, animals, and humans, which enables propagation. The word "zera" (seed) in the biblical verse alludes not only to the physical seed that nourishes humans but also to the spiritual seed or "Seed Consciousness," which facilitates conscious development.

The letter Zayin is both an intellectual and practical letter. It is the first letter in the alphabetical sequence that introduces the cycle of karma, reminding humans that the seed of their intentions, actions, and deeds has consequences. It encourages the use of intellectual power to sow peace rather than war. This letter marks the beginning of experiential earthly trials related to human interactions aimed at fostering high self-awareness and awakening consciousness. These experiences are intended to guide individuals in developing a proper approach to life and people.

Pronunciation

The letter Zayin is pronounced as "Za-yin" and is represented in English as Z.

The pronunciation of the letter Zayin closely mirrors its name, Zayin, and it carries multiple meanings that are embedded in this name. Firstly, it denotes a weapon or fighting tool, derived from the word "kli zayin" (כלי זין), highlighting its association with combat or defense. Secondly, the letter signifies nourishment, a meaning derived from the word "zan" (זן), indicating its connection to sustenance. Thirdly, Zayin is associated with the male reproductive organ, also referred to as "zayin" (זין), a physical organ in a male's body through which animals and humans procreate, linking the letter to the theme of continuation of life.

Graphic Shape

As illustrated in the sketch, the shape of the letter Zayin resembles a weapon, such as an arrow or a spear, and is akin to a reaper sickle, a tool used for harvesting crops.

The keywords associated with the letter Zayin are struggle and warfare, be it physical, verbal, or intellectual. This letter symbolizes the spiritual and earthly challenges individuals face in their earthly lives, encapsulating the struggle for both spiritual and material nourishment. This concept resonates with the biblical verse, *"By the sweat of your face you shall eat bread."* (*Genesis*, Chapter 3, Verse 19)

Diagram 42: Zayin's Graphical Shape / Reaper Sickle

The energy of Zayin is bold and combative, which may explain its infrequent use in names. Individuals with Zayin in their names are endowed with a daring and militant spirit, tending to assert themselves vigorously and are willing to fight for their principles through verbal confrontation.

While this tendency can manifest as constructive assertiveness, its negative aspect may lead to aggression, confrontation, and potential harm toward others. The position of Zayin in the alphabetical order, preceding the letter Khet, symbolizes, among other things, the potential fall into sin due to emotional dysregulation.

The graphical form of Zayin displays a partially open and partially closed structure, featuring a roof above its head and a dividing wall. This configuration signifies its closure to spiritual matters and the wisdom embodied in the preceding letter, Vav, and its openness to the maters of the material world and the energy of the subsequent letter, Khet. The letter stands on one leg on the line, hinting at its instability, fluctuation, and the inherent difficulty of maintaining internal equilibrium.

Zayin's level of openness suggests a tendency for those associated with this letter to behave in two distinct ways, depending on the circumstances. They may exhibit a dynamic, pleasant, and light-hearted personality, expressing a desire to connect with others, engage in conversations, and initiate social connections. Conversely, they may also show a propensity to stand their ground and assert their tone.

Gematrical Value

The gematrical value of the letter Zayin is seven, a number replete with symbolism and mystical meanings tied to metaphysics, spirituality, and eternity.

We encounter the significance of the number seven in various contexts: the seven days of the week, notes on musical scales, continents, firmaments, oceans, seas, colors of the rainbow, and the openings in the human head. The seventh day, representing God's rest, symbolizes the completion of one creative cycle and the commencement of another.

In Judaism, the number seven is significant in observances such as the Sabbatical year, the seven menorahs in the Temple, the seven weeks of counting the Omer, the seven seals of King Solomon, the seven blessings in wedding ceremonies, and the seven days of mourning.

In the Bible, the value of seven is notably encountered in the context of waiting, such as in Jacob's service for Rachel, and in the story of Joseph, the king of dreams, where it relates to seven years of famine and abundance. The number seven also appears in the seven commandments given to all descendants of Noah and, more broadly, to all the nations of the world. This value is exemplified in the context of the walls of the City of Jericho, illustrating how spiritual power influences material reality (Joshua, Chapter 6, Verses 3-4).

The value of seven encourages humans toward spiritual and ideological development arising from social collaboration. It advocates for an understanding that spiritual power enables effective control over materiality. The gematrical value of the preceding letter, Vav, is six, representing the earthly realm and its limitations in six directions. The letter Zayin, following Vav, guides humans toward understanding that beyond the defined and confined earthly dimension exists a higher spiritual dimension, rich with countless directions and aspects.

The Zodiac Sign Associated with Zayin

Sefer Yetzirah associates the letter Zayin with the zodiac sign of Gemini, providing a deeper understanding of its prominent characteristics. Notably, Gemini is the first zodiac sign symbolized by a human figure.

The Gemini symbol, depicting two heads facing or opposing each other, hints at several concepts. Firstly, it represents the duality within the human soul. Secondly, it emphasizes the importance of developing a perspective that considers both sides of an issue. Thirdly, it suggests that what we see in others often reflects aspects of ourselves.

Gemini is characterized by intellectual agility, abstract understanding, logic, sociability, excellent communication skills, personal charm, humor, and wit. Its dualistic nature propels individuals toward intellectual adventures, encapsulated by the defining phrase, "I think, therefore I exist."

In Judaism, Gemini is associated with the interplay between light and darkness, positive and negative forces, and a rapid, slick tongue. Rabbi Chaim Vital, in his book *Sha'arei Kdusha*, emphasizes the importance of using the gift of verbal expression to promote peace rather than instigate argument or conflict.

Diagram 43: Gemini Zodiac Sign

The letter Zayin, associated with Gemini, encapsulates positive qualities such as intellect and intelligence, characterized by high cognitive skills. It signifies communicativeness, agility, good short-term memory, spatial orientation, coordination, and technological aptitude.

However, in an imbalanced state, individuals associated with this letter may exhibit mental restlessness, fickleness, a constant search for new stimuli, indecisiveness, and impatience with deeper exploration, leading to superficiality. For these individuals, everything, including emotions, is often perceived through the lens of logic.

The Groups the Letter Zayin is Associated With

Air Element Letter

The letter Zayin is associated with the air element. In relation to this letter, the air element is characterized as warm, light, flexible, versatile, and swift. It signifies a dynamic movement that keeps the human intellect in a constant state of receptiveness and motion. This results in a mental state where the mind is continuously thinking, calculating, showing interest in a wide array of topics, and engaging with multiple subjects simultaneously.

Practical Letter

Zayin is the third letter in the group of twelve simple letters, representing the practical and applied aspects of a person's character. This letter endows individuals with the ability to establish themselves in earthly life through their high communicative skills.

The Measure of Mercy

The letter Zayin embodies the measure of mercy, expressed through qualities such as consideration, generosity, understanding, and forgiveness. This measure reflects the energy awakened in a person in response to another's distress, compelling them to be considerate, helpful, and ease the suffering of others.

However, the inhibiting aspect of this measure can manifest in providing assistance based on considerations of personal profitability and gain. It involves evaluating whether helping is beneficial for oneself, what personal gain can be derived from it, and potentially manipulating the person or situation for personal gain.

Karma and Rectification Letter

Zayin is the first letter in the alphabetical sequence that marks a transition from the group of 'Soul" letters to "Karma and Rectification" letters. It signifies a shift from intentions and actions rooted in a consciousness of unity to those based on a consciousness of separation. As a letter intrinsically linked to communication, Zayin suggests that the rectification process for individuals associated with this letter lies in the relationships they form with others and in their interpersonal communicationwith them.

Strengths

The strengths associated with the letter Zayin encompasses qualities such as intellect, curiosity, lightness, adaptability, spontaneity, flexibility, communication, humor, cleverness, playfulness, persuasive power, friendliness, a rational approach to facts and events, and excellent expressive ability. Additional attributes include wit, vigilance, assertiveness, dynamism, mobility, vitality, sharpness, sophistication, and tactical and strategic thinking.

Weaknesses

Conversely, the weaknesses linked to Zayin include duality, instability, inconsistency, jealousy, insincerity, irritability, restlessness, superficiality, detachment, lack of grounding, easy distraction, impatience, a tendency to jump from topic to topic, difficulty in taking a stand, shallowness, and detachment from feelings, things and people.

Zayin is associated with concepts like a two-edged sword: poor communication, impatience, and a desire for quick, immediate results. Its inhibiting aspect is manifested in characteristics such as fickleness, dishonesty, hypocrisy, trickery, cunning, espionage, scheming, unreliability, and the use of aggressive, sharp language akin to a knife.

אבגדההוזה**ח**טיכלמנסעפצקרשת

"Your soul is often a battlefield, upon which your reason and your judgment wage war against your passion and your appetite."

Kahlil Gibran

Uniqueness and Purpose

The letter Khet (חֵית), the eighth letter in the Hebrew alphabet, represents the seed of emotions embedded in humans. It symbolizes the capability that allows them to engage emotionally and experientially with life and its challenges, forming a foundation for self-awareness. The purpose of the letter Khet is to evoke in individuals the remembrance of being autonomous entities with free choice.

The Letter in Creation Stories

The first encounter with the letter Khet in the creation stories occurs alongside the letter Vav in the word "v'khoshech" (וחושך), meaning "and darkness," in verse, *"And the earth was a formless and desolate emptiness, and darkness was over the surface of the deep."* (*Genesis*, Chapter 1, Verse 2) However, the letter Khet first appears independently in the Bible in the word "khayah" (חיה), meaning "living creature," in the verse, "Then God said, 'Let the waters teem with swarms of living creatures." (*Genesis* Chapter 1, Verse 20)

The word "Khoshech," meaning "darkness", does not necessarily imply something negative. Life itself begins in a dark, watery place - the womb's dark waters. Interestingly, by reversing the letters of the Hebrew word for "darkness" (חשך), we get the word for "forgot"

(שכח). Thus, "darkness" signifies a state of forgetfulness, a state in which a person has forgotten the divine spark within them.

The letter Khet is an emotional letter, associated with water element, which endows humans with the ability to feel, contain, merge and emotionally identify with others. This element descends downward and turns inward, delving into the world of emotions in all its shades. Water can vibrate at high or low frequencies; it can lift a person on a wave, placing them on solid ground, or generate emotional storms within them, leading to an emotional flood.

Khet is the second practical letter in the group of karma and rectification letters. It speaks about the rectification of an emotional approach required from a person. Here, I invite you to think with me. Could it be that the name and position of the letter in the stories of Genesis hint to us that in a state where we forget the divine spark within us, this forgetfulness is what leads us to sin? This implication seems to arise from the pronunciation of the letter Khet's name.

Pronunciation

The letter Khet is pronounced as "Khet" or "Chet" and is represented in English as KH or CH, depending on its position in a word or name and its pronunciation.

In terms of sound, the pronunciation of the letter Khet can be represented in two different writing forms. The first is "חטא," and the second is "חית." The meaning of the first writing form (חטא) signifies transgression, sin, or an offense against the will or laws of God—an act that contradicts a law or moral principle. Sin represents the violation of a commandment or moral norm, a state in which a person intentionally harms another through thought, speech, or action. In Judaism, a distinction is made between two types of sins: those between a person and the divine (God) and those between a person and their fellow human beings.

The meaning of the second writing form emerges when the letter is written with missing spelling (without mater lections) as

"חת" instead of "חית." In this form, it is associated with a word synonymous with awe—a feeling of fear. Fear is an unpleasant emotional and physiological sensation that arises from exposure to a threatening stimulus. In Hebrew, the phrase "He is made without Khet" (הוא עשוי ללא חת) is used to indicate that a person is fearless, meaning "He is inherently fearless."

The name, pronunciation, and writing forms of Khet, as well as the context in which it appears in the creation stories, symbolize its dual aspects and characteristics: life and vitality versus sin and animality (**inclinations**[27]).

Graphic Shape

The graphic shape of the letter Khet resembles a wedding canopy, a structure consisting of two pillars with a spread cloth on top. Under this canopy, Jews perform the wedding ceremony (chuppah) and betrothal (kiddushin), symbolizing unity and oneness, both personally and collectively. During this ceremony, the couple receives blessings and unites their destiny, while their families also gather beneath the canopy. The value of Khet resonates with the importance of unity and oneness, mirroring its graphical shape and gematrical value.

The shape of the letter Khet is closed from three directions in both its handwriting and print writing forms. It resembles a fenced structure, akin to a house with a roof and walls. The letter is closed at its upper base, symbolizing a closure to the maters of the spiritual world, and is open at its lower base, indicating openness to the maters of the material world. It stands on a line with two stable legs, reflecting its ability to maintain internal balance over time. The

---

[27] Inclination is an inner, instinctual urge of a person or animal to behave or react in a certain way without conscious thinking, planning, or deliberation.

letter turns its back to the wisdom of its preceding letter, Zayin, and to the wisdom of its subsequent letter, Thet.

Diagram 44: Chuppah (Canopy)

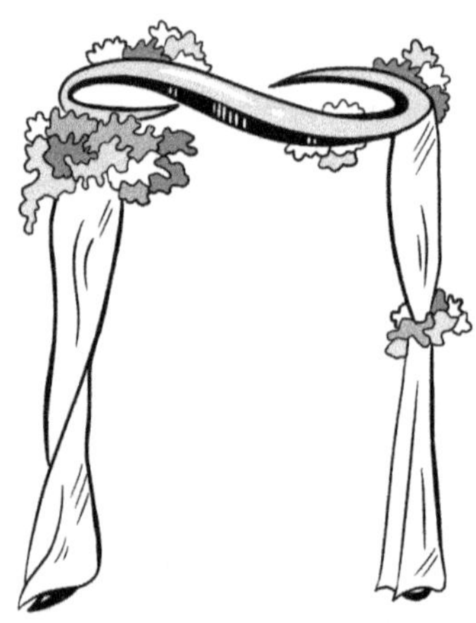

According to Kabbalistic teachings, a letter closed from three directions suggests a raw tendency toward self-centeredness and a desire to receive for oneself. It represents the boundaries and limitations individuals impose on themselves and others, and the tendency to close off and store emotions, things, and situations. These primal tendencies tend to narrow an individual's perspective, distort self and other perception, and hinder their ability to see the big picture and the half-full glass.

Diagram 45: The Handwritten and Printed Letter Chet

Gematrical Value

The gematrical value of the letter Khet is eight, a value imbued with profound esoteric and mystical significance. Across various cultures, this number symbolizes the transcendent or supernatural—the power that enables humans to transcend the material realm and allows the spirit to navigate matter. Considered one of the most potent numbers, eight embodies both constructive and inhibitory aspects.

The shape of the number eight is circular, specifically, composed of two interconnected circles. This formation, reminiscent of human DNA and the symbol of infinity when flipped on its side in a balanced position, signifies the energy connecting humans to multidimensionality and realms beyond their sensory experiences.

Diagram 46: Number Eight and DNA

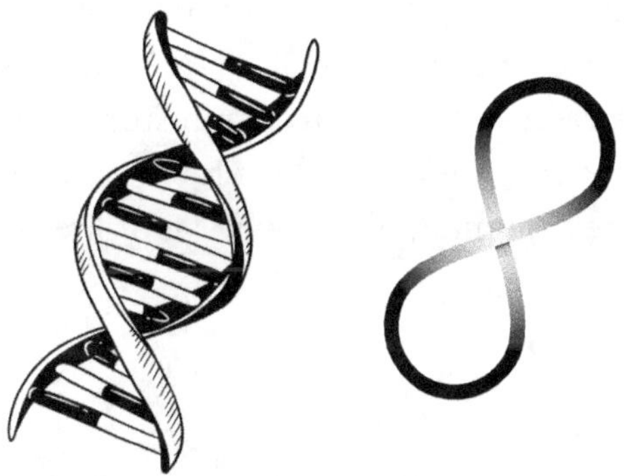

The gematrical value of Khet is associated with concepts such as abundance, power, strength, rare courage, magic, passion and influence. It also relates to the law of karma and its influence on human actions.

Eight encapsulates various forces, abilities, skills, and talents in both the spiritual and material realms. It represents the power of creation and destruction, relating to magic, mysticism, morality, ethics, and primarily the law of cause and effect. This number speaks of karmic equality and the spiritual law stating, "As one sows, so shall they reap."

In the Hebrew name for the number "eight," (שמונה) the word "Soul" is hidden. Rearranging the letters of "Eight" in its missing spelling form (שמנה) yields the word "Soul" (נשמה).

In Judaism, eight is associated with the covenant between man and God, encompassing both verbal (speech) and physical (circumcision) covenants. It also appears in observances like **Shemini Atzeret**[28] and **Simchat Torah**[29], the **eight fringes of the Tzitzit**[30], and the **eight days of the Hanukkah miracle**[31].

This gematrical value of eight is mentioned in biblical stories, scriptures, and Christianity in contexts dealing with resurrection and new beginnings, life after death, and the onset of a new order, era, or cycle, which is essentially its core meaning.

The symbolism of these values is reflected in the eight types of covenants mentioned in the Bible: the covenant of the rainbow with Noah, the covenant of the pieces, the covenant of circumcision with Abraham, and covenants with Isaac, Jacob, Moses, Aaron, and David. It is also present in the resurrection story of Jesus, who rose on the first day of the week after his crucifixion, symbolizing the eighth day and the beginning of a new form of life.

---

[28] Shemini Atzeret is a Jewish holiday celebrated on the eighth day after the Sukkot festival, marking the end of the harvest season. It is a day of solemn assembly and reflection, characterized by special prayers for rain in the coming year.

[29] Simchat Torah is a joyous celebration that marks the completion and restart of the annual cycle of Torah readings. The holiday carries themes of spiritual renewal and gratitude, signifying the transition from the festive Sukkot to a more introspective and prayerful atmosphere.

[30] The eight fringes of the Tzitzit are strings on Jewish prayer garments, reminding wearers of God's commandments. Each corner has four strings, creating eight ends, tied to symbolize religious principles based on Torah directives for mindfulness of God's laws.

[31] The eight days of Hanukkah celebrate a miracle where a day's worth of oil lasted eight days in the Holy Temple after the Maccabees' victory over the Greeks. It symbolizes the triumph of light and spirituality, observed by lighting candles on a menorah for eight nights.

The Zodiac Sign Associated with Khet

Sefer Yetzirah links the letter Khet to the zodiac sign Cancer (crab), providing insights into its prominent characteristics.

Cancer, a water sign, is primarily characterized by strong empathy—the ability to sense and empathize with the emotions of others. This sign imbues individuals with grace, affection, kindliness, and a strong sense of domesticity and sociability. It emphasizes emotionality, gut feelings, a need for the security of home and family, a sense of belonging, emotional tranquility, and a desire for assimilation. People born under Cancer are known for their strong intuition, which enables them to feel others.

The emotional energy associated with this zodiac sign endows individuals with sensitivity, vulnerability, intuition, and reactivity. Their reactions often originate from deep-seated instincts within the unconscious and subconscious realms. On the inhibitory side, this influence may lead to sentimentality, indulgence, fickleness, mood swings, self-pity, a sense of victimhood, and the development of abandonment anxiety.

Diagram 47: Cancer Zodiac Sign

Cancer is symbolized by the Crab, an aquatic creature primarily found in shallow and fresh waters, such as small rivers, coastlines, and pools. The Crab can survive outside water but only for a limited time. Its body is covered by a hard shell, serving as a defense against predators. When threatened, the Crab withdraws into this shell for protection. This behavior symbolically reflects how individuals, akin to the Crab, guard their emotionally vulnerable selves in times of threat.

The Crab's powerful pincers serve as a weapon for defense. When threatened, it stands on its hind legs and opens its pincers to appear larger. Its eyes, located on stalks, provide panoramic vision necessary for hunting and defense. The Crab moves sideways, unable to walk directly forward or backward.

Individuals of the Cancer zodiac sign, similar to the Crab, may withdraw into their shells when feeling insecure or sad, often taking circuitous paths and avoiding direct approaches. When they fixate on something, much like the Crab's pincers, they tend to hold onto it tightly, particularly regarding past memories, and struggle to let go.

Human Emotions

The letter Khet holds a unique position as the first letter in the sequence, connecting individuals to the emotional and sentimental aspects. It also opens the group of watery letters known as "kheneq-met" (חנק-מת), translated as "choking-dead." This term directs our attention to the realm of human emotions, which evoke psychological and emotional responses, both pleasant and unpleasant, alongside instinctual physiological reactions.

To illustrate the power, strength, potency and influence of human emotions and their governance over our lives, let's consider the biblical story of Cain and Abel, where we first encounter the realm of human emotions.

The narrative of Cain and Abel is one of the most captivating biblical stories that allude to the power of choice. It tells of two brothers, one spiritual and the other materialistic, each offering a sacrifice to God. God accepts Abel's offering but rejects Cain's. This rejection triggers intense bitterness, shame, and anger in Cain, emotions he struggles to bear and regulate. Unable to manage his emotions, Cain's turmoil drives him to the violent act of murdering his brother.

God, recognizing the inner struggle and emotional turmoil within Cain, sees his inability to manage his emotions, which leads to distressing thoughts. Perceiving the potential for destructive actions, God appeals to Cain's intellect, urging him to think rationally and master his emotions. God warns him against the temptation of sin, saying, *"Sin is lurking at the door; and its desire is for you, but you must master it."* (*Genesis*, Chapter 4, Verse 7)

Diagram 48: Cain and Abel

This biblical story vividly portrays the human soul, filled with a variety of emotions, including those with low vibrational frequencies that evoke irrational anxieties and fears. These fears include the fear of rejection, abandonment, and not feeling good enough, worthy enough, or loved enough. Such anxieties give rise to frustration, anger, jealousy, hatred, and an inclination toward sin, often followed by feelings of guilt.

The Groups the Letter Khet is Associated With

Water Element Letter

The letter Khet is the first letter that draws our attention to our "inner child"—an inner aspect within us yearning for attention and recognition. As an emotional and sentimental letter, it encapsulates emotional vulnerability. Those associated with the letter Khet should remain mindful of this emotional aspect, which tends to manage them subconsciously and influence their actions. The letter urges those individuals to connect with their inner child and, if necessary, initiate a healing process.

Practical Letter

Khet is the fourth letter in the group of twelve simple letters, representing the practical and applied aspects of a person. It endows individuals with the ability to establish themselves in earthly life through their fertile and creative watery power.

The Measure of Mercy

The letter Khet embodies the measure of mercy, expressed through qualities such as consideration, generosity, understanding, and forgiveness. This measure reflects the energy awakened in a person in response to another's distress, compelling them to be considerate and helpful and to ease the suffering of others.

However, the inhibiting aspect of this measure can manifest as providing assistance based on considerations of personal profitability and gain. This involves evaluating whether helping is beneficial for oneself and what personal gain can be derived from it rather than acting purely for the sake of the person or situation in need.

Karma and Rectification Letter

The letter Khet is part of the group of karma and rectification letters, signifying the inner waters within a person that seek purification, balance, and rectification.

Strengths

The strengths associated with the letter Khet include qualities such as willpower, assertiveness, realism, practicality, efficiency, determination, and seriousness. These are complemented by an ability to focus on goals and objectives. Additional strengths encompass caring, mediumship, motherhood, a therapeutic sense, authoritativeness, the need to care and protect, heartfelt warmth, identification, solidarity, sentimentality, rich imagination, memory, empathy, understanding, listening ability, and sensitivity. These qualities enable individuals to comprehend and empathize with others.

Weaknesses

Conversely, weaknesses associated with Khet include heightened sensitivity, intense emotionality, lack of confidence, excessive caution, doubtfulness, dependency, clinginess, possessiveness, and emotional turmoil. A compulsive desire to give excessively and emotionally suffocate others is also common, along with restlessness, frequent mood swings, irritability, excessive worry, numerous fears, daydreaming, lack of grounding, hesitation, and emotional rigidity. The inhibiting aspect manifests in an inability to withstand pressure, a tendency toward nostalgia, and the preservation of emotionally charged memories.

א ב ג ד ה ה ו ז ח ט י כ ל מ נ ס ע פ צ ק ר ש ת

"Human behavior flows from three main sources:
desire, emotion, and knowledge."

Plato

Uniqueness and Purpose

The letter Thet (טֵית), the ninth letter in the Hebrew alphabet, symbolizes the law of the eternal cycle in the wheel of life and the creative ability that enables humans to leave a unique imprint on their lives. Thet also highlights the notion of hidden good within the human soul.

Kabbalistic teachings suggest that the name of the letter Thet reveals a hint of the dual inherent qualities in every individual: purity and impurity, along with a natural inclination toward both goodness and evil.

Humans, as living souls, embody these inclinations. The "good inclination" (yetzer hatov) represents the higher, divine aspect of humanity, symbolizing tendencies toward goodness, purity, moral conscience, empathy, and altruistic acts. It is the inner light guiding ethical behavior. Conversely, the "evil inclination" (yetzer hara) reflects our lower, animalistic side, often leading to impurity and characterized by selfish or instinctual drives, such as survival, pleasure, and personal gain.

These concepts are pivotal in Jewish psychology and moral philosophy, illustrating the internal struggle between contrasting aspects of human nature. The interplay between the good and evil inclinations is fundamental to the human experience, influencing behavior and decision-making.

The letter Thet serves a twofold purpose: to guide individuals in revealing their inner light and the concealed goodness within, enabling them to share this divine essence with others and to foster authentic inner strength and inner forcefield. These qualities emerge as individuals recognize and engage with the dual forces within them. By fully experiencing, accepting, and respecting these inclinations, without repression or denial, and acknowledging that they represent two sides of the same coin, individuals can consciously choose between them from an informed and mindful state of mind.

The Letter in Creation Stories

The first mention of the letter Thet in the Genesis narratives is in the word "tov" (טוב), meaning "good," in verse: *"God saw that the light was good; and God separated the light from the darkness."* (*Genesis*, Chapter 1, Verse 4) The word "good" is emphasized numerous times throughout the creation process, underscoring the importance of making distinctions between things.

Pronunciation

The letter Theth is pronounced as "The-t" and sometimes as "Te-t" and can be represented in English as T or TH.

The pronunciation, name, and meaning of the letter Thet provide profound insights into its essence and energetic influence. The pronunciation of the letter can be written as "טית" or "טיט." When Thet is written in the form "טיט," it embodies a dual interpretation. The first is that of clay—cement and material in the hands of the creator, the substance from which a sculptor molds form. The second interpretation is mud and dirt—the elemental matter from which humans originate and to which they eventually return.

The name and pronunciation of Thet imply that the human soul can be shaped according to an individual's free will and choice. To achieve this, one must first recognize the dual forces within their soul—the inclinations toward good and evil. To mold the lower aspects of the soul, akin to clay in the hands of a creator, a person needs to develop discretion and inner strength, as described in Kabbalistic studies as "the power of resistance" (כוח ההתנגדות).

Diagram 49: Clay

The interplay between these two inclinations can be metaphorically compared to that of a sheep and a shepherd Metaphorically speaking, within each of us exists both a sheep and a shepherd. Free choice enables us to choose which of the two we wish to embody, and to which of these two we assign our power.

Graphic Shape

The graphical shape of the letter Thet is a closed form on three sides, sealed at its lower part and on both sides, with only a narrow and small upper opening. This configuration resembles a vessel, a pitcher, or a container with a small lid, limiting the entry of external elements.

The letter is uniformly closed in three directions in both its handwritten and printed forms. It is closed downward to the matters of the earthly realm and partially closed upward toward the spiritual realm. It turns its back to the wisdom of the preceding letter, Khet, and the following letter, Yod.

The graphical shape of Thet embodies multifaceted symbolism. First, it signifies a person's ability to receive divine light and conceal it within. Second, it denotes the individual's capacity to contain and hold within. Third, it suggests a predisposition toward closure and the accumulation of emotions, things, and experiences. This graphical shape draws individuals inward, guiding them toward their inner center, enabling the revelation and integration of the concealed divine light into their essence.

Additionally, the graphical shape of the letter bears a resemblance to an Ouroboros, a mystical serpent that bites its tail. This symbol of the Ouroboros consuming its tail to sustain life represents the perpetual cycle of renewal within the circle of life—embodying the continuous cycle of birth, death and rebirth.

Diagram 50: Thet in Print and Handwriting

Diagram 51: Ouroboros

Gematrical Value

The gematrical value of the letter Thet is nine, a number with profound significance in both spiritual and material realms. This value symbolizes the conclusion of a cycle, the achievement of goals, and the end of a journey, while also heralding new beginnings and the potential for rebirth every nine lunar months. It embodies the power of transformation, turning the old into the new while preserving its essence.

Diagram 52: The Uniqueness of the Value Nine

$1 \times 9 = 9, 2 \times 9 = 18 (1 + 8 = 9), 3 \times 9 = 27 (2 + 7 = 9)$ **and so on**

Nine is the final one-digit number before the leap to two-digit numbers, where the accompanying zero magnifies each characteristic of the adjacent number, dramatically enhancing its attributes and pushing it toward its purest expression. This process is reminiscent of a caterpillar's metamorphosis into a butterfly.

The number nine is associated with transformative energy, symbolizing profound internal change. It represents a state in which individuals learn to perceive things from a new perspective, adopt significant viewpoints, and, as a result, change their fundamental beliefs about themselves and the world. This transformative process enables individuals to become personal role models, demonstrating how change and evolution are possible.

In Judaism, this numerical value is linked to the nine rhythms of life, suggesting that every nine years, a person alters the rhythm of their life. This concept is encapsulated in the saying, *"Nine steps he will walk and nine steps he will rush."*

In nature, the number nine symbolizes the plowing period, a time during which the earth undergoes preparation before new sowing. In humans, it represents the slow maturation stage that occurs during the nine months of pregnancy.

The value of the letter, symbolizing transformation, beginnings, and endings, corresponds to the stages of pregnancy and the rhythm of life. It encourages individuals to let go of the past and embrace the transformative power within them for complete self-evolution.

The vibrational frequencies of the letter Thet guide a person to move beyond their bubble— their individual story and drama—and propel them to release their attachment to the past and the old, thereby opening up to the new, similar to a fetus leaving its mother's womb and breaking free from the placenta.

Diagram 54: Number Six

Diagram 53: Number Nine

Diagram 55: Fetus in Mother's Womb

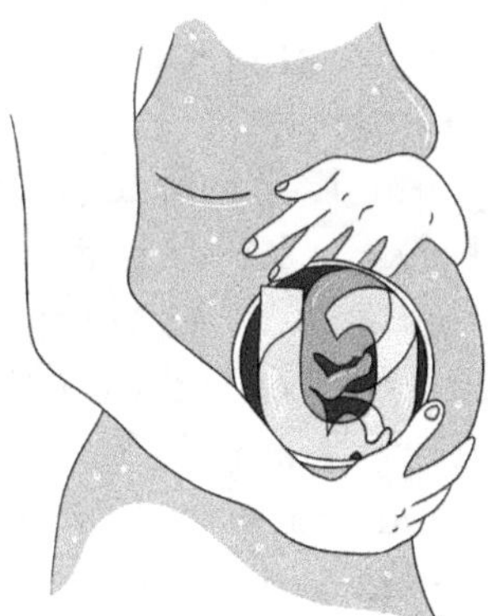

The graphical shape of the letter Thet, in both its handwritten form and its numerical value, bears a striking resemblance to a fetus nestled within its mother's womb. The numerical value of nine aligns with the advanced stages of pregnancy, mirroring the intricate position of the developing fetus. Interestingly, inverting the number nine transforms into six, reminiscent of the early stages of pregnancy and remarkably akin to the graphical shape of the handwritten Thet.

Among the twenty-two letters comprising the Hebrew alphabet, Thet stands alone in having a graphical shape that precisely corresponds to its numerical value. This unique alignment underscores the symbolic connection between the visual representation of the letter, its numerical value, and the evocative imagery of a fetus in both its early and advanced stages within the mother's womb.

The Zodiac Sign Associated with Thet

Sefer Yetzirah associates the letter Thet with the Leo zodiac sign, providing insights into its prominent characteristics. The Leo sign, ruled by the element of fire, is marked by a compelling need for creative self-expression and a strong desire to impress and be at the center of attention. Notable traits include creativity, passion, and lust.

The lion is a large predator belonging to the feline family and is a highly sophisticated terrestrial predator. The lion is more skilled at hunting than any other terrestrial predator and is considered the king of the animal kingdom. Lions spend the majority of their time resting, conserving energy for hunting, and using their powerful roar for communication and to establish territory. This roar metaphorically represents the Leo individual's desire to be noticed and acknowledged, embodying a flair for dramatic self-expression that seeks to captivate and charm audiences. Astrologically, Leos are believed to possess innate acting skills and creativity.

In Judaism, the lion embodies dual aspects of both benevolence and malevolence, representing both good and evil.

Diagram 56: Leo Zodiac Sign

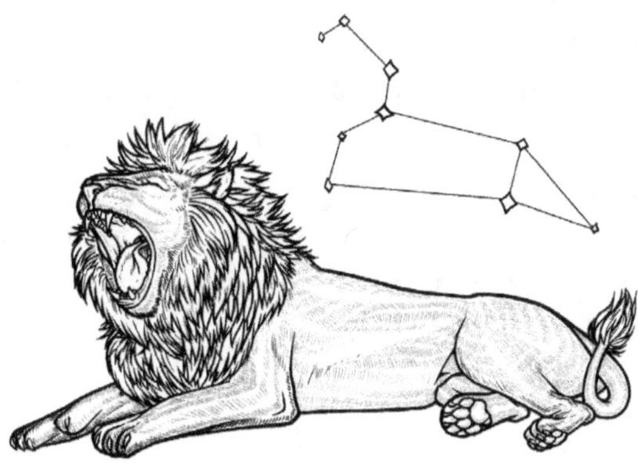

The Leo sign, corresponding to the Hebrew month of Av (July-August), aligns with the scorching heat of the summer season. Thus, the fire element symbolized by Thet represents a warm, dry, and intense fire. Its vibrational frequencies instill qualities such as energy, vitality, vigor, enthusiasm, spontaneity, boldness and self-confidence in individuals, coupled with a competitive spirit. This dynamic blend encourages readiness to challenge anything that restricts movement, space, and creative self-expression.

Such characteristics forge an active and assertive personality, unwavering in goal pursuit. However, when faced with real or perceived threats, based on their subjective feelings, their response is immediate and unequivocal, often leading to sharp verbal attacks. At these moments, they are primed to vigorously defend their stance or fight for victory.

The Groups the Letter Thet is Associated With

Fire Element Letter

The letter Thet is associated with the fire element, symbolizing a potent creative and driving force. This element grants an individual's creativity, self-reliance, and motivation. In the context of this letter, the fire element is expressed through traits such as self-confidence, willpower, an inherent sense of ability, enthusiasm, and dynamism, emphasizing a significant need for expansive opportunities for action and self-expression.

Aspirational Letter

Thet is the first letter in the group of ThLQ'Tz letters, symbolizing the aspirational aspect of human nature. Individuals who associated with this letter often strive to highlight their uniqueness in some way, seeking avenues to underscore their individuality.

As a rectification letter featuring a graphical shape that rises above the baseline in both written forms, Thet embodies an ambitious spirit marked by a deep yearning for recognition and distinction. This drive may be expressed overtly or through nuanced behaviors, leading individuals to embrace specific identities or philosophies, evidenced by declarations like "I am spiritual," "I am environmentally conscious," "I am vegan," etc.

Practical Letter

The letter Thet is the fifth letter in the group of twelve simple letters, representing the practical and applied aspects of a person. The letter endows individuals with the ability to establish themselves in earthly life through their creative and inventive power.

The Measure of Mercy

Thet embodies the measure of mercy, characterized by consideration, generosity, understanding, and forgiving nature. This measure reflects the energy awakened in a person in response to another's distress, compelling them to be considerate and helpful and alleviate the suffering of others.

However, the inhibiting aspect of this measure tends to manifest in providing assistance based on considerations of profitability and gain, evaluating personal benefits rather than acting purely for the sake of the person or situation in need.

Karma and Rectification Letter

The letter Thet belongs to the group of karma and rectification letters, and it embodies the measure of mercy. This energetic blend may foster in individuals a strong desire to receive for oneself, challenges in adapting to change, new people, and situations, as well as tendencies toward attachment, accumulation, possessiveness, and a domineering nature. Giving may often be motivated by self-gain rather than altruism. The rectification process for individuals associated with this letter involves addressing these tendencies.

Strengths

Individuals associated with the letter Thet often exhibit strengths such as intuition, vitality, vigor, courage, optimism, joy, warmth, enthusiasm, creativity, independence, self-confidence, bravery, dynamism, aspiration, ambition, determination, improvisation, verbal ability, generosity, stubbornness, perseverance, connection to passion, and visionary foresight.

Weaknesses

Conversely, weaknesses may include closeness, self-centeredness, egocentricity, overt or covert domineering, self-importance, stereotypical thinking, excessive stubbornness, pride, arrogance, a strong desire to impress, leading inauthenticity, a relentless quest for admiration and respect, and uncontrolled ambition. The inhibiting aspect of the letter could manifest in power struggles, a lack of tact, theatricality, melodramatic reactions, and tendencies toward idolatry. When faced with unpleasant or inappropriate situations, individuals associated with this letter or its corresponding zodiac sign might instinctively resort to verbal aggression, characterized by a blunt and forceful approach.

אבגדההוזחטי׳כלמנסעפצקרשת

*"Silence brings forth answers; silence is the
language of God, all else is poor translation."*

Jalal ad-Din Rumi

Uniqueness and Purpose

The letter Yod (יוד) is the tenth letter in the Hebrew alphabet, imbued with both spiritual and earthly energetic power that serves to protect and shield individuals from harm.

The letter Yod appears in the word "Shaddai" (שדי), inscribed on Mezuzahs (doorposts in Hebrew homes), symbolizing the feminine divine power that protects and guards humans. The letter expresses the concept of an inner compass, guiding individuals toward their higher selves. It signifies the path leading to the initial acquaintance with their "I am" consciousness.

The letter Yod is considered a blessed letter, whose vibrational frequencies endows individuals with important qualities such as cleverness, innovation, ambition, enthusiasm, productivity, efficiency, control, organizational capabilities, practicality, and pragmatism.

Yod aims to foster a connection to one's inner core and awaken a deep yearning for absolute truth and the quest for life's meaning. This meaning should provide purpose and clear direction. The overarching purpose of the letter is to propel individuals toward a higher developmental stage, enabling them to shine as beacons of light amidst darkness.

The Letter in Creation Stories

The first appearance of the letter Yod in the Genesis stories is in the word "yehi" (יהי), which means "let there be." This is seen in the phrase: *"Then God said, 'Let there be light;' and there was light."* (*Genesis*, Chapter 1, Verse 3)

The term "yehi" indicates a state of existence, occurrence, and development. As a verb, it conveys command and future tense in biblical language, signifying that divine creation commenced through the spoken word, initiated by the word "yehi."

Pronunciation

The letter Yod is pronounced "Yod" and can be represented in English as I, J or Y, depending on its position in a word or name and its punctuation marks.

The pronunciation of the letter Yod, its name and its significance offer insights into its essence and energetic power. Its name and pronunciation have various interpretations. The first relates to iodine, a chemical mineral crucial for the proper functioning of the human thyroid gland. Iodine is an essential component in producing hormones that regulate the body's metabolism. Insufficient iodine, especially during pregnancy and early childhood, can impede brain growth and development, physical growth, motor and cognitive function, and, in some cases, result in intellectual disabilities.

The second interpretation relates to the word "yad" (יד), meaning "hand." This refers to the physical organ extending from the shoulder to the forearm, used by a person for action and doing and is present on both sides of the body.

Diagram 57: Hand

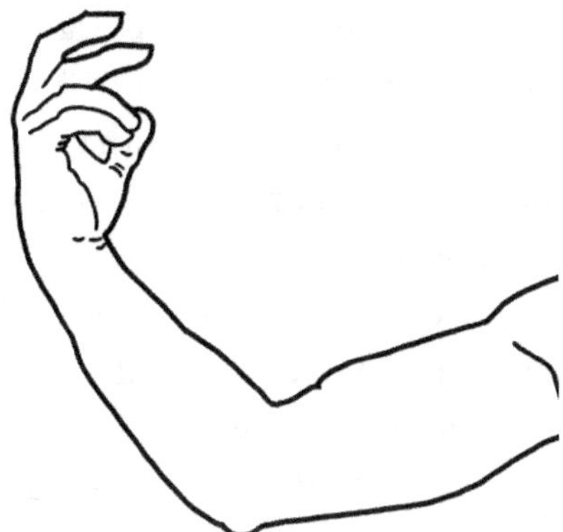

Graphic Shape

The graphical shape of the letter Yod is small and minimalistic, composed of two short lines resembling two floating dots in space or akin to a comma and a period. Despite being the smallest letter among the twenty-two letters of the Hebrew alphabet, Yod constitutes a significant portion of most spiritual letters.

The letter Yod possesses a diminutive body and a short leg that appears to hover in the air. This shape symbolizes qualities such as lightness, flexibility in movement, and the capacity to effortlessly rise above things. However, its limiting aspect signifies a level of stability that can make it easily swayed and lose its balance. When this happens, it may lead a person to develop issues such as arrogance and a condescending attitude.

Gematrical Value

The gematrical value of the letter Yod is ten, a strong and meaningful number that embodies divine order and conveys the concept of perfection. It is a value often used to describe something that approaches perfection or the highest degree of quality.

We encounter the value ten in various significant contexts: the Ten Commandments, the ten divine Sefirot of the Tree of Life, the ten utterances that created the world, the tithe – the custom practiced by Israelites of giving one-tenth of earnings to charity, the ten trials that the Israelites underwent in the desert as described in the Bible, and the ten trials endured by Abraham, the father of all nations, starting with the command "Go to yourself" (לך לך) and culminating with the story of the binding of Isaac.

The number ten combines the characteristics of the number one, which include primacy, originality, and individualism, and those of the number zero, which enhance the qualities of the number one.

The number zero is a highly powerful value associated with the frequencies of divine creation. It represents the eternal life force, the concept of unity, and the infinite possibilities available to humans. Its primary characteristic is amplifying the frequency of the number it accompanies, multiplying the quality and energy of that number, and propelling it toward its purest expression.

The vibrational frequencies of the number zero encourage individuals to transcend from their illusionary selves—their personal drama, ego, personality, and the **Qliphoth**[32] accumulated throughout their life incarnations—toward their true, authentic nature.

This value prompts individuals to pause, assess their current situation, reflect on their journey, examine their actions and achievements, consider their development, and decide what they want to learn and become moving forward.

---

[32] Qliphoth refers to the forces of impurity, negativity, evil, and spiritual corruption. It is intricately linked to the shells or husks that envelop the divine spark.

The Zodiac Sign Associated with Yod

Sefer Yetzirah connects the letter Yod to the zodiac sign Virgo, thus offering us additional insights into its prominent characteristics. Virgo is associated with the earth element from which humanity was created. Key characteristics of Virgo include survival skills, order, organization, efficiency, process optimization and efficient, practical implementation.

Diagram 58: Virgo Zodiac Sign

The astrological sign of Virgo is symbolized by a maiden holding a sheaf of wheat. Wheat holds significant symbolism in **Midrash**[33] and the Bible. Wheat, according to Judaism, symbolizes spiritual nourishment (Torah), material sustenance (bread), and

---

[33] Midrash is an ancient commentary attached to sections of the Hebrew scriptures, used extensively by Jewish scholars. It provides interpretation, explanation and elaboration of the biblical text, often revealing deeper insights, ethical teachings, and moral lessons that may not be immediately apparent in the text itself.

the Tree of Knowledge. Like wheat, which grows from the earth, humans are born from it, nourished by it, and eventually return to it.

To derive nourishment from wheat, one must engage in a chain of agricultural actions related to the earth, including sowing, harvesting, gathering, binding sheaves, threshing, grinding, and baking. Similarly, the spiritual process requires a person to undergo ten stages of developmental growth before they can reap divine bounty.

Among the earth signs, Virgo is the lightest and most adaptable. Its characteristics include a strong sense of responsibility, keen perception, and practicality. Virgos are known for their flexibility, clear-mindedness, and rationality, with notable attention to detail. They prioritize efficiency and quality over quantity, often preferring supportive roles where they can focus on delivering high-quality results. Their critical thinking and meticulous approach allow them to excel in roles that contribute to the greater system.

Consciousness and the Introspection

The letter Yod symbolizes the stage in which recognition and complete self-consciousness develop within a person - a consciousness that evolves through processes such as introspection and inner reflection.

The letter Yod is associated with a period in nature when individuals reap what they have sown and grown. In Judaism, this period corresponds to the Hebrew month of Elul, a time for repentance, deep self-examination, summarizing the events of the past year, and preparing for improvements in the upcoming year.

From a psychological perspective, the letter Yod directs individuals toward introspection, encouraging them to go inward, disconnect from the noisy and tumultuous external world, and engage in a deeply reflective process. The aim is to hear the insights emerging from within, guiding individuals to find their internal compass and "inner lantern" to illuminate their path, first for themselves and then for others. In the esoteric tradition, the inner lantern represents higher wisdom and is associated with King Solomon's seal.

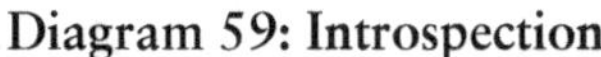

Diagram 59: Introspection

The letter Yod prompts individuals to turn inward, to connect with their intuition and inner guidance, to assess their core beliefs and values, and all those elements that define their 'self.' It encourages examining how well they live their lives in accordance with their inner and moral truth. This includes scrutinizing their thoughts, emotions, and behavioral patterns, enabling them to recognize and break free from unconscious patterns that seek external validation.

As long as this introspective process does not occur, a person remains under the influence of unconscious forces that tend to throw them off balance and away from their inner center. The ability to hear our truth arises only when we are in a stable inner center.

In Kabbalah, the letter Yod embodies the principle of "In its smallness is its greatness" (בקטנותה גדולתה). The purpose of Yod is to guide individuals to cultivate humility, uniqueness, authenticity, self-discipline, and precision in their being.

However, individuals associated with this letter may become confused. Instead of focusing on the exactness of their being, they might pursue "perfection," paying critical attention to everything they perceive as not "perfect," both in themselves and others.

The Groups the Letter Yod is Associated With

Earth Element Letter

The element associated with the letter Yod is earth, representing material and solid energy. This element connects humans to the Earth, endowing them with physical strength, patience, caution, moderation and high endurance. The vibrational frequencies of the letter tend to evoke in individuals a desire to assimilate and root themselves in the earthly realm, to hold onto the tangible, and to preserve the existing.

Karma and Rectification Letter

The letter Yod belongs to the group of karma and rectification letters. It embodies vibrational frequencies that lead individuals to experiential interactions, aiming to develop an awakened consciousness, strengthen the sense of unity within, and guide them toward a corrected approach to life and people.

The letter Yod is a supreme letter, implying that the rectification required from individuals associated with this letter relates to their haughty attitude, where they tend to view others from an 'ivory tower' and conduct themselves from a sense of entitlement.

Mercy Letter

The letter Yod embodies the measure of mercy, expressed through qualities such as consideration, generosity, understanding, and forgiveness. This measure reflects the energy awakened in response to another's distress, compelling them to be considerate and helpful and alleviate the suffering of others. However, the inhibiting aspect of this measure tends to manifest in providing assistance based on personal profitability and gain, evaluating whether it is beneficial for them and what personal gain can be derived from it.

Practical Letter

The letter Yod is the sixth letter in the group of twelve simple letters, representing the practical and applied aspects of a person. It endows individuals with the ability to establish themselves in earthly life through their high capability to optimize processes and implement projects in a practical and efficient manner. As a warm and earthy letter that encompasses both material and spiritual aspects, it draws people toward actions rooted in both spirit and matter.

Strengths

Individuals associated with the letter Yod exhibit strengths that include responsibility, practicality, efficiency, grounding, solidity, inner peace, self-satisfaction, analytical thinking, discernment, humility, modesty, patience, endurance, caution, order, organization, attention to detail, precision, perseverance, as well as and monitoring, evaluation and survival skills.

Weaknesses

Conversely, weaknesses may include criticality, skepticism, poor self-concept, shyness, hypochondria, perfectionism, an excessive focus on minor details, restlessness, irritability, excessive worry, conservatism, possessiveness, difficulty in letting go, a tendency toward victimization, and masochism. In a state of imbalance, the vibrational frequencies of the letter Yod can lead a person toward meticulousness, focusing on small details, feeling superior over others, and observing others from a critical standpoint.

אבגדההוזחחטיכךלמנסעפצקרשת

"There are three good things: to be bent but upright, to cry out silently, and to be alone in the midst of a marketplace."

Menachem Mendel of Kotzk

Uniqueness and Purpose

The letter Caf (כַּף) is the eleventh letter in the Hebrew alphabet. It symbolizes the **alchemical power**[34] inherent within a person and the energetic movement that connects an individual to the **unified field**[35]—the realm where all human soul potentials exist. The letters' purpose is to foster humility and attunement.

Positioned centrally in the Hebrew alphabet, Caf is adjacent to the letter Lamed, which immediately follows it. Together, they form the word "col" (כל), meaning "all." This signifies completeness, wholeness, and permanence. Caf echoes the concept that enlightened creations originate from a stable connection to the inner center and the "I am" presence. Its vibrational frequencies offer individuals the opportunity to 'restart' their life's path.

----

[34]   Alchemical power encapsulates the transformative process of converting challenges into opportunities for self-discovery and enlightenment. This process is analogous to the alchemical transformation of base metals into gold, symbolizing personal growth. It involves stages like purification, shedding old patterns, confronting challenges, and integrating newfound wisdom.

[35]   The term "Unified Field" refers to a metaphysical unified field that encompasses the full spectrum of human soul potentials and capabilities. Within this expansive and interconnected domain, emotions, intellect, intuition, and spirituality coexist harmoniously. Connecting with this field enables individuals to delve into deeper dimensions of consciousness, transcend limitations, and attain a higher state of being.

The Letter in Creation Stories

The first encounter with the letter Caf in the *Genesis* stories occurs in the word "Ci" (כִּי), meaning "that it," as seen in the verse: *"God saw that the light was good; and God separated the light from the darkness."* (*Genesis*, Chapter 1, Verse 4)

In Hebrew, the word Ci (כִּי) functions as a conjunction, connecting sentences, words, and paragraphs. Its primary roles are to clarify the writer's messages and assist the reader in navigating and understanding the text. Each conjunction word establishes a logical connection, guiding the reader through contradictions, goals, reasons, or consequences. Ci (כִּי) indicates a "cause-and-effect" relationship and can take various forms, such as because, since, as, due to, following, and for that.

The letter Caf appears again in the creation stories in the word "Ken" (כֵּן), paired with "Vaehi" (וַיְהִי), together meaning "It was so" (ויהי כן), as illustrated in verse: *"God made the expanse, and separated the waters that were below the expanse from the waters that were above the expanse; and it was so."* (*Genesis*, Chapter 1, Verse 7)

Ken (כֵּן) signifies approval or agreement, akin to the English word Yes. This verse highlights, among other aspects, a distinction between light and darkness and between the upper and lower waters, suggesting that this distinction is intentional and positive. The created world aligns with God's plan and fulfills His will.

The phrase "Ci-Tov" (כי טוב), translating to "As it is good," is mentioned seven times during the creation process. Each instance follows a stage of creation, paired with "Vaehi-Cen" (ויהי כן), suggesting that God paused after each stage to assess His creations before proceeding.

Biblical commentators interpret this to teach two key lessons: Firstly, the practical meaning of "good"—something that fulfills its purpose and is beneficial. Secondly, it emphasizes the importance of discernment, specifically the ability to separate the wheat from the chaff. This metaphorically signifies the distinction between truth and falsehood and understanding the interplay between cause and effect. The ability to recognize the difference between two things and how one thing leads to another is a necessary skill that enables exercising discretion.

Pronunciation

The letter Caf is pronounced as "Caf", or "Cha-f" and can be represented in English as C, CH, K, KH or X, depending on its position in a word or name and its hard or soft pronunciation.

The pronunciation, name, and meaning of the letter Caf provide additional insights into its essence and the energetic encoding it carries. The pronunciation of Caf's conveys significant functions. The first meaning refers to a "spoon"—a curved tool used for stirring and consuming primarily liquid foods, consisting of a small elliptical or round bowl connected to a long handle.

Diagram 60: Spoon

The second meaning pertains to the "palm" of the hand, an external organ located at the end of each arm, essential for gripping and holding. The palm plays a critical role in various activities such as touching, feeling, caressing, sensing, receiving, grasping, containing, holding, arranging, and manipulating.

The functionality of our palm is closely linked with the "Hand," the physical organ discussed in the context of the previous letter, Yod. These two letters, Yod and Caf, form the Hebrew word 'Ci,' which appears repeatedly in the creation stories as a symbol of goodness, exemplified in Genesis, Chapter 1, Verse 4.

Diagram 61: The Palm

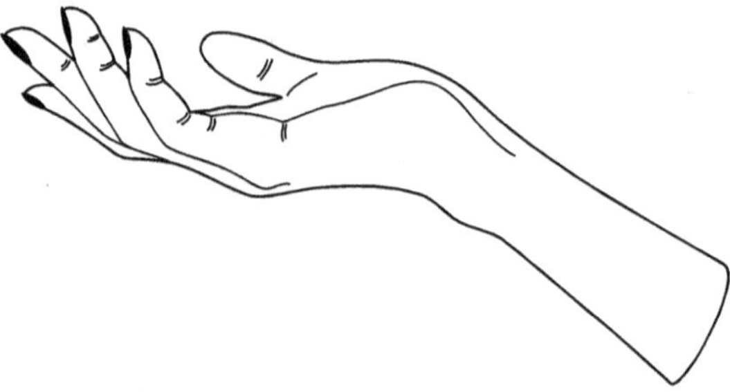

The human palm is capable of both verbal and non-verbal communication. The positioning of our hands can reflect our mental state—whether open to receiving and giving or closed; whether gentle or firm, whether holding onto something or being held. Hand movements, including gestures and sign language, are potent forms of communication. For example, a clenched fist might express emotions such as anger or frustration. With our palms, we can write, draw, sculpt, and create lasting impressions.

In Kabbalistic interpretation, the pronunciation of Caf is linked to the "Scales of Justice" (כף המאזנים), a biblical concept denoting a state of decision-making, where actions are weighed, tipping the scales toward right or duty. This concept is encapsulated in the phrase, *"Man's fate hangs on the scales."*

Diagram 62: Scales

Graphic Shape

The letter Caf has a closed shape from three sides. It is closed upward, symbolizing its closeness to spiritual matters and unity consciousness, and closed downward, representing its closeness to earthly matters, while turning its back to the wisdom of the previous letter, Yod.

The circular trajectory of Caf symbolizes perpetual motion, echoing the ecliptic plane that encompasses Earth's orbit around the sun. As we will explore later, Caf is associated with the sun, the central celestial body around which the moon and stars orbit, mirroring Caf's central placement among the twenty-two letters.

The shape of Caf also resembles a dome, similar to a celestial dome (sky), and a **Kippah**[36], a thin, round piece of fabric worn on the heads by Jews. The round shape of Caf is reflected in sacred structures such as churches, mosques, or dome houses.

---

[36]   Kippah is a small fabric covering or rounded skullcap worn by Jewish men as a sign of reverence and a reminder of the presence of God.

Diagram 63: Spiral Diagram

Diagram 64: Logarithmic Spiral

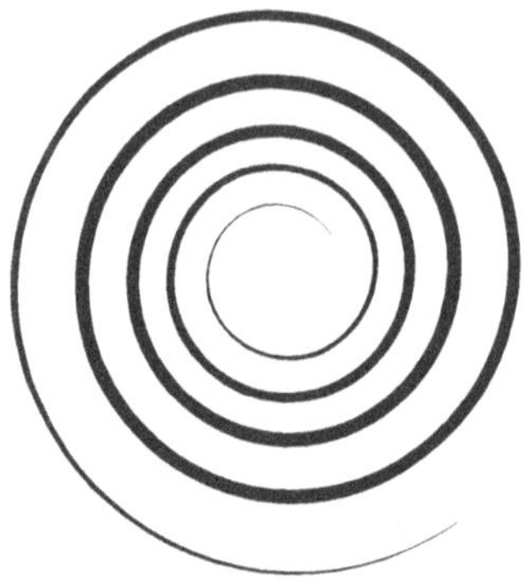

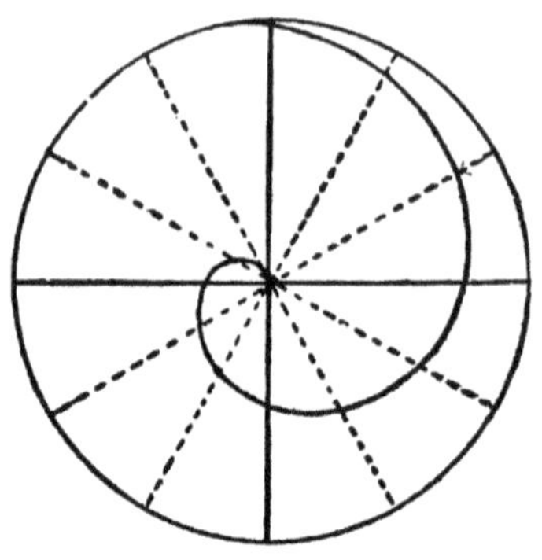

Diagram 65: Archimedean Spiral

Diagram 66: Snail Shell

Symbolizing the concept of eternity, Caf embodies the circularity and eternal nature of human life. It reminds us that life is not a linear journey, as we often perceive it. Rather than moving forward and leaving things behind, Caf suggests that life involves constant repetition, revolving around the same roles and patterns until full self-awareness is achieved.

In the game of life, we transition from one incarnation to another with our soulmates, who are our partners in life's journey. In each incarnation, what changes is our external physical appearance and the roles of our soulmates. Life lessons will repeat in a circular manner until we develop unity consciousness at its core.

Diagram 67: Kippah

Diagram 68: Sky Dome

Diagram 69: Dome House

The concept of life's cyclic nature is not new and has been explored by many philosophers and spiritual teachers. Friedrich Nietzsche, an existentialist philosopher, along with figures like George Gurdjieff, Peter Ouspensky, Osho and others, have discussed this idea. These philosophers liken life's repetition to a prison, asserting that until a person undergoes a transformative developmental process that changes their consciousness and emotional world, they remain "asleep," perpetually rolling in the circle of life and encountering the same lessons in each incarnation.

Gematrical Value

The gematrical value of the letter Caf is twenty, a number representing qualities such as sensitivity, empathy, caring, diplomacy, negotiation, relationships, and partnerships. On the negative side, it can signify impatience, instability, and hastiness.

In biblical narratives and scriptures, this value often symbolizes cyclicality and a fresh start, typically following a period of waiting or anticipation. It signifies the release from a burden, leading to self-liberation, the completion of one life cycle, and the beginning of a new one.

One of the biblical stories that connects us to the wisdom of Caf is the story of Jacob. After fleeing from Canaan and his brother Esau due to deceit and theft of blessings, Jacob spends twenty years freeing himself from the grip of his father-in-law Laban. This is expressed in *Genesis*, Chapter 31, Verse 41: *"For these twenty years I have been in your house; I served you fourteen years for your two daughters, and six years for your flock, and you changed my wages ten times."*

The value of twenty appears again in the Book of Judges, Chapter 4, which describes societal anarchy. Due to a lack of self-leadership and external spiritual guidance, the Israelites deviated from their spiritual obligations made at Mount Sinai, turning to worship Canaanite deities: Baal, the god of rain, and Asherah, the goddess of fertility. This led to twenty years of servitude under the Canaanites until their liberation from the Canaanite king.

The number twenty combines the attributes of the number two and zero. The corresponding letter to Caf in the unit's digit is Bet, with a numerical value of two. The addition of zero amplifies these attributes, encouraging individuals to transcend their illusionary selves—their dramas, egos, and conditioned selves - toward their true, authentic nature and the inner center connecting them to their field of potential.

The Planet Associated with Caf

"He made the letter Caf king, and He bound a crown to it, and He combined one with another, and with them, He formed the sun..." (*Sefer Yetzirah*, Chapter 4, Verse 8)

Sefer Yetzirah connects the letter Caf to the sun, illuminating the qualities embodied within the letter. The sun, a giant ball of hot gas, serves as the central body in our solar system, around which various celestial bodies, including Earth, orbit. It is a crucial source of light, energy, and heat, influencing seasons, periods, and eras. Without the sun's light, trees would not grow, water would freeze, and life on Earth would cease.

In Western astrology, the sun is classified as one of the five personal planets, representing a person's characteristics, tendencies, personal needs, and desires. It symbolizes the energetic force driving individuals toward the "self"—self-expansion, self-building, and heightened self-awareness. This force provides strength, inspiration, purpose, and a desire for activities that bring honor and appreciation. It fosters the development of a unique, well-defined, and authentic self-identity, or as it is termed in psychological language, "self-individuality."

The sun symbolizes the ego, pride, and identity—the essence one projects to the world. Based on the position of Caf in a person's name and their astrological maps, one can gain insights into their character, personality, fundamental behaviors, adopted beliefs, and areas where their personality requires redemption.

The solar consciousness imparts a strong, dominant, and ruling energy. On the positive side, it bestows warmth, heartfulness, strength, creativity, vitality, dynamism, drive, self-confidence, strong willpower, independence, and leadership. However, on the negative side, this energy can lead to power complexities, including excessive self-centeredness, selfishness, tyranny, pride, lack of self-restraint, uncontrolled ambition, and a craving for honor, power, and control.

The warm vibrational frequencies of Caf encourage individuals to develop a distinct "personal identity" and an awakened awareness of their "I am" presence.

Furthermore, the Hebrew name for the sun, "Shemesh," provides additional insight into Caf's characteristics. The words "Shemesh" (שֶׁמֶשׁ), meaning "sun," and "Shamash" (שַׁמָּשׁ), meaning "service," are written similarly in Hebrew but with different vowel markings. This similarly underscores the service theme intrinsic to those associated with this letter—to serve, assist, and give generously.

The Groups the Letter Caf is Associated With

Fire Element Letter

The element associated with the letter Caf is fire. This letter expresses the fire element as a warm, burning, and kindling fire that, in its constructive expression, awakens qualities such as vitality, liveliness, vigilance, movement, vigor, and initiative in a person. However, when unbalanced, it can ignite impulsive behaviors, ego, and pride, along with a craving for recognition and admiration. Fire, by its nature, seeks drama and a stage. Therefore, unbalanced inner fire can be hazardous, posing a risk to both the individual and those around them. While fire can provide warmth, unchecked it can also cause destruction.

Karma and Rectification Letter

The letter Caf belongs to the group of karma and rectification letters. It contains vibrational frequencies that guide individuals toward experiential interactions, aiming to awaken consciousness and strengthen the sense of unity within. It directs them toward a correct approach to life and people.

As a karma and rectification letter, Caf's goal is to foster an understanding of one's core inner qualities that require refinement and precision. This understanding is intended to lead to better experiences on personal, interpersonal, and societal levels, enabling a smoother life flow and allowing the manifestation of divine abundance.

Creational Mind Letter

The letter Caf is a creational mind letter, carrying within its energetic coding motives linked to the authentic self. It encourages individuals to gain awareness of their intentions and become more conscious of how they express their thoughts, emotions, desires, and needs, especially concerning motives related to power, authority, and control.

Hard and Soft Sound

Caf can be pronounced with either a hard or soft sound, influencing its characteristics. As a creative mind letter, Caf can intensify or weaken its vibrational frequencies. A hard sound gives the letter a masculine (yang) and more intense tone, while a softer sound imparts a feminine (yin) and gentler tone. When pronounced hard, it suggests difficulty in becoming flexible when needed. Conversely, soft pronunciation represents the ability to be flexible and dissolve the ego.

When Caf appears with a hard sound, as in the word "kavod," meaning "honor," it exhibits greater strength and presence but also a higher risk of ego-driven actions. Conversely, in its soft form, Caf reduces its vibrational frequency, diminishing the ego's influence and fostering a greater capacity for actions rooted in humility.

For example, the hard sound is encountered in words such as caas (anger), cele (prison), cvedut (heaviness), cachash (deception) and cazav (false), words that can subdue others. In contrast, soft sounding words include hachala (containing), michal (vessel, container), smicha (blanket), malchut (kingdom) and nesichut (princesses).

The Measure of Compassion and Judgment

The letter Caf is written in two different forms: as an initial or middle letter in a name or a word and as a final letter. These forms indicate the dual measures that characterize it. As an initial or middle letter, Caf represents the expression of compassion. Conversely, as a final letter, it signifies the expression of judgment.

Redemption Letter

Belonging to the group of redemption letters, Caf endows a person with the power and opportunity to create significant change in their life. It offers the possibility to cleanse the "Qlipoth" – the negative influences accumulated over lifetimes.

Strengths

The strengths associated with Caf include vitality, warmth, courage, vigor, enthusiasm, optimism, confidence, strength, independence, dynamism, initiative, fearlessness, generosity, resourcefulness, wit, ambition, determination, creativity, inspiration, and perseverance.

Weaknesses

Conversely, the weaknesses tied to Caf encompass false self-confidence, lack of focus, resistance to change, a desire for power, and a tendency to avoid personal responsibility. In an imbalanced state, positive qualities like determination, initiative, enthusiasm, and courage can devolve into reckless outbursts, impulsiveness, arrogance, lack of tact, haughtiness, ostentatiousness, stubbornness, egotism, dominance, and fanaticism.

א ב ג ד ה ה ו ו ז ח ח ט י כ ל מ נ ס ע פ צ ק ר ש ת

"From all my teachers I have learned."

Psalms, Chapter 119, Verse 99

Uniqueness and Purpose

The letter Lamed (לְמֶד) is the twelfth letter in the Hebrew alphabet and represents the path of learning at the heart and soul level. It holds the secret to reaching the true purpose of things and embodies the quality of learning—a desire to understand, know, acquire new knowledge, explore, examine, scrutinize, and intellectualize.

Lamed signifies a mental attribute that fosters self and spiritual development, aiding individuals in acquiring wisdom and knowledge. The quality of learning enriches a person with inner content and meaning, fostering noble virtues and moral values such as fairness, justice, and integrity.

The wisdom within Lamed highlights the concept of learning and guides us in understanding how wisdom is acquired at the soul level. It delineates a significant difference between studying out of necessity and studying driven by a heart's desire to understand and know.

Studying out of necessity is often motivated by external factors, often focusing on completing tasks for tangible rewards, such as a certificate or qualification. In contrast, studying driven by internal motivation and genuine interest leads to profound intellectual comprehension and personal growth. It engages both the emotional and intellectual parts of the brain, resulting in a deeper, more holistic understanding.

When a person enjoys studying a particular subject, they develop an emotional connection to it. This connection increases focus and engages both the emotional and intellectual aspects of the brain, leading to a deeper and more comprehensive understanding. Conversely, when a person does not enjoy studying a specific subject, they often struggle to engage with it, remember its content, or delve into its depths. The key to learning is invariably linked to the feelings and the heart. This is encapsulated in the saying, *"A person only learns in a place where his heart desires." (Tractate Avodah Zarah,* page 19).

Kabbalistic teachings associate Lamed with the heart. Our physical heart, situated at the center of the body, facilitates deep learning when one engages with a subject through love and passion. When a person loves what they study, their body aligns in harmony, allowing the learning to penetrate the heart and become ingrained in the soul. This concept is reflected in Judaism regarding Lamed: *"Just as the heart sustains the body, so does learning from the depths of the heart sustain the soul."*

Lamed is linked to qualities like ideals, fairness, decency, moral sensitivity, and broadening horizons. It holds the secret to reaching goals and destinations. In biblical stories, Lamed appears in the names of purposeful kings, prophets, and angels, such as King Solomon, King Saul, prophets Samuel, Ezekiel, Zadkiel, and angels like Uriel, Raphael, Gabriel, Michael, and more.

Lamed implies that the path to reaching goals, purpose, and life's objectives, begins primarily with learning.

The Letter in Creation Stories

The first encounter with the letter Lamed in the Bible is in the Hebrew word "Lilah" (לילה), meaning "night," as stated in *Genesis, "God called the light "day," and the darkness He called "night." And there was evening and there was morning, one day."* (Genesis, Chapter 1, Verse 5)

This verse speaks to the existence of two types of light and energetic forces sustaining divine creation: light and darkness, day and night. These concepts symbolize states of brightness.

In this context, Lamed plays a dual role. Firstly, it acts as a connecting letter that joins "light" and "darkness," creating a link between them. Secondly, it signifies that the word "Li-lah" (לי-לה) embodies a perfect balance between two divine principles: the masculine and the feminine. Lamed connects the letter Yod (י), representing the masculine principle, with the letter Heh (ה), representing the feminine principle.

The word "lilah" encompasses opposite lights and forces that complete each other, expressing wholeness akin to a two-sided coin. It considers both the individual "li" (לי), meaning "me" and the other "lah" (לה), meaning "for her" or "the other." Thus, in one word Lamed demonstrates its main attribute: the ability to bridge and connect opposites, bringing them into balance. This includes linking intellect and emotion, matter and spirit, male and female, while considering both the self and the other simultaneously.

In the Ten Commandments, Lamed is prominent in the moral and social commandments within the word "lo" (לא), meaning "not": "You shall not have," "You shall not bear false witness," "You shall not murder," "You shall not commit adultery," "You shall not steal," "You shall not torture," "You shall not covet."

Pronunciation

The letter Lamed is pronounced as "La-med" and is represented in English as L.

The name, meaning, and pronunciation of the letter Lamed encapsulate its inherent characteristic of the capacity for learning. It represents a level of eclectic learning—the ability to absorb knowledge from any source, situation, or person.

Kabbalistic teachings highlight that Lamed is blessed not only with the ability to learn but also with the capacity to teach and instruct others. This dual capacity is emphasized by its graphic form, the element it is associated with, and its position in alphabetical order.

The letters Lamed and Alef are both associated with the air element. When combined, they form the word "El" (אל), a term rich in meaning, signifying superior power and direction. Together, Alef and Lamed symbolize the educational roles they embody, each uniquely and especially guiding and leading in teaching and instruction.

In the order of their appearance in the Hebrew alphabet, each letter assumes a unique leadership role. Alef leads the first group of ten letters (from Alef to Caf), while Lamed takes charge of the second group of ten (from Lamed to Tav). While Alef guides the learning of simpler letters, Lamed oversees the instruction of more complex letters.

Graphic Shape

The graphic shape of the letter Lamed is closed from three directions: upward toward spiritual matters, downward toward earthly matters, and turning its back on the wisdom of the preceding letter, Caf.

In both print and handwriting, Lamed possesses a unique graphical structure executed in a single stroke, featuring a long antenna at the top that enhances its receptivity. This structure enables Lamed to stretch its boundaries, developing a higher level of openness akin to that of an open-closed letter. This stretching allows it to grasp both the holistic and the individualistic perspectives. However, its narrow and unstable base suggests a tendency for a quick loss of internal balance.

Lamed belongs to the group of uplifting letters known as ThLQ'Tz (טלק-צ), characterized by their graphical form rising above the line. Uniquely, Lamed is the only uplifting letter that ascends above the line in both printed and handwritten forms, as if peering into the distance. The name, graphical shape, and aspirational nature of Lamed signify the human heart's desire to acquire knowledge and wisdom from higher realms, broaden horizons, transcend earthly matters, and seek direction and purpose in life.

Diagram 70: Lighthouse

The shape of Lamed resembles a tall lighthouse shining into the distance, hinting at a person who, like someone standing atop a tower, looks far ahead to discern their path, both physically and in terms of personal development.

The graphical shape of Lamed also resembles a cattle prod, a tool used by shepherds to guide their flock and ensure they stay on course. In Scripture, the cattle prod symbolizes a guiding tool that directs people toward a specific, accurate path. An example of this is found in the Book of Judges: "*Who struck and killed six hundred Philistines with an ox goad.*" (Judges, Chapter 3, Verse 31)

Diagram 71: Lamed's Graphical Form

ל

Diagram 72: Cattle Prod

Gematrical Value

The gematrical value of the letter Lamed is thirty, a number symbolizing endless optimism, boundless creativity, wisdom, sociability, and an elevated worldview. In scriptural and other writings, the value of Lamed is associated with the soul's process of maturing, particularly in developing wisdom and engaging in spiritual activities. It also represents the soul's dedication to a specific mission and the stage of life when a person energetically begins a purposeful task.

In Judaism, the number thirty holds significant meaning, signifying the age at which priests were traditionally accepted for the priesthood. Similarly, in Christianity, it represents the age for ordination as a priest. This age is also biblically significant, as King David ascended to the throne at around thirty years old. This period in life is noteworthy for Joseph, the king of dreams, who began his prominent role in Egypt at this age. The prophet Ezekiel received his enlightenment and prophetic abilities at around this time as well.

In the New Testament, this age marks a pivotal point: John the Baptist commenced his spiritual activity at thirty, and Jesus, son of Mary and Joseph, began spreading his message among his followers in his thirtieth year, coinciding with the thirtieth year of the counting.

The Zodiac Sign Associated with Lamed

Sefer Yetzirah connects the letter Lamed to the zodiac sign Libra, offering deeper insight into its qualities. Libra, an air sign, is linked to intellectual, logical, and rational elements, characterized by the ability to receive, connect, and form links between things. It is marked by intuition, intellect, creative thinking, and communication, embodying a desire for equality, non-discrimination, and consideration.

The symbol of Libra is depicted as a female figure with her eyes covered by a scarf, holding scales in one hand. These scales symbolize law and justice, highlighting that each issue has two sides that require equal examination and weighing. The scarf over the figure's eyes suggests that while human justice may be blind, cosmic justice is all-seeing, governed by inescapable cosmic laws where every action has consequences and outcomes.

The scales, an instrument with two pans on either side, resemble two inverted Caf letters hanging on a rod or chain, used for weighing by comparison. In the Hebrew name for the Libra zodiac sign, "moznaim" (מאזנים), meaning "scales," the word "ozen" (אזן), meaning "ear" and the word "azen" (אזן), meaning "balance" and "equilibrium," is embedded, further emphasizing the theme of balance and fairness inherent in Libra.

Diagram 73: Libra Zodiac Sign

Lamed is the first letter marking a shift in focus from "I" to "you and I." From this point, the energetic focus in the Hebrew alphabet turns to connections, relationships, partnerships, and companionship.

Lamed embodies the desire to please and delight others, along with a willingness to compromise and accommodate, aiming to create harmony for all involved. This inclination also fosters a talent for hospitality, driven by a strong desire to please.

However, the tendency to adjust and please others can lead to a habit of pleasing, which can hinder personal development. Pleasing involves acting against one's true will for external approval, recognition, appreciation, and sympathy, indicating conditional love and giving. This habit can lead to a form of "surrender"—the annulment of personal will, equating to mental-emotional death. The energy of pleasing and self-deprecation gradually leads to mediocrity, monotony, and stagnation.

The zodiac sign Libra, associated with Lamed, corresponds to the month of Tishrei, a period significant in Judaism for repentance, forgiveness, and rectification of harmful habits. Tishrei typically occurs in September and October on the Gregorian calendar and represents a time when an individual's actions are measured and weighed on the scales. It is a period of soul reckoning, emphasizing forgiveness, pardon, and love, both toward oneself and others.

The Groups the Letter Lamed is Associated With

Air Element Letter

The element associated with the letter Lamed is air, a light and swift element that facilitates energetic connections and the transmission of information. The air element is associated with qualities like communication, ideas, inventions, technology, and science, highlighting the significance of interaction and social life. In Lamed, this element is manifested through quick thinking, physical and mental agility, speech, conversation, the written word, and skills in diplomacy and persuasion.

Aspiration Letter

The letter Lamed is the second letter in the ThLQ'Tz (טלק-צ) alphabet group, embodying the aspirational aspect of a person. It characterizes the eternal student, representing individuals who are eager to learn from all sources. They often prefer emotional privacy and the warmth of home, which can make them the driving force behind others rather than being in the spotlight themselves.

Formative Letter

Lamed is one of the seven formative letters that are used in verbs to indicate time, place, purpose, direction, and belonging.

This letter appears in Hebrew words that emphasize direction, such as "next to" (ליד), "up" (למעלה), "down" (למטה), "toward" (לעבר), "forward" (לפנים), "backward" (לאחור), "there" (לשם), and "here" (לכאן). These words express the inherent aspiration within a person to reach various spiritual and physical goals and objectives, representing the ability to move from one place to another.

Lamed is also used to indicate purpose and goals, whether constructive or hindering, as seen in verbs like "to love," (לאהוב)

"to hug," (לחבק) "to understand," (להבין) "to feel," (להרגיש) "to help," (לעזור) "to listen," (להקשיב) "to think," (לחשוב) "to learn," (ללמוד) "to educate," (לחנך) "to delay" (לעכב), "to envy" (לקנא), "to be angry"(לכעוס), and "to hate" (לשנוא).

Practical Letter

The letter Lamed is a practical letter signifying the pragmatic aspect of a person. Its various combinations endow individuals associated with this letter with diplomatic and strategic abilities, openness to new ideas, the capability to view things from a higher perspective, and the skill to connect with individuals who are not easily accessible to everyone. These qualities make those associated with Lamed effective advisors adept at promoting processes such as mediation and diplomacy.

The Measure of Mercy

Lamed embodies the measure of mercy, expressed through qualities like consideration, generosity, understanding, and forgiveness. This measure reflects the energy awakened in response to another's distress, compelling individuals to be considerate and helpful and alleviate the suffering of others. However, the inhibiting aspect of this measure may manifest in providing assistance based on self-interest, evaluating actions more in terms of personal gain rather than focusing solely on the well-being of others.

Karma and Rectification Letter

The letter Lamed belongs to the group of karma and rectification letters. It carries vibrational frequencies that lead individuals through earthly trials associated with human interactions, aiming to develop awakened consciousness, strengthen unity, and guide toward a corrected approach to life and interpersonal relationships.

As a supreme letter, Lamed suggests that the necessary rectification process for individuals associated with it relates to their elevated approach, viewing others from an ivory tower, and conducting oneself with a sense of righteousness. Following the bent letter Caf, Lamed symbolizes that bending the ego is essential for learning humility.

Strengths

Individuals associated with Lamed exhibit strengths like intellect, high learning ability, developed thinking, understanding, spirituality, idealism, inventive capability, diplomatic and strategic skills, conversational prowess, negotiation skills, communication, interactivity, synergy, lightness, grace, charm, pleasantness, kindness, friendliness, caring, empathy, generosity, hosting skills, aesthetics, and hospitality.

Weaknesses

Weaknesses linked to Lamed may include difficulty refusing others, procrastination, tendency to give up, self-indulgence, haughtiness, arrogance, criticality, and indecisiveness, often stemming from an intellectual source—seeing all points of view but struggling to make decisions. The inhibiting aspect manifests in a tendency toward developing inner conflicts and constant internal warfare between desires and reality.

א ב ג ד ה ו ז ח ט י כ ל מ נ ס ע פ צ ק ר ש ת

"I am the carrier of the divine information and the source of infinite wisdom. I am the womb of the cosmic creation in which the divine creation takes place, which You humans are my raw material."

Letter Mem

Uniqueness and Purpose

The letter Mem (מֶם) is the thirteenth letter in the Hebrew alphabet, embodying the path of unconditional love—a path enabling the transition from one state of consciousness to another. Mem is a high spiritual letter that symbolizes holiness. It originates from the "Yetzirah" world, a higher spiritual realm where divine light reveals itself openly and without concealment. Mem contains divine information that forms the cornerstone of physical and material creation.

Mem is a spiritual, material, intuitive and emotional letter. It represents the energy of "being"—the divine feminine force that grants all things the right to exist unconditionally. Mem embodies receptive energy, nurturing, calming, supportive, and nourishing, characterized by a quiet inner strength. Its purpose is to instill in a person complete devotion and dedication to an ideal.

The Letter in Creation Stories

The first appearance of the letter Mem in the Genesis narrative is in the words "merachefet" (מרחפת), meaning "hovering," and

"Mayim" (מים), meaning "water." These words are accompanied by the letter Heh as an informative letter. The verse illustrates this: *"In the beginning God created the heavens and the earth. And the earth was a formless and desolate emptiness, and darkness was over the surface of the deep, and the Spirit of God was hovering over the surface of the waters."* (*Genesis*, Chapter 1, Verses 1-2)

The Hebrew word for hovering, "merachefet" (מרחפת), suggests floating in the air. This word encompasses within it the word "rachefet," meaning "floating boat"—a vessel or a boat that remains afloat above the water's surface without sinking. Such a vessel is propelled and glides on an air cushion it creates over the water's surface, simulating the motion of floating.

Pronunciation

The letter Mem is pronounced as "Mem" and is represented in English as M.

The pronunciation of the letter Mem emits a deep, calm, and soothing sound, often used for relaxation (mmmm...mmmm...). In esoteric teachings, the sound of Mem is associated with prophecy, and its chanting is believed to induce deep meditation.

Mem is a feminine letter imbued with the essence of motherhood. This letter manifests in many languages worldwide in various forms of the word "Mother," such as Em, Ima, Mama, Mah, Mater, Mommy, Madre, Mare, Ma, Mutter, Amma, Um, Mza'ah, Mza'zi, Mamama, Mor, Matka, Matushka, Meme, Mai, and more.

The name Mem derives from the ancient term "mayim," which translates to "water." It is named after the element fundamental to all life forms. Water possesses an alchemical quality—the ability to transform matter at a molecular level. The Hebrew word for water, "ma-yim" (מ-ים), includes the letter Mem (מ) and "yim" (ים), meaning "sea," signifying large bodies of both fresh and saltwater linked to oceans and seas.

Mem is unique in the Hebrew alphabet for symbolizing the ancient spiritual root of water, biblically referred to as "tehom." Tehom represents the purest form of water in higher realms, the source from which the initial stage of matter originates. From this primordial state emerges the fundamental substance that gives rise to the tangible reality we perceive and interact with.

Water is a tangible, physical, and malleable energy that lacks the solidification of the earth. It constitutes a major component of our cells, playing a critical role in growth and developmental processes. Over seventy percent of our physical body is fluid, and our brain cells consist of about eighty-five percent fluid. Water's molecular memory endows humans with alchemical and transformative abilities, allowing the conversion of internal water from a lower to a higher vibrational frequency.

Graphic Shape

The letter Mem is a watery letter, and its graphic shape is closed from three directions: upward toward spiritual matters, downward toward earthly matters, and turning its back on the wisdom of both the preceding letter, Lamed, and the wisdom of the following letter, Nun. Mem stands on a broad and stable base, indicating its capacity for maintaining internal balance and equilibrium over time.

Reversing the shape of Mem—turning it upside-down—yields a form akin to a container or vessel, similar to a woman's womb. This form, capable of containing and nurturing within its watery framework, illustrates the secure environment where a fetus develops. The fetus, inverting before birth, emerges through a narrow passage, symbolized by the shape of Mem.

Birth, representing a profound act of creation, is intrinsically linked with "love," a concept numerically aligned with thirteen—the gematrical value and the position of Mem in the Hebrew alphabet.

Diagram 74: The Two Forms of the Letter Mem

Mem exhibits two distinct graphical forms. In the beginning or middle of a word, it appears as a letter closed from three sides, while at the end of a word, it takes a fully closed form. Its closed form, resembling an impenetrable wall, symbolizes preservation and protection but can also indicate emotional closure and accumulation of emotions. The partially closed Mem (מ) represents the measure of mercy, whereas the fully closed Mem (ם) embodies the measure of absolute judgment.

These graphical forms of Mem mirror an important aspect of our life's journey. We begin our life journey as recipients, akin to a vessel, effortlessly receiving divine abundance during infancy and childhood. As we mature, we learn to reciprocate by sharing our abundance, thus making space for new blessings to flow into our lives.

Failing to distribute this abundance to others can lead to an energetic overload, a consequence of excessive receiving, which can result in imbalance and, potentially, illness. Illness often serves as a signal and a kind of a wake-up call—an opportunity for the person to stop and reflect on the changes they need to make in their lives and the rectification required of them, both themselves and others.

As the final letter of rectification, Mem emphasizes the importance of learning to give, release, forgive, and forget. This understanding is crucial for a more harmonious and enjoyable life journey.

Gematrical Value

The gematrical value of the letter Mem is forty, imbued with unique qualities and vibrational frequencies that prepare a person for **soul initiation**[1] and establish the presence of the "I am" in their daily life.

The term "I am" is a profound spiritual concept with multiple meanings and roles. It denotes the core of human existence—the highest spiritual and soulful aspect closest to the divine light—God. This divine spark, residing in the center of our higher heart—the seat of the soul, embodies our "true self" and the highest qualities of our being. Activation of this divine spark initiates our journey toward spiritual elevation.

In Kabalistic teachings, the gematrical value of Mem is associated with the concept of "a new creation." A prime example of this is pregnancy. For the fetus to mature and develop into a human form, a period of forty days is essential, and the fetus stays in the mother's womb for forty weeks. Mem, as the final letter in the Hebrew word for mother, "em" (אם), which comprises Alef and Mem, underscores the transition of a woman to motherhood. This transformation occurs on the forty-first day following childbirth, with the newborn having developed in the womb until birth. The gematrical value of the Hebrew word for "mother" (אם) is forty-one, and that of "fetus" (ולד) is forty.

In the Scriptures, the value of Mem is linked to mystical themes of purification and initiation. According to the Midrash, the necessary period for a person to internalize insights so profoundly that they become an integral part of their being, enabling divine realization, is forty days and forty nights.

This gematrical value is notably present in the story of Moses the Prophet, particularly during the Mount Sinai event, where Mem's value is mentioned twice. The first instance is when Moses

---

[1]   Soul initiation refers to a transformative journey of self-discovery and spiritual awakening. It involves a deep exploration of one's inner self, often accompanied by challenges and insights. This concept is rooted in various spiritual traditions, where individuals undergo a profound process of personal growth and inner transformation. Soul initiation may include facing fears, confronting aspects of oneself, and ultimately leading to a heightened sense of self-awareness and purpose.

ascends the mountain for the first forty days and nights, undergoing a process of purification and sanctification. This process was crucial for preparing him to receive and comprehend the written and oral Torah, along with the secrets and teachings of mystical Kabbalah.

"It came about at the end of forty days and nights that the Lord gave me the two tablets of stone, the tablets of the covenant." (Deuteronomy, Chapter 9, Verse 11)

The second instance at Mount Sinai occurs when Moses ascends the mountain again for another forty days and nights, praying for the peace of Israel and seeking God's forgiveness for their sins.

The value of forty is also associated with the process of "autosuggestion," a psychological technique where, over forty days, a person repeats positive affirmations aimed at altering their mindset. This repetition ingrains the affirmations in their consciousness.

In both Judaism and Christianity, the number forty holds significant importance in several key events described in the Old and New Testaments. For instance, in the biblical story of the Flood, it rained for forty days and forty nights. *"The rain fell upon the earth for forty days and forty nights."* (*Genesis*, chapter 7, verse 12) The purpose of the flood was to cleanse the earth of the impurity and corruption that had overtaken its inhabitants, ending the old-world order and initiating a new one.

This value is evident again in the Bible during the forty years of the Israelites' journey through the desert. To transition from the mentality of slavery, ingrained in them in Egypt, to one of unity and freedom, required forty years.

In Christianity, the number forty symbolizes the period necessary for spiritual preparation. According to the Holy Gospel of Matthew, Master Jesus fasted for forty days and forty nights before facing temptations. *"And after He had fasted for forty days and forty nights, He then became hungry."* Chapter 4, Verse 2)

Similarly, the Gospel, according to Luke, mentions, *"Now Jesus, full of the Holy Spirit, returned from the Jordan and was led around by the Spirit in the wilderness for forty days, being tempted by the devil. And He ate nothing during those days, and when they had ended, He was hungry. And the devil said to Him, "If You are the Son of God, tell this stone to become bread. And Jesus answered him, "It is written: Man shall not live on bread alone."* (Gospel of Luke, Chapter 4, Verses 1-4)

The Hebrew language is considered a scientific language. Biblical names act as codes containing alphanumeric ciphers that provide insights into how the energy of a letter manifests in a person. The powerful force of the letter Mem and the ascension power it contains are evident in biblical figures who were guided by spirituality, prophecy, and spiritual leadership. These include the prophet Moses, a highly spiritual leader; the prophet Samuel; and King Solomon, known for his wisdom.

The Planet Associated with Mem

The letter Mem is associated with the planet Neptune, symbolizing supreme love and enlightenment. Neptune represents the soulful need for unwavering faith in a higher power and guides individuals through profound transformative processes. It governs the unconscious mind, encompassing memories and dreams.

Neptune's vibrational frequencies imbue individuals with intuition, creativity, sensitivity, receptivity, identification, responsiveness, containment, and dissolution. These qualities facilitate an emotional understanding of people, situations, and processes. They enable empathy, comprehension, accommodation, and, when necessary, the subdual or even relinquishment of personal will. Such qualities, marked by a high therapeutic capacity, are exemplified prominently in motherhood.

The energy of Neptune is pure and innocent, often evoking a longing for ideal love and an unconscious desire for absolute truth. This yearning is often inexplicable, even to the individuals themselves. It encourages idealization, a tendency to view people and situations through rose-colored glasses and to experience objective reality subjectively. Neptune's energy instills a desire to escape material limitations, detach from daily troubles, and delve into imagination, fantasies, and daydreams.

In a constructive aspect, Neptune's vibrational frequencies bestow upon individuals artistic and creative expression, as seen in the works of Michelangelo, spiritual enlightenment, as exemplified by the prophet Moses, or a spiritual vision, as observed in Mahatma Gandhi.

While a rich imagination and heightened sensitivity are valuable, they can, in an underdeveloped personality, lead to a lack of grounding and a retreat into a world of daydreams, clouding consciousness. This can result in emotional confusion, a distorted perception of reality, unanchored hopes, and judgment errors, culminating in feelings of inadequacy, deep escapism, and various addictions.

In its inhibiting aspect, the receptiveness, sensitivity, and high empathy bestowed by Neptune can become a conduit for negative external energy influences, leading to subconscious absorption of surrounding events in a hypnotic manner. As a watery letter that receives, absorbs and internalizes the content it encounters, this energy may cause individuals to lose their unique identity and personal boundaries, becoming easily swayed by others. In dense and challenging environments, this can potentially lead to physical or mental issues.

It is highly recommended that individuals with this letter in their name engage in daily grounding practices, learn to set personal boundaries, and continuously seek what truly brings them happiness and fulfillment.

The Groups the Letter Mem is Associated With

Water Element Letter

The element associated with the letter Mem is water, symbolizing the emotional aspect hidden within us. It directs our attention to the world of emotions and our inner child, highlighting an internal aspect that seeks acknowledgment and attention. Mem is the highest water element letter in terms of vibrational frequency and embodies high sensitivity, sentimental empathy, and emotional vulnerability.

For individuals with this letter, it is crucial to be conscious of the emotional aspect that tends to manage them unconsciously. They should learn to connect with their inner child and heal it if necessary.

Spiritual Letter

The letter Mem belongs to the group of AM-SH letters (אמ-ש), comprising three high spiritual letters characterized by nobility, faith, wisdom, understanding, spiritual power, vision, and the purpose of creating a new reality from nothingness. Mem instills in a person the willingness to transcend oneself and everything that limits one's uniqueness and freedom. It encourages disconnecting from situations that do not serve one's higher good and from all that restricts and confines, empowering the individual, if necessary, to start anew from a zero point.

Karma and Rectification Letter

Mem is the last letter in the group of Karma and rectification letters. It contains vibrational frequencies leading individuals through experiential earthly trials related to emotional interactions. The aim is to develop an awakened consciousness, strengthen the awareness of unity, and guide them toward a refined approach to people and life.

The letter Mem is a spiritual letter symbolizing the upper and pure waters, hinting that the required rectification for those who possess this letter involves the **transformation**[2] of both their materialistic perspective and their victimization aspect. Starting from the next letter, the letters become more consequential and intense in their energy.

Redemption Letter

The letter Mem belongs to the group of five letters of redemption. Unique in this group, Mem, in its two forms of writing, symbolizes the feminine and maternal principles. In its constructive aspect, as a letter of redemption, it endows a person with tenderness and a high capacity for giving. Conversely, in its inhibiting aspect, it may draw individuals toward emotional closeness, difficulty in expressing emotions, resistance to change, and a propensity for stagnation, dependence, and victimhood.

As a letter of redemption, Mem emphasizes to individuals associated with this letter the importance of embracing openness to spiritual processes, learning to give and receive in a balanced manner, developing a unique and distinct personal identity, and becoming acquainted with the full range of their emotions.

The Measure of Mercy and Absolute Judgment

The letter Mem embodies the measure of mercy and absolute judgment. When appearing at the beginning or in the middle of a

---

[2]   Transformation refers to a fundamental, profound, and long-term internal and external change.

name or a word, it signifies the measure of mercy. As a final letter, it indicates the measure of absolute judgment.

Formative Letter

The letter Mem is formative, serving as a preposition. It abbreviates the word "min" (מן), meaning "out of" or "from," indicating departure from a certain place. This is evident in Hebrew words such as "from" (מתוך), "out of" (מתוך), "from within" (מעצמו), "from his room" (מחדרו), "from his home" (מביתו), "from his city" (מעירו), "from his country" (מארצו), and "from his birthplace" (ממולדתו).

Following Lamed, another formative letter, Mem draws our attention to the concept of "the existing reality versus the ideal one." They encourage individuals to reflect on their life journey, assessing their developmental stages. This involves recognizing their starting point, acknowledging their achievements so far, and identifying the developmental stage they aspire to attain. As wisely stated in *Pirkei Avot: Ethics of the Fathers*, "*Know from where you come and to where you are going.*"

Strengths

The strengths associated with the letter Mem include spirituality, creativity, a rich imagination, inspiration, artistry, mysticism, sensitivity, receptiveness, acceptance, responsiveness, and the capacity to hold and understand. Additionally, caring, empathy, devotion, humility, the ability to receive and contain, sympathize with others, give and support, and a willingness to forgive and pardon. Mem is capable of elevating a person to high levels of mediumship and channeling.

Weaknesses

The weaknesses associated with the letter Mem can manifest as a lack of grounding, absence of boundaries, escapism, confusion, lack of logic, internal disorganization, a tendency to indulge in fantasy and daydreaming, emotional dispersal, escaping from reality, a tendency toward isolation and worries. The inhibiting aspect of the Mem is characterized by a propensity for melancholy, developing fears and anxieties, difficulty in decision-making, as well as a tendency toward giving up and self-sacrifice. These traits can lead to issues such as an inferiority complex and feelings of worthlessness and victimhood, often resulting in an internal dialogue echoing thoughts like, "I am a failure, messed up, unworthy."

אבגדהוזחטיכלמנ**נ**סעפצקרשת

*"Love means to reach for the sky and with every breath
to teara hundred veils. Love means to step away from
the ego, to openthe eyes of inner vision, and not
to take this world so seriously."*

Jalal ad-Din Rumi

Uniqueness and Purpose

The letter Nun (נון), the fourteenth letter in the Hebrew alphabet, symbolizes the path toward spiritual enlightenment and self-renewal at the cellular level. It carries vibrational frequencies that facilitate transformation and regeneration processes—profound experiences that enable one to shed their old form and assume a new one, reminiscent of the mythical Phoenix.

The letter Nun is among the most fascinating and challenging letters. It encompasses a wealth of spiritual, mental, and emotional strengths, paving the way for rejuvenation and rebirth. Nun aims to ignite spiritual enlightenment and foster mental and emotional growth.

It underlines the importance of letting go of control over opinions, people, and situations, emphasizing the need for flexibility—being adaptable yet steadfast. This principle reflects the wisdom of ancient spiritual traditions, capturing the essence of being bent but upright. The letter highlights the unique capacity of individuals to deeply and emotionally experience life's events in a manner that reaches into their very core and induces fundamental transformation.

The Letter in Creation Stories

The first instance of the letter Nun in the Genesis stories appears in Chapter 1, within the phrase "nefesh haya," (נפש חיה) meaning "living soul" as a part of the verse, *"Let the waters teem with swarms of living creatures."* (*Genesis*, Chapter 1, Verse 20) Here, "nefesh haya" refers to small water creatures capable of rapid reproduction and generating many offspring.

The second occurrence of the letter Nun in *Genesis* is in Chapter Two, in the word "neshmat haim" (נשמת חיים), meaning "breath of life," as noted in the verse, *"Then the Lord God formed the man of dust from the ground, and breathed into his nostrils the breath of life; and the man became a living person."*(*Genesis*, Chapter 2, Verse 7) This verse signifies the creation of human beings and represents an evolutionary development where a human, an entity with a living soul, receives the living spirit.

In these two verses, the letter Nun is associated with two pivotal concepts essential for deep understanding—"Soul" (נפש) and "Spirit" (נשמה). In Kabbalistic teachings, while the soul represents the past, the spirit symbolizes the future.

Pronunciation

The letter Nun is pronounced as "Nun" and is represented in English as N.

The name of the letter Nun is derived from the Aramaic word Nun, meaning "edible fish." This term is commonly used as a suffix in the Hebrew names of many fish, such as amnon (tilapia), tamanun (octopos), zehavnun (Alaska pollock), leshonun (Atlantic halibut) and karpion (carp), symbolizing the aquatic creatures that nourishment to humans.

In its pronunciation, the letter Nun encapsulates the letters of its name—two Nun letters with a Vav in between. This arrangement creates a connection between the feminine aspect represented by the initial Nun (נ) and the masculine aspect symbolized by the final Nun (ן).

Graphic Shape

The letter Nun is written in two distinct graphical forms, each signifying the letter's dual role. When it is written at the beginning of a name or a word, Nun's is shaped as a curved and bent letter (נ), while at the end of a name or word, it is represented as an upright letter (ן).

Diagram 75: Nun's Graphical Shape

ן　　נ

The curved and round shape of the letter Nun (נ) symbolizes feminine qualities in a person, characterized by reciprocity, equality, submission, reconciliation, appeasement, and a willingness to bend for mutual good, such as household peace. This curved form resembles a submissive posture, like someone sitting in contemplation with their legs stretched out in front, focusing inward on the depths of their soul.

Conversely, the upright shape of the letter Nun (ן), used as a final letter, signifies masculine qualities like taking a stand, power, control, and the need for discharge. Its graphic upright form resembles a racquet or a long stake, akin to a war weapon such as an elongated spear or a rocket, ready to engage in battle the moment it is ignited.

The curved shape of Nun (נ) has a closed structure on three sides. It is closed downward toward earthly matters, slightly closed upward toward the spiritual realm, and turns its back to the wisdom of the preceding letter, Mem (מ), while being open to the energy of the following letter, Samekh (ס).

The broad foundation of the bent Nun provides mental stability, internal balance, the ability to rely on something constant within oneself, faithfulness, determination, anchors and grounding. It enables maintaining internal balance and equilibrium over long periods. In its inhibiting aspect, this closed form can lead to closure, self-centeredness, and emotional accumulation, marked by difficulty in release and letting go.

The upright shape of Nun (ן), standing on a point or a single long leg, signifies a desire to plant itself firmly into the earthly realm. In its inhibiting aspect, this form can indicate a rapid loss of internal balance and equilibrium.

The two forms of Nun teach us the importance of being both bent and upright. This involves educating oneself to yield, bend when needed, and give up for the common good while also maintaining an upright posture—standing firm and stable, not allowing others to step on or trample upon them.

Gematrical Value

The gematrical value of the letter Nun is fifty, a number associated with charisma and multidimensional communication—cosmic, spiritual, and earthly. It embodies the qualities like love, giving, self-efficacy, determination, perseverance, commitment to a goal, inner strength, and mental and emotional courage. In its constructive aspect, this value propels a person to progress and improve at all levels of their being.

The gematrical value of Nun also symbolizes the number of chapters in the book of Genesis, reflecting the stories of creation. In Kabalistic teachings, this value is linked to the fifty gates of holiness and understanding (שערי בינה) against the fifty gates of impurity (שערי טומאה). In the Scriptures, "impurity" signifies opacity and lack of flow. The root letters of the Hebrew word "impurity" (טומאה) are

T.M.A. (ט.מ.א), which, when reversed, form the word "sealing plug" (אטם), denoting a valve that blocks flow.

In the Bible and scriptures, the value of fifty is associated with redemption and liberation from states of hopelessness and destruction. This is exemplified in the biblical story of Sodom and Gomorrah, where God intends to destroy four cities for the sins of their inhabitants. Abraham, the father of world nations, negotiates with God to spare the righteous, starting with the number fifty: *"Abraham approached and said, Will You indeed sweep away the righteous with the wicked? 24 Suppose there are fifty righteous people within the city; will You indeed sweep it away and not spare*

the place for the sake of the fifty righteous who are in it?" (*Genesis*, Chapter 18, Verses 23-24)

In the Bible, the value of fifty is also highlighted in the Book of Esther, which recounts the salvation of the Jewish people from mass genocide. It focuses on the attempts of Haman the Agagite, a high-ranking official under King Ahasuerus of Persia, to incite the king against the Jewish population and orchestrate a massacre. This plan culminates with Haman hanging on a gallows fifty cubits high, underscoring the principle that those who seek harm for others and lay traps for them often fall into their snares. (Book of Esther, Chapter 5, Verse 14)

The number fifty combines the qualities of the number five and zero, amplifying its characteristics. A notable attribute of the number five is movement and motion, which is why many individuals with the letter Nun in their names tend to be very active and restless. However, this trait depends on the letters adjacent to Nun in a name.

This intensive numerical value propels individuals to integrate the different aspects of their "self"—body, soul and spirit. It represents an energy that seeks to follow the soul's path, operating from a place of heightened self-awareness. This state of being involves a deep connection to oneself and one's emotions in all their shades, recognizing the various vibrational frequencies of these emotions and understanding how to regulate them. The vibrational frequencies of Nun function like a transformer in a person, facilitating the transition from one state to another, enabling the movement from point A to point B.

Diagram 76: Transformer

Corresponding to Nun in the unit's digit is the letter, Heh. Both Heh and Nun possess feminine qualities along with great inner strength and power. Heh represents a singular feminine force in the unit's digit numbers, while Nun represents a plural feminine force in the tens digit numbers. When Nun and Heh appear together in a person's name, they bestow abundant fertility, both creative and physical.

The Zodiac Sign Associated with Nun

The letter Nun belongs to the water element, characterized by emotional feelings and gut sensations. It possesses strong empathy and the ability to perceive the emotions of others and to identify with them. Nun symbolizes the ocean waters—deep groundwater located beneath the earth's surface and flowing slowly through an almost impermeable layer known as an "aquiclude."

Sefer Yetzirah connects the three water-related letters KhNQ (חנק) to aquatic animals that humans consume, such as "fish" associated with the letter Qof, "crab" associated with the letter Khet, and "scorpion" associated with the letter Nun, although the scorpion is not an aquatic animal, from which we derive sustenance.

Diagram 77: Scorpion

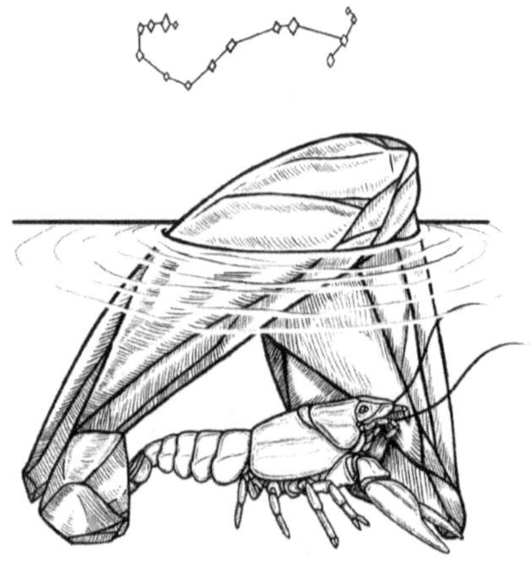

Diagram 78: Lobster

The land scorpion, known to us today, is not an aquatic creature but an invertebrate that lives on land and belongs to the arachnid family.

The land scorpion is primarily active at night. During the day, it hides in dark and concealed places, often suddenly revealing itself. When threatened, it attacks and then retreats to hide again. Its attacks are fast, powerful, and paralyzing, affecting the nervous system and, at times, even causing death. The scorpion's venom, a means of self-defense, is potent and has both positive and negative uses, with numerous medical and agricultural applications.

I must admit that this issue has troubled me for a long time, leading me to investigate whether the relation of Nun is actually associated with the land scorpion or with some other aquatic creature that resembles it in shape and appearance and nourishes humans, similarly to fish and crab. This research revealed that in the past, there indeed was an aquatic scorpion, a mythical creature that lived in deep waters and was physically enormous. This creature is linked to an ancient and largely unknown lineage, with limited knowledge about it in our times.

As seen in the sketch, the external shape of the scorpion is very similar to that of another aquatic creature, the lobster. The lobster lives in deep waters, resembling the land scorpion in size and shape, and belongs to the arthropod family, similar to crabs and fish, which coexist with us and are a source of human nourishment. The lobster provides us with a deep understanding of the uniqueness of the zodiac sign and the characteristics of the letter Nun. Here, I invite those of you who are associated with Nun to see if they relate to the traits of the lobster.

The lobster mostly dwells on the ocean floor and has a hard outer shell that serves as its defense. In order to grow, the lobster must shed its outer shell. During the process of shedding the hard shell, the lobster becomes extremely vulnerable, similar to an octopus, and therefore, to protect itself, it retreats to a hidden place, such as a rocky crevice or cave, where it sheds its old shell. It takes several months for the lobster's outer shell to harden again.

The lobster swims forward and backward, and when threatened, it retreats backward. Additionally, it can regenerate complete limbs even in adulthood. Furthermore, when the lobster is cooked, it turns red, a color associated with the planet Mars, which rules over this zodiac sign. The season in which this zodiac sign occurs is autumn, when nature is surrounded by trees displaying various vibrant colors, including red.

The lobster symbolizes the hidden and deep aspects inherent in human beings and the desire to delve into the depths of things beyond the surface. This is also one of the reasons why many individuals with this letter in their name can be found in fields such as research, investigation, intelligence, and cybersecurity roles or are deeply connected to water.

It is characterized by processes of regeneration—renewal and rebirth. It represents the interconnectedness of death and birth, shedding the old and wearing a new form, similar to a snake shedding its old skin or a phoenix rising from its ashes.

The prominent characteristics of the zodiac sign Lobster are a strong character with emotional depth and sensitivity, curiosity, wisdom, empathy, mental and emotional strength, mediumship, gut feelings, and strong intuition, combined with a tough external shell and a soft interior. This sign characterizes sensitive, devoted, loyal, and determined people who are driven by an internal barometer that motivates them into action. These people have challenges in trusting others and revealing their deep emotions to others until they have earned their trust. They are individuals who do not succumb to difficulties and, thanks to their strong and determined nature, are capable of facing challenges and obstacles that others would have long given up on.

One of the main fears that characterizes this sign and this letter is abandonment—an ancient fear deeply rooted in the collective consciousness of human beings. The fear of abandonment generates in individuals a strong desire to hold on, difficulty in letting go, releasing and parting, alongside an almost desperate need for warmth, touch, encouragement, support, and understanding. The letter Nun echoes the understanding of the importance of this aspect within us.

The fear of abandonment is complex and manifests in various aspects of our lives, including emotional, psychological, or physical forms. Many people, whether consciously or unconsciously, harbor this ancient fear to varying degrees based on their life experiences. However, individuals associated with the letter Nun tend to experience this fear more profoundly.

This fear significantly influences our thinking and behavior, serving as the hidden yet most potent driving force behind various mental and emotional challenges. Without awareness, it can lead to issues such as restlessness, perpetual dissatisfaction, a sense of emptiness, psychological distress, dependency issues, and difficulties in maintaining healthy relationships.

The letter Nun encourages individuals to engage in deep self-awareness processes, particularly concerning their emotional selves and their inner child, which tends to be trapped in their emotional experiences. It underscores the importance of undergoing transformative processes on cognitive, emotional, physical, and spiritual levels, highlighting that embracing the new requires shedding the old.

The Groups the Letter Nun is Associated With

Beginning with the letter Nun, there is a pivotal shift in the vibrational frequencies of the letters. From this point onward, the frequencies become denser, more complex, and more intense, guiding individuals toward actions that align with their soul's path. Although the complexity of these frequencies increases, they nevertheless contain the energetic strength required to overcome the challenges they present. As mentioned in the Bible, God will never give you more than you can handle.

Water Element Letter

The element associated with Nun is water, linking individuals to a world of deep feelings and emotions. Among the three watery letters KhNQ (חנק), Nun stands as the most profound, embodying a significant emotional intensity. It is oriented toward fostering relationships based on deep, intimate connections. Nun encourages individuals to explore the depths of their feelings and emotions, to understand their full spectrum—with all their colors, shapes, and vibrational frequencies—and to learn how to navigate them.

Following the letter Mem, which represents the upper and pure waters of the heavens (as indicated in the Hebrew word for "heavens" (שמים), meaning "there-sea," Nun symbolizes the lower waters, characterized by dense vibrational frequencies that seek transformation. Nun epitomizes the human capacity to deeply and emotionally engage with people, situations, and earthly life events in a profound manner, enabling transformation at the very essence of one's being.

Practical Letter

Nun holds the position of the eighth letter in a group of twelve simple letters, symbolizing the practical and applied aspects within an individual. Nun draws individuals toward both spiritual and practical implementation.

As a feminine letter, Nun embodies the power of fertility. The secret of femininity and the power of childbirth inherent in Nun are revealed through the changes it induces when added to words. For instance, adding Nun alongside Heh (the corresponding letter in the unit digits) to masculine Hebrew words like "תבוא" (come), "תצא" (go out), "תיקח" (take), "תשתה" (drink), transforms them to their feminine and plural forms: "תבאנה" (they will come), "תצאנה" (they will go out), "תיקחנה" (they will take), "תשתנה" (they will drink).

Similarly, adding Nun to verbs changes them from singular to plural and the future tense, as seen in the transformation of words such as "דיבר" (speak), "אכל" (eat), "שתה" (drink), "ישן" (sleep) to "נדבר" (we will speak), "נאכל" (we will eat), "נשתה" (we will drink), "נישן" (we will sleep).

The Measure of Mercy and Absolute Judgment

The letter Nun is associated with both the measure of mercy and absolute judgment. When it appears as an initial or middle letter in a name or word (in its bent and curved form), it signifies mercy. Conversely, as a final letter (in its upright form), it represents absolute judgment

Consequential Letter

Nun is the first consequential letter, hinting at lessons the incarnated soul has taken upon itself to learn in this life journey, especially those not learned in previous lifetimes. The purpose of Nun's intense vibrational frequencies is to push individuals to the edge, awakening awareness of their soul lessons. This awareness enables them to perceive the hidden outcomes behind their life experiences and events.

As a consequential letter, Nun directs individuals toward enhanced initiation processes, introspection, uprooting false beliefs, and eliminating elements that do not serve their higher good. It encourages individuals to devote themselves to these transformative processes.

Redemption Letter

Nun is one of the five letters of redemption, typically appearing as a final letter in a word or name. In its constructive role as a final letter, Nun bestows upon a person an enhanced ability to survive and adapt. However, in its inhibiting aspect, it can foster tendencies toward extremism, fixation, resistance to change, and stagnation. As a redemption letter, Nun highlights the significance of connecting with high spiritual values and cultivating an openness to transformative processes, which is essential for rejuvenating the inner waters.

Strengths

Individuals associated with Nun possess strengths such as wisdom, sensitivity, emotional depth, mental strength, inner power, mediumship, acceptance, responsiveness, empathy, loyalty, gentleness, a therapeutic and maternal sense, identification, self-confidence, passion, humility, a deep understanding, attention to detail, discernment, goal-oriented focus, determination, perseverance, dynamism, certainty, independent thinking, unwavering belief, resourcefulness, resilience, the ability to influence, cope with difficulties, and renew.

Weaknesses

Nun's weaknesses may include tendencies toward closure, suspicion, secrecy, envy, intense emotional involvement, attachment, difficulty in communicating deep emotions, stubbornness, obsessiveness, and excessive dominance. Its inhibiting aspect manifests in possessiveness, manipulativeness, intrusion into others' affairs, difficulty in forgiveness and letting go, quarrelsomeness, combative tendencies, and conflict-proneness.

אבגדהוזחחטיכלמנ **ס** עפצקרשת

"Be still, and know that I am God."

Psalms, Chapter 46, Verse 10

Uniqueness and Purpose

The letter Samech (סָמֶך) stands as the fifteenth letter in the Hebrew alphabet. It symbolizes the path of mental and emotional evolution as well as spiritual upliftment. Samech is imbued with alchemical vibrational frequencies that enable the integration of the various aspects of one's soul. Its primary purpose is to cultivate the willingness to be a supportive and reliable factor and to walk the path of life with trust and faith.

The mental evolutionary journey that Samech guides includes a process of awakening and a shift in consciousness. It involves developing higher self-awareness and a more profound understanding of one's spiritual nature and connection to something greater than oneself. This journey fosters a deeper connection to divine power, coupled with a purpose and willingness to actively contribute to positive change, both in one's own life and in the lives of others.

The Letter in Creation Stories

In a thorough reading of the *Genesis* stories, we note that the letter Samech is absent in the initial creation narratives of Chapter One. Its first appearance is in Chapter Two, paired with the letter Heh, in the word "sovev" (סובב), meaning "around" and "surround": *"Now a river flowed out of Eden to water the garden; and from there it divided and became four rivers. The name of the first is Pishon; it flows around the whole land of Havilah, where there is gold."* (*Genesis*, Chapter 2, Verses 10-11) The term "surround" (סובב) implies a circular motion, revolving around something.

The next occurrence of Samech is in Chapter Four, alongside Alef, in the word "asater" (אֶסָּתֵר), meaning "be hidden": *"Behold, You have driven me this day from the face of the ground; and I will be hidden from Your face, and I will be a wanderer and a drifter on the earth, and whoever finds me will kill me."* (*Genesis*, Chapter 4, Verse 14) "Asater" (אסתר) is derived from the root word "seter" (סתר), meaning "hide" and "conceal."

Samech appears independently for the first time in Chapter Five, in the word "sefer" (סֵפֶר), meaning "book." Chapter Five discusses the generations of Adam, the first biblical human being: "This is the book of the generations of Adam. On the day when God created man, He made him in the likeness of God." (*Genesis*, Chapter 5, Verse 1) The Hebrew word "sefer" has multiple meanings. Firstly, it is a written text containing information for knowledge, understanding, teaching, and guidance. For instance, the term "Ish Sefer" refers to an educated person, while "Beit Sefer" refers to a place of education.

Kabbalistic teachings regard a book as a spiritual tool that awakens awareness and insights about oneself and the world—a tool that aids individuals in their progress and evolution. The second meaning of "sefer" (סִפֵּר) is to tell a story, whether real or fictional, while the third meaning (סָפַר) refers to counting or enumerating.

In Hebrew, one word, written with the same letters but different punctuation, can significantly change its meaning. In this instance, a single word encompasses both the value and quantity aspect. This concept is emphasized in Chapter Two.

The placement of Samech in the Genesis stories exemplifies its three main qualities: firstly, to revolve (סובב) or move around something without a direct approach; secondly, as hiding or refuge

(אסתר), denoting concealment; and thirdly, to tell (ספר) or possess the ability to narrate a story, whether it is real or imagined.

Pronunciation

The name and pronunciation 0 inof the letter Samech offer insights into its nature and purpose. The first meaning of its name is "semech" (סֶמֶךְ), meaning "support" and "protection," signifying a point of fulcrum and security. The verb semech means to establish and to support, representing the innate human ability to be a reliable and supportive factor, one that others can trust and lean on. The second meaning, "samach" (סָמַךְ), pertains to the act of "trusting," the state in which a person relies on something and places their trust in it.

When the letters of its name are reversed, we get the word "masach" (מָסַךְ), meaning "cover" or "curtain," signifying a buffer that separates two entities. With different vowel markings, this word becomes "misech" (מְסֵךְ), which means "disguise" or "concealment." The root of Samech appears in various words such as "סכום" (sum), "סיכום" (summary), "סמיכה" (trust, rely upon, support), "מסך" (screen), "מסכן" (poor thing), and "מסכה" (mask).

The letter Samech is pronounced as "Sa-mech" or "Sa-mekh" and can be represented in English as C or S, depending on its position in a word or name.

Graphic Shape

The graphical shape of the letter Samech, both in handwriting and print, is distinctive: it is round and closed from all directions. Notably, it is the only letter in the Hebrew alphabet that is entirely closed, with no opening in its circumference. This unique shape symbolizes the letter's closure and sealing, both upward toward spiritual matters and downward toward earthly realms.

It also implies its closure toward the wisdom of the preceding letter, Nun, and toward the letter that follows it, Ahyin. The round, closed structure of Samech represents a form that is impenetrable and sealed, embodying both its constructive and inhibiting aspects.

Diagram 79: Alphabet Letters in Order

א ב ג ד ה ו ז ח ט י כ ל מ נַ ס עַ פ צ ק ר ש ת

The position of the letter Samech in the order of letters is between Nun, which symbolizes the importance of emotional transformation, and Ahyin, which symbolizes the importance of mental transformation. The letter turns its back to both of them and remains closed in itself, showing a reluctance to open up to mental and emotional transformational processes.

The letter Samech is powerful, both in its constructive and inhibiting aspects. In its constructive aspect, it provides a person with protection and defense against energetic attacks, or as referred to in Judaism, (השגחה פרטית) meaning, "personal providence."

The inhibiting aspect of the letter signifies the inherent tendency in humans toward closure, isolation, and creating a barrier between oneself and others and between oneself and the world, alongside self-centeredness, a strong desire to receive for oneself, and the accumulation of anger.

The degree of its closure indicates tightness, fixation, the dimming of consciousness, and difficulty in opening up to changes, issues that may lead a person to stagnation, pessimism, melancholy, bitterness, victimhood, and the development of diseases resulting from **excess in receiving**.[3]

---

[3] The phrase "excess in receiving" denotes a condition where an individual receives more than they contribute. Such an imbalance can result in various health complications. Kabbalistic teachings, alongside Eastern philosophies, emphasize the significance of moderation and equilibrium in the interplay of giving and receiving. They suggest that sustaining a balanced energy exchange is essential for holistic well-being.

The shape of the letter Samech is round, and it lacks a stable base on which to rely. This round shape is characterized by constant rolling, being able to move non-stop, here and there, or being in constant motion, and it depends to some extent on what it is supported by or the letters it is adjacent to in a person's name.

The graphic shape of the letter Samech resembles an astronaut's suit helmet. This round, closed shape is similar to a bubble that surrounds a person's consciousness, making them unaware of the events that take place outside of them. Although every person perceives the world through their bubble, this letter emphasizes this issue even more and invites the letter's owner to examine how closed they are in their bubble and how willing they are to break its boundaries and move beyond it.

Diagram 80: Astronaut Helmet

Gematrical Value

The gematrical value of the letter Samech is sixty, a number that symbolizes the conceptual ideal of nurturing harmonious relationships. These relationships are characterized by foundational elements such as love, equality, mutual support, protection, open communication, responsibility, and care.

It is a numerical value that holds significance in various fields, including astronomy (with time measured as sixty seconds in a minute and sixty minutes in an hour), geometry (sixty degrees in each of six equal-sided triangles), and music (sixty beats per minute in a measure).

In Judaism, the value sixty is associated with the "Priestly Blessing" (Birkat Kohanim), an ancient sixty-letter blessing used for protection and defense against harm.

In the Bible (*Genesis*, Chapter 25, Verses 23-26), the number sixty is contextualized in the story of Isaac's birth, Abraham's son, and the subsequent birth of his twin sons, Esau and Jacob. From these twins, two diverse and rival nations emerged, engaged in constant conflict, characterized by themes of inequality, deception, and ethical injustice.

The equivalent letter to Samech in the unit digit is Vav, which has a gematrical value of six. This value signifies the importance of personal qualities such as ethics, moral values, humanity, personal responsibility, and service from a pure and clean place. Samech, as an expansion of Vav, amplifies this energy, emphasizing the need to examine one's core beliefs and values and their manifestation in the present moment.

The intense vibrational frequencies of Samech drive individuals toward their inner center. These frequencies encourage individuals to develop a deeper and more meaningful internal dimension within themselves and engage in processes that enable them to shed inhibiting aspects that hinder humility, compassion, and authenticity. Samech guides individuals to embrace values like integrity, personal responsibility, self-respect, and respect for others, ultimately fostering spiritual growth and purification of the soul. These processes allow a greater amount of surrounding light to penetrate and illuminate their inner being.

Maimonides, a prominent Jewish philosopher, notes that physical and spiritual nourishment significantly impacts spiritual development. He posits that the type of food consumed can either promote or hinder this development. Maimonides advocates a plant-based or vegetarian diet, suggesting that it renders the body and soul less dense, thus facilitating spiritual upliftment and the absorption of higher-level information.

The Zodiac Sign Associated with Samech

Sefer Yetzirah associates the letter Samech with the zodiac sign of Sagittarius, offering additional insights into the letter's qualities.

Sagittarius, belonging to the fire element, is characterized by a strong desire for freedom, akin to being a free bird, alongside a penchant for movement and renewal. Those born under Sagittarius often exhibit an eagerness to explore and lead diverse lives.

Sagittarius is a philosophical sign, aspiring toward spiritual ideals. It imparts qualities such as intuition, broad horizons, and a pursuit of wisdom and the ultimate truth that unites all things.

In its constructive aspect, Sagittarius is marked by individuals who are the ultimate philosophers with expansive spiritual horizons. They are guided by principles of truth and justice. The sign resonates with themes of freedom, independence, exploration, affinity for nature trips, and self-discovery. It signifies adventurous spirits who crave space, activities, action, and adrenaline and are often recognized for their candidness in speaking their minds.

The astrological symbol of Sagittarius is represented by an arrow and a bow, and at times as a Centaur—a mythical creature with the lower body of a horse and the upper body of a human, holding an upward-aimed bow and arrow. The bow and arrow, as historical tools for target accuracy, symbolize the dual aspects of this astrological sign: the philosophical (human) and the instinctive (animal).

Diagram 81: Sagittarius Zodiac Sign

The emphasis in Sagittarius is on connections, relationships, partnerships, and interactions with the external environment. It encourages individuals to cultivate unique skills and exert influence. This sign instills qualities such as optimism, the joy of life, vitality, enthusiasm, an adventurous spirit, a love for socializing and entertainment, attraction to different religions and cultures, excitement, social involvement, and a willingness to take risks.

Individuals born under Sagittarius are vibrant and possess a constructive aspect of kindness, generosity, and a readiness to help others. Their high adaptability allows them to adjust to evolving conditions and situations. Naturally generous, especially in social settings, Sagittarians often avoid commitments and constraints that restrict their independence and freedom.

Typically, Sagittarians are averse to routine and find repetitive tasks challenging. They possess an inner, restless fire reminiscent of **ADHD**[4] characteristics. This fiery nature can lead to impulsive enthusiasm and taking risks without careful consideration. Their directness and impulsiveness sometimes result in expressing thoughts without prior consideration, leading to later regrets.

These restless energies can also lead to mental and energetic dispersion. The defined boundaries set by the letter Samech, which Sagittarians may try to escape, are vital for constructively channeling their inner fire. Samech offers support and a foundation, assisting Sagittarians in directing their energies toward well-defined goals and achievements.

---

[4]   ADHD stands for Attention Deficit Hyperactivity Disorder, a condition characterized by difficulties in attention, concentration, impulsivity and hyperactivity. These challenges often interfere with daily functioning and can significantly impact the quality of life for those affected.

The Groups the Letter Samech is Associated With

Fire Element Letter

The element associated with the letter Samech is fire, symbolizing a creative and driving force. This element bestows upon a person creative abilities, self-sufficiency, and motivation. The fire element manifests in this letter as self-confidence, willpower, inner strength, enthusiasm, dynamism, and a need for extensive action and broad self-expression.

Practical Letter

Samech, the ninth letter in the group of twelve simple letters, represents the practical and applied aspects of humans. It embodies a unique combination of both spiritual and material elements. However, the qualities inherent in Samech, coupled with its characteristic of being closed from all directions, often lead individuals associated with this letter to gravitate toward actions that are primarily focused on material manifestations.

Consequential Letter

Samech is the second consequential letter, offering insights into the soul lessons that an individual's soul has undertaken to learn in this lifetime, particularly those not mastered in previous lifetimes. As a consequential letter, Samech propels individuals back to their inner center and guides them through a process of completion and liberation from all that does not align with truth or serve their soul's path. It is an intensive letter that encourages individuals to fully dedicate themselves to the transformative processes it signifies.

The Measure of Mercy and Judgment

The letter Samech embodies both the measure of mercy and judgment, representing a synthesis of these two perspectives. It holds potential energy for consideration, understanding, generosity, mercy, and forgiveness. However, as a dense and completely closed letter, Samech can incline individuals toward a judgmental state, where they judge others based on their actions without empathy. It may also reflect a mindset where assistance to others is conditional, offered only when convenient or beneficial. This measure of judgment resonates with the cosmic law of "like attracts like."

Samech is a powerful and energetically elevated letter. However, its characteristics can lead to deviations toward high levels of ego, pride, and hubris. For those with this letter in their name, success is found in connecting to spirituality and showing a willingness to support others. Engaging in projects aimed at benefiting others is key. Actions should ideally stem from a pure intention to benefit society rather than seeking personal gain or public accolades.

The measure of judgment embodied by Samech can lead individuals associated with this letter toward harsh self-criticism, a critical view of others, arrogance, and a sense of superiority. These tendencies can result in consciously or unconsciously harming others, humiliating them directly or indirectly, casting reproach, and diminishing their worth to feel superior. Samech encourages its bearers to open up intellectually, emotionally, and spiritually, to release rigid beliefs, and to trust that life's events ultimately contribute to their higher good.

Strengths

Individuals associated with Samech demonstrate strengths like intuition, wisdom, broad-mindedness, a welcoming nature, faith in goodness, vigor, humor, adaptability, and generosity. They are characterized by a love for learning, experimenting, wandering, traveling, exploring new places, meeting new people, and acquiring experiences and wisdom. They value personal space and freedom in relationships and have an aversion to limitations on their freedom.

Weaknesses

The weaknesses linked to Samech include anger, envy, irritation, pride, judgment, arrogance, blame, failure to take personal responsibility, complacency, cynicism, rigidity, lack of focus, mental distraction, aimlessness, a strong desire to receive to oneself, avoidance of obligations, and difficulty in listening and giving space to others. Its inhibiting aspect manifests in confusion, belief in the infallibility of one's opinion, fickleness, lack of tact, self-righteousness, grandiosity, a penchant for glamour, disrespect for others' privacy, impulsiveness, and reactivity.

א ב ג ד ה ו ז ח ט י כ ל מ נ ס עַ פ צ ק ר ש ת

"Beauty is in the eye of the beholder."

Uniqueness and Purpose

The letter Ahyin (עַיִן) is the sixteenth letter in the Hebrew alphabet. It symbolizes the power of vision inherent in a person and emphasizes the correct use of this power. This letter represents the all-seeing, observing eye and the perspective from which a person views the world.

In its spiritual sense, Ahyin embodies the eye of reason—the capacity for full and comprehensive observation, merging both the physical and metaphysical (spiritual) aspects of sight inherent in the human soul. Ahyin seeks to connect individuals to the wisdom of observation and cultivate within them the ability to peer into the depths of things to discern their true meanings. It aims to refine and enhance the individual's vision, transitioning from mere physical sight to the sight of the heart—spiritual and three-dimensional vision. Furthermore, it encourages a transition from sensory (visual) perception to a supersensory inner vision, which enables the reorganization of mental understandings and thought patterns.

The Letter in Creation Stories

The first mention of the letter Ahyin in the creation stories appears with the words "al-pney" (עַל פְּנֵי), meaning "over the surface of," in the biblical verse, *"And the earth was a formless and desolate emptiness, and darkness was over the surface of the deep, and the Spirit of God was hovering over the surface of the waters."* (Genesis,

Chapter 1, Verse 2) The Hebrew phrase "over the surface of" suggests a vision that transcends mere surface appearance, hinting at a depth of human eyesight capable of seeing beyond the externality of things, into a realm of three-dimensional vision.

Another biblical verse that mentions the mystical power of vision associated with Ahyin is, "Then the eyes of both of them were opened, and they knew that they were naked." (*Genesis*, Chapter 3, Verse 7) This verse reveals a new level of eyesight bestowed upon Adam and Eve after consuming the fruit from the Tree of Knowledge. While Adam and Eve could see before eating the fruit, it was after this act that a new inner vision, a profound type of eyesight, was unveiled to them.

The letter Ahyin, with its inherent wisdom, alludes to the immense ability hidden within humans: a unique "inner metaphysical eyesight." This extraordinary capability enables the perception of images, forms, and visions conveyed from a higher source through metaphysical and spiritual vision, facilitating the communication of these insights to humanity. Historically, this ability was inherent in prophets and seers. The letter Ahyin appears in the biblical Hebrew names of figures such as Elisha (אלישע), Amos (עמוס), Joshua (יהושע), Ada (עדו), and Jesus (ישוע). The Hebrew meaning of the name Jesus (ישוע) is "salvation."

On an earthly level, Ahyin pertains to the physical eye, a sensory organ that bridges the external world with the internal. The eye, located in the head at the center of the face, is a perceptual, sensory organ through which humans not only perceive tangible reality and electromagnetic radiation (light photons) but also transfer this external information to the brain. This process connects the inner world of an individual with the outer realm.

In its metaphysical aspect, the letter Ahyin alludes to the human capacity for "super-vision"—the ability to delve into the essence of things and unveil hidden truths. A profound example of this concept is depicted in the movie *Avatar*. The short expression, "I see you," is uttered repeatedly throughout the film, echoing the profound essence of eyesight not merely as a physical act but as a deep, comprehensive understanding of it—its ability to see love, emotions, and the soul of the other.

We encounter the spiritual power of eyesight in the biblical story of Mount Sinai, where the Israelites received the Torah. Remarkably, they were able to "see" voices and sounds, as documented in Exodus in the Hebrew version, *"And all the people see the voice."* (Exodus, Chapter 20, Verse 14) This phenomenon underscores the profound spiritual ability to perceive things beyond the physical realm and experience synesthesia—a sensory crossover where one type of sensory input is perceived as another.

Rabbi Berg, the founder of the Kabbalah Centre and an esteemed author on Kabbalistic teachings, emphasizes in his works that the Israelites attained this metaphysical vision through the spiritual diligence they practiced over the forty-nine days preceding the divine revelation at Mount Sinai, a period known as the "Count of the Omer." During this time, they engaged in a comprehensive purification process, shedding all ego and negativity. This preparatory work culminated in an elevated state of consciousness, enabling them to experience the divine in an unprecedented way, where sight transcended its conventional boundaries to encompass the realm of sound.

Pronunciation

The letter Ahyin is pronounced "Ah-yin," though it is sometimes articulated as "A-yin" or "A-yeen," mirroring the name of the organ after which it is named. To accurately reflect its phonetic sound, I am presenting the letter phonetically as Ah-yin. In English, Ahyin can be represented as A, E, AH, EY or O, depending on its position in a word or name.

The pronunciation of the letter Ahyin mirrors its Hebrew name, which translates to "Eye."

Ahyin is the fourth letter in the alphabet, which, in its pronunciation, alludes to a bodily organ with a powerful influence. Ahyin underscores the notion that eyesight is not as passive as commonly believed but is instead an active and initiating force. The eye is more than a mere receiver; it is a sensory organ that acts as a transmitter, sending signals across distances and exerting a significant influence on reality. The human eye is a creative and tangible organ capable of shaping or altering reality.

Our vision governs how we see and perceive the world. It is a complex perceptual experience that involves receiving information from the environment and transferring it to the brain, where it is processed, assigned value, and meaning. A crucial aspect of vision is the interpretation individuals give to the stimuli received by the eye, influenced by their accumulated knowledge.

The eye does more than receive (absorb) light frequencies from outside; it also radiates and transmits inner energy from inside to outside continuously. According to Kabbalistic teachings, vision can be likened to a form of touch, where the invisible radiation emanating from the eye affects both the observer and the observed with its power. In this way, the human eye can uplift or demean others. The eyes serve as the mirror of the soul, reflecting a person's inner state, health, and purity.

Beyond two physical eyes, humans also possess a "spiritual eye," known in esoteric teachings as the "third eye." This spiritual eye is located in the center of the forehead, where the red Tika of Hinduism is applied. It is an energetic organ responsible for metaphysical vision. It enables supersensory vision, allowing for the reception of inner knowledge through shapes, images, and the reception of mental or metaphysical impressions. Through our spiritual eye, we can understand the nature of objects without relying on physical sight or logical reasoning.

The letter Ahyin conveys that our physical eyes, which are engaged in external vision, have their limitation. An example of that is our inability to see bacteria without a microscope. However, spiritual vision transcends these limits, uncovering depths and meanings not visible to our physical eyes. This form of vision, incredibly powerful, can manifest desired realities. When we vividly imagine something with intense emotion, seeing it through our spirit's eyes, we endow it with the potential to materialize.

Graphic Shape

The graphic shape of the letter Ahyin is a closed form from three sides. It is closed on its right and left sides and at the bottom, thereby creating a barrier in three directions. Ahyin is closed downward toward the matters of the earthly realm and turns its back on the wisdom of the preceding letter, Samech, as well as from the letter that follows it, Peh. This level of closure indicates an inherent inclination toward self-centeredness, closure, and a desire to receive for oneself.

The letter Ahyin also lacks a base or legs to lean upon and stands in an inherently unstable posture, signifying its inherent challenge to maintain balance and equilibrium over time.

In both its handwritten and printed forms, the letter Ahyin features an upper opening and two arms that extend upward, as if reaching to draw something from the higher planes into itself.

The handwritten form of Ahyin is particularly noteworthy. As depicted in the sketch below, its two arms intersect in a manner akin to two optic nerves, creating a shape reminiscent of the optic chiasm, the area in the brain where the optic nerves cross.

Gematrical Value

The gematrical value of the letter Ahyin is seventy, a number laden with significant implications in both its constructive and inhibitory aspects. This value represents a vibrational frequency that urges an individual to uncover the hidden through introspective processes such as inner observation. It encourages one to transcend their illusory ego and the "Qliphoth" (impurities) accumulated over their life cycles, enabling them to navigate their life with authenticity, integrity, humility, and honesty.

Diagram 82: Optic Chiasm

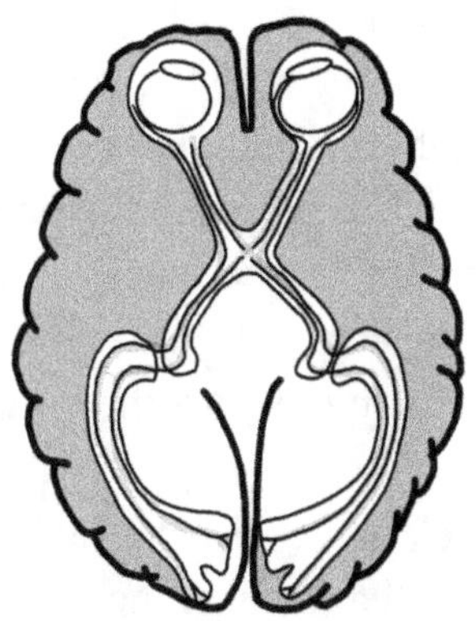

In Judaism, the value of Ahyin is linked to the concept of wholeness of consciousness. The corresponding letter in the unit digit to Ahyin is Zayin, which holds a numeric value of seven. This number, in its constructive aspect, is associated with spirituality, intellect, curiosity, abstract thinking, sensitivity, and deep understanding. Conversely, in its inhibitory aspect, it signifies confusion, obscurity, concealment, internal chatter, incessant thoughts, loneliness, and escaping from dealing with reality.

Ahyin, essentially an expansion of Zayin, magnifies Zayin's energy tenfold, pushing it toward its fullest expression. These two letters are connected by their similar endings and numerical values.

The Bible mentions this value in various contexts. It appears in relation to the number of Noah's sons, the seventy descendants who survived the flood and from whom new humanity emerged. (*Genesis*, Chapter 10, Verse 32)

We encounter this value in the context of the number of souls who went down to Egypt—seventy souls were the core of the future Israelite souls, the children and grandchildren of Jacob—when the family of Jacob descended to Egypt as a fragmented family. From the seed of seventy souls, the nation of Israel was formed, as stated in the verse: "*All the people of the house of Jacob, who came to Egypt, were seventy.*" (*Genesis*, Chapter 46, Verse 27)

The value of seventy is emphasized multiple times in the prophecies of the prophet Jeremiah and the prophet Daniel. In the book of Jeremiah, which contains prophecies, warnings, and moral teachings aimed at awakening people to repentance, the value is mentioned in the context of the seventy years of exile that were decreed upon the people due to their sins. (Jeremiah, Chapter 25, Verses 11-12)

In the book of Daniel, which also contains prophecies, warnings, and moral teachings aimed at awakening people to the awareness of their sins and transgressions, the value of seventy is mentioned in the context of the number of weeks given to the people for the completion of their sins and transgressions. (Daniel, Chapter 9, Verse 24)

We also encounter the value of seventy in the mysterious story of the Tower of Babel (*Genesis*, Chapters 10-11), a story that takes place several generations after Noah. The story describes a process of "language confusion" resulting from the sin of hubris, ego, and pride among a certain group of people. As a result, one nation speaking one language is split into seventy nations with seventy different languages. This division created distinct linguistic groups, rendering them unable to understand each other.

Today, the number of nations and languages is greater than ever before, as the mixing of languages and peoples has led to a situation where there are no clear boundaries between languages and nations.

The story of the Tower of Babel provides us with an understanding of the **perfection of consciousness**.[1] It describes a stage in humanity where human consciousness reached a level of perfection, allowing them to create great makings. This was a developmental state in which humans were connected to high-dimensional consciousness, experienced spiritual upliftment, and could communicate telepathically. It was an era when technology was at its peak, and there was no need for verbal language, as communication between individuals could occur through thought.

Diagram 83: Tower of Babel

This mythological story signifies a period of spiritual enlightenment followed by a fall in consciousness. It contains many facets of wisdom, which, in my opinion, are very important

---

[1]   Perfection of consciousness is a spiritual and philosophical concept highlighting a state of advanced self-awareness, a keen understanding of one's thoughts and emotions, and an enriched connection to the world and a higher reality.

to understand for accurate self-development and the expansion of consciousness, both individually and socially.

The story of the Tower of Babel conveys two important and intriguing meanings. The first highlights the reason for the fall in consciousness—the sin of hubris and the misuse of the divine light frequencies and wisdom. It describes a state in which humans began to develop creations based on their personal light, disconnected from the divine light, thus exploiting their free will for evil purposes. Consequently, they were punished, fell, and were scattered into seventy nations.

The second insight from this ancient tale is the fall of humans into the hands of negative forces that have since been dominating, manipulating, and managing humans. These forces are not interested in human progress and development and strive to keep humans in a state of "survival consciousness"—a state of sleepwalking to facilitate their control over humanity.

It is important to note that the constructive aspects of Ahyin enable a person to transform the negative traits embedded within themselves, thereby attaining personal freedom. The term "embedded," as used in Kabbalistic teachings, refers to the compressed, negative, and rigid mental traits that are ingrained in a person's soul. These traits carry over from one incarnation to another through their 'base body." Such traits can disrupt a person's inner harmony, negatively impact their mental well-being, and hinder their success in life until they learn to shed them. Understanding this concept is crucial, especially for those associated with the letter Ahyin or the zodiac sign linked to this letter. I discuss this issue in detail in my subsequent books.

The Zodiac Sign Associated with Ahyin

Sefer Yetzirah connects the letter Ahyin to the astrological sign of Capricorn, providing additional insight into its attributes.

Capricorn, an earth sign, is symbolized by the goat—a member of the Bovidae family. This animal, the offspring of the she-goat and he-goat, is known as a kid in its youth. Domesticated by humans more than ten thousand years ago, goats were among the earliest animals to be sacrificed on altars in ancient times.

The goat is renowned for its endurance, agility, and curiosity. It thrives in nature and is adept at climbing mountains and peaks. Methodically ascending mountainous trails, it navigates rocky and treacherous paths filled with obstacles. These challenging terrains serve not only as a test but also as a means for the goat to progress and reach higher elevations, where it can bask in the purity of clean and fresh air. Exploration is a primary instinct for goats; they use their lips and tongue to interact with the unknown. This intelligence and inquisitiveness often lead them to escape their pens, driven by a desire to explore their surroundings and all that is new and unfamiliar.

The Capricorn zodiac sign embodies qualities such as seriousness, strictness, diligence, perseverance, mental maturity, conservatism, frugality, and a forward-looking concern for the future. It also signifies a deep desire to initiate practical measures that lay the foundation for a stable material base. Capricorns are driven by the ambition to build a stable professional, social, and economic status. This drive propels them to master their destiny through tireless, patient, and persistent efforts, focusing intently on achieving their set goals.

For individuals born under this sign, concepts like hierarchy, structure, status, and bureaucracy hold significant importance, as do clearly defined schemes and patterns. These elements play a crucial role in their lives, influencing their actions and decisions both consciously and unconsciously.

The letter Ahyin stands as one of the most densely compressed earth letters, embodying a level of density that often leads individuals toward a sense of victimhood, whether conscious or unconscious. It evokes feelings of a lost childhood or a lack of sufficient support from fate, family, or society. Those born under this sign may feel deprived or neglected, a sentiment that, in the unconscious realm, steers them toward a survival consciousness and prompts them to blame external factors. While these feelings are inherently subjective, they are, nonetheless, undeniable and impactful.

Within these individuals resides a profound internal commitment to efficiency and control. They are adept at bearing burdens, responsibilities, and obligations, demonstrated through their relentless hard work and determination to achieve their goals. There is a deeply held belief that success is attainable only through long, persistent, and strenuous effort.

Judaism offers a perspective on individuals of this sign, noting that from early childhood, they often engage in struggles for control and power. Frequently, they grapple with 'stardust' until they learn to alter their life's perspective, embrace self-responsibility, assimilate their spiritual lessons, and cultivate deep self-awareness and an awakened consciousness.

Diagram 84: Capricorn Zodiac Sign

The Groups the Letter Ahyin is Associated With

Earth Element Letter

The element associated with the letter Ahyin is earth, which endows individuals with stability, resilience, physical strength, and the ability to survive while also fostering a strong connection to the tangible aspects of their lives. The earth element, symbolized by Ahyin, represents the cold and dense ground, akin to the cold and rainy winter season that turns the earth into mud. This state tends to draw individuals toward focusing excessively on materialistic concerns, with a potential risk of becoming entrenched in the quest for material success.

The Measure of Mercy and Judgment

The letter Ahyin encapsulates both the measure of mercy and judgment, representing a complex interplay of these two dynamics. It harbors potential energy for consideration, understanding, generosity, mercy, and forgiveness. However, its nature as a dense and inwardly closed letter from three directions predisposes individuals toward a stance where assistance to others is extended not from pure intention but rather out of convenience or suitability. The inclination to consider and support others often emerges not from proactive generosity but in response to explicit needs or requests.

The dense vibrational frequencies of Ahyin incline those associated with this letter or its corresponding zodiac sign to be driven by self-interest, questioning, "What will I benefit from this?" or "What is the easiest and most profitable option for me?" In its restrictive aspect, these frequencies may lead bearers of the letter to engage in the manipulation and exploitation of others for personal gain.,

Consequential Letter

Ahyin is a consequential letter that offers insights into the soul lessons an individual has committed to learning in this lifetime—lessons that remain unmastered from past lives. This letter tends toward harsh judgment and criticism, both self-directed and toward others, by assigning scores and labels to each individual and situation. Its vibrational frequencies, particularly in their inhibitory aspect, tend to foster a consciousness of separateness.

When this consciousness of separateness encounters judgment, it only strengthens the sense of division, creating barriers rather than fostering unity among differing opinions, ideas, and people.

As a consequential letter, Ahyin guides individuals toward shedding all that does not align with their higher good and soul's purpose. It encourages a focus on introspective processes designed to return them to their inner core and uncover their true spiritual mission. This journey allows them to navigate life with a heart-centered approach characterized by kindness and compassion. Ahyin is a powerful letter that urges individuals to embrace and surrender to the transformative processes it speaks about.

Practical Letter

Ahyin is the tenth letter in the group of twelve simple letters that represent the practical and applied aspects of a person. As an earthly and material letter, it tends to draw individuals toward actions primarily focused on material achievements.

Strengths

The strengths associated with the letter Ahyin include qualities such as realism, pragmatism, grounding, patience, mental maturity, responsibility, seriousness, conservatism, ambition, loyalty, caution, perseverance, determination, and a goal-oriented mindset, methodology, organization, order, resourcefulness, endurance, excellent cognitive abilities, purposefulness, moderation, and self-discipline. It characterizes individuals as calculated, reasonable, efficient, and committed to their endeavors.

Weaknesses

Conversely, Ahyin's weaknesses include solemnity, over-meticulousness, excessive criticism, judgmental attitudes, rigidity, a lack of uplifting imagination, possessiveness, controlling nature, arrogance, pride, obstinacy, cynicism, envy, emotional and physical stinginess, patterned thinking, dominance, difficulty in opening up, resistance to accepting conventions and compromise, resistance to change, and an overemphasis on conformity and tradition.

Its inhibitory aspect can lead to insolence, unbridled ambition, boldness, political maneuvering, manipulation, a desire for quick results, and exploiting others for personal gain.

אבגדההוזחחטיכלמנס ע **פ** צקרשת

"The tongue has the power of life and death"
Proverbs, Chapter 15, Verse 21

Uniqueness and Purpose

The letter Peh (פֶּה) is the seventeenth letter in the Hebrew alphabet, symbolizing the mouth—the physical organ responsible for speech, verbal expression, and human language.

Following the letter Ahyin, which represents the human eyes capacity to observe divine reality and interpret it through inherent eyesight, Peh joins in to manifest a potent energy capable of altering current and future events. Vision and speech act as two dynamic forces with a profound impact on our actions and reality.

The letter Peh is considered a creative mind letter, denoting the organ capable of forging new realities or annihilating them. Through speech, an individual holds the power to uplift others to great heights or cast them into the depths of despair and destruction.

The purpose of the letter Peh is to draw a person's attention to the proper use of the mouth, speech, and language. Its goal is to transform the aggressive communication frequencies typically associated with this letter into ones of compassion, making individuals aware of the power of their speech. It aims to guide them to speak from the heart—with sincerity, directly and authentically, devoid of fear or reverence, and free from shame or embarrassment.

The Letter in Creation Stories

The first mention of the letter Peh in the Genesis stories occurs in the phrase "al-pnei" (עַל-פְּנֵי), meaning "over the surface of," in verse, "*And the earth was a formless and desolate emptiness, and darkness was over the surface of the deep, and the Spirit of God was hovering over the surface of the waters.*" (Genesis, Chapter 1, Verse 2)

In this profound verse, Peh is articulated twice, each instance seamlessly intertwined with the letter Ahyin within the phrase "over the surface of" (עַל-פְּנֵי). This linguistic pairing unveils the superficial aspect of existence, delving into how things appear on the surface—their external appearance, visual semblance, and, potentially, the visible expression of their inner essence.

Pronunciation

The pronunciation of the letter Peh hints at its essence and the secret it conceals within. Peh is a labial letter pronounced with the lips. Its name and sound carry dual meanings: "peh" (פֶּה), signifying "mouth," and "po" (פֹּה), indicating "here" or "present." These interpretations, though spelled with the same letters as Peh, are distinguished by different diacritical marks within the letter itself.

The human mouth acts as a gateway for two primary processes and transitions. Physically, it is an opening for absorption and emission: we consume food that sustains us, breathe air that vitalizes our bodies and produce sounds that form the language conveying our thoughts. Metaphysically, it symbolizes the passage through which the incarnated human soul both descends into the body and ascends.

The mouth wields considerable power and influence as a tool of communication, expressing thoughts, emotions, and inner truths. It represents the capacity to articulate thoughts, feelings, emotions, and sensations and to describe phenomena, conveying insights and messages.

The words emanating from the mouth possess immense power—they can heal or harm, uplift or demean, unify families, nations, and peoples, or sow discord and division. The mouth's power of speech enables humans to create or destroy, as encapsulated in Proverbs: *"Death and life are in the power of the tongue."* (Proverbs, Chapter 18, Verse 21)

The power of speech extends beyond audible words. The link between the letter Peh, a physical organ, and presence at the moment is profound. Humans, as thinking and expressive beings, generate a continuous internal dialogue that can sometimes disrupt our peace of mind. For example, inner speech of a low vibrational frequency often leads to confusion and mental turmoil, akin to a bug-ridden computer program.

Diagram 85: Computer Screen with Bugs

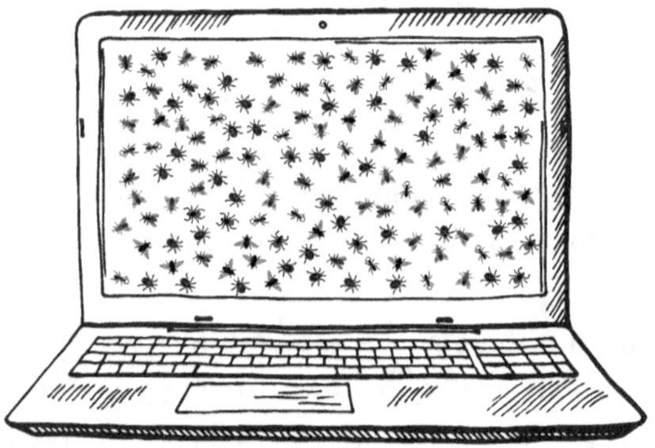

Our thoughts often drift toward the past or future, rarely anchoring in the present. Reflections on the past usually evoke feelings of sadness, anger, or regret over past decisions or mistakes. Similarly, thoughts directed toward the future can stir up resistance, fear, and anxiety about what lies ahead, leading us to identify more with our thoughts than with the present moment. This identification causes us to lose ourselves in excessive worry and overthinking about the past, which has already concluded, or the uncertain future.

Eckhart Tolle, an inspiring teacher and the author of "The Power of Now," highlights this crucial aspect in his work. He teaches us to recognize and neutralize incessant mental chatter, enabling us to inhabit the present moment in a state of inner peace.

The letter Peh serves as a reminder of the importance of being present in the here and now, fully grounded in our earthly existence—with our bodies, emotions, and thoughts—while connecting to our inner core. It also underscores the importance of directing our speech toward the present moment rather than dwelling on the past or speculating about the future.

The letter Peh can be represented in English as P or F, depending on its position in a word or name and its hard or soft pronunciation.

Graphic Shape

The graphic shape of the letter Peh provides us with additional insight into the qualities it embodies. The graphical shape of Peh in both print and handwriting, is closed in three directions: upward, toward the matters of the spiritual realm; downward, toward the matters of the earthly realm; and it turns its back on the wisdom held by the preceding letter, Ahyin, while being partially closed to the wisdom of the letter that immediately follows it, Tzadi.

The graphic shape of Peh resembles a spiral, extending inward toward the inner center. This shape emphasizes the importance of being at the inner center—a center that serves as an anchor, a protective and serene space where all noises fade away, allowing a person to connect with their inner essence.

The spiral represented by Peh exhibits two modes of expression: convergence from the outside to the inside and expansion from the inside to the outside. This shape signifies an energetic flow upward or downward, similar to an energetic vortex that serves as a gateway through which spiritual energy enters inward, into the earth that absorbs the energy, and through which energy is emitted outward, from the earth into the world.

Both in the universe—the macrocosm, and in humans—the microcosm, energetic processes are activated. In a state where the heart and mouth of a person are aligned, a strong, energetic spiral is activated within them, extending into space and connecting them to the "Unified Field"—the energy field of the universe, allowing heartfelt desires to manifest in the blink of an eye.

Diagram 86: Bent Letter Peh   **Diagram 87: Upright Letter Peh**

פ   ף

The letter Peh is written in two different forms. When it appears at the beginning or middle of a word or a name, it is written as a bent and curved letter (פ), embodying an inward inclination that encourages introspection. This form guides one toward the depths of their soul—toward the essence of their being, prompting the realization that struggles for power, honor, ego, and pride are fundamentally illusory.

Conversely, when it appears at the end of a word or a name, it stands upright (ף), resembling a long stake or a supportive walking stick. This upright form symbolizes the redemption attained through personal rectification, marking a journey of soul purification, overcoming personal and spiritual hurdles, fostering forgiveness toward oneself and others, and acknowledging life's challenges as opportunities for growth and development.

As depicted in the sketches, the bent shape of Peh features a broad base that offers a stable foundation, unlike the upright form, which features a long leg extending below the baseline, indicative of grounding. This graphical difference suggests that the upright form is more susceptible to losing internal balance compared to its bent counterpart.

Gematrical Value

The gematrical value of Peh is eighty, a value imbued with significant meanings, chiefly symbolizing the triumph of the spirit over matter.

This value embodies a potent, energetic force that represents qualities such as inner strength and courage. These traits empower individuals to transcend their materialistic nature and courageously deal with the challenging trials of earthly life. Transcendence becomes possible when individuals open themselves up to transformative change processes.

The gematrical value of eighty also represents a pragmatic approach oriented toward material achievement and the acquisition of property. It symbolizes a practical and logical approach focused on effective solutions that lead to desired final results, granting a person a sense of accomplishment and material security.

Symbolically, eighty is associated with structures, particularly structural legality, and addresses themes of oppression, slavery, and subjugation.

The vibrational frequencies of this gematrical value compel a person to live a life rooted in honesty (with oneself and others), integrity, authenticity, humility, gratitude, self-respect, and respect for others, alongside determination and dedication to a goal. It urges individuals to build stable and long-term structures in all areas of their lives based on high moral values and a true and complete connection to their heart's desires and feelings of love and compassion.

The value of eighty signifies the infinite abundance a person attains when they liberate themselves from their illusory ego and strong attachments to the material aspects of life.

We encounter this gematrical value in biblical contexts related to leadership, including self-leadership (self-discipline and self-management) and the leadership of others, as well as in matters pertaining to causes and actions that lead people into bondage and their subsequent liberation.

Furthermore, we encounter this value in the context of Moses, the prophet's age, in the story of the Exodus of the Israelites from their slavery in Egypt. Moses, after undergoing profound transformative processes throughout his life journey—from being a prince of Egypt to becoming a fugitive and eventually the leader of the entire nation—returns to Egypt at the age of eighty to redeem his people from bondage. "*And Moses was eighty years old.*" (Exodus, Chapter 7, Verse 7)

Moses stands as the inaugural leader of the Jewish people, and it is said about him in the scriptures, "*Since that time no prophet has risen in Israel like Moses, whom the Lord knew face to face.*" (Deuteronomy, Chapter 34, Verse 10) He is the first biblical leader who illustrates the value of the process of change and the outcome obtained when a person dedicates themselves to deep transformative processes.

Moses becomes an exemplary leader, not because of his Egyptian lineage but through his own merits. He stands at the apex of law and legislation, holding traditional authority. Mose's leadership is characterized by a lack of hierarchy. Around him, a system of priesthood, legislation, and justice was established, not dependent on him but drawing its power from his wisdom and greatness.

We also encounter the value of eighty in the Book of Judges, which describes the slavery that the Israelites fell into as a result of sins associated with idol worship. This slavery lasted for eighty years, and the judge Ehud ben Gera, the son of the Benjamite, delivered the people and judged them for eighty years. "*And the land was at rest for eighty years.*" (Judges, Chapter 3, Verses 12-30)

The letter that corresponds to the letter Peh in the unit digit is the letter Chet, with a gematrical value of eight, a powerful number in itself, which speaks about metaphysical processes related to abundance and influence. These processes aim to develop high self-awareness in a person and a connection to the multi-dimensionality that exists within them.

Peh is an expansion of Chet. It multiplies the value of Chet by ten, granting it highly energetic potential, allowing a person to change the underlying operating system with which they entered their current life incarnation. It pushes a person to step out from the illusory ego and toward their unique and authentic self, guiding them back to their inner center. It urges them to develop a heightened awareness of how they use their speech abilities and the way they communicate with themselves and with others.

The intense vibrational frequencies of Peh, similar to the letter Ahyin, grant a person mental and emotional strength that enables them to transform the negative aspects embedded within them, so that they can gain personal freedom.

The Planet Associated with Peh

"He made the letter Peh king, and He bound a crown to it, and He combined one with another, and with them, He formed Venus in the Universe." (*Sefer Yetzirah*, Chapter 4, Verse 9)

Sefer Yetzirah connects the letter Peh to the planet Venus, known in Hebrew as "Noga." This association provides deep insights into how Peh's vibrational frequencies shape our reality.

In Western astrology, Venus is part of the group of five planets known as personal planets. Being closest to Earth and possessing high speed, Venus directly influences an individual's character. It symbolizes one's attitude toward life and the way one gains experience and provides insights into one's essential traits, tendencies, needs, and personal desires.

When you look at the sky early in the morning, just before sunrise, or toward the evening, shortly after sunset, you can see a shining celestial body glowing in the sky, kind of like a spot of light, which is why Venus is known as the "Morning Star" and the "Evening Star."

Historically, Venus has been linked in various mythologies to the goddess of beauty, love, magic, and sensuality. It supports those who accept unconditional love and presents challenges to those who resist or spurn genuine affection. Various mythologies suggest that this radiant planet was hijacked by "the other force"—the force of impurity and evil. These stories associate Venus with the "beloved angel of God," the fallen angel, whose Hebrew name is Hillel ben Shahar, and whose English name is Lucifer.

This luminous planet is associated with feelings, aesthetics, and sexuality, as well as possessions, wealth, and material comfort. Venus symbolizes the source of power behind emotional expression, the expression of love, and identification with inner and collective values. Its vibrational frequencies attract into individuals lives people, relationships, events, and situations through which they can learn to conduct themselves fairly, with integrity and reliability in interpersonal and financial situations. These frequencies aim to develop within individuals the ability to love unconditionally.

The vibrational frequencies of Venus encourage individuals to form close connections and establish relationships based on appreciation, fairness, mutual respect, and true love. They prompt individuals to balance and unite the contradictions and contrasts within their souls and to create inner and outer harmony. This is achieved through the development of high self-awareness and recognition of how they express their love-hate emotions, whether in a loving and compassionate manner or a dismissive and hostile manner.

The Groups the Letter Peh is Associated With

Earth Element Letter

The element associated with the letter Ahyin is earth, which endows individuals with stability, resilience, physical strength, and the ability to survive while also fostering a strong connection to the tangible aspects of their lives. The earth element, symbolized by Ahyin, represents the cold and dense ground, akin to the cold and rainy winter season that turns the earth into mud. This state tends to draw individuals toward focusing excessively on materialistic concerns, with a potential risk of becoming entrenched in the quest for material success.

The Measure of Mercy and Judgment

The Earth element, associated with the letter Peh, grounds humans, endowing them with formidable physical strength. As the densest of all elements, Earth, when combined with Peh's closed pattern from three directions—encompassing harsh, critical, and judgmental vibrational frequencies—narrows an individual's consciousness, limits their understanding, and draws them toward a separate consciousness with a tendency to see the differences in everything.

This inherent challenge in recognizing the inherent value on both sides of any issue complicates the ability of those connected to Peh to reconcile the contradictions born from complex realities. Such a struggle often results in a closed-off stance, clinging to illusory self-perceptions, and an overreliance on defense mechanisms. This reliance can foster conditional behavior, leading individuals to navigate life in a state akin to sleepwalking.

The letter Peh harbors an ancient fear, a primal fear of release and letting go—of beliefs, relationships, and opinions. Despite its power, Peh poses significant challenges due to its intensity, housing numerous conditional behavioral patterns and an inner resistance to change. It also reveals a tenacious hold on achievements, even when this grip results in profound mental and emotional distress.

We must not forget that our body serves as a vessel for the divine spirit, the vessel through which the soul connects with its creator. This vessel cannot remain closed for a long time. James Watkins aptly said, "*A river cuts through a rock not because of its power but because of its persistence,*" and the same goes for the inner voice of the soul. In a state where the vessel is closed, and the light struggles to enter the body, eventually, a crack will form in the vessel to create a window for the light to enter. For those associated with the letter Peh, this moment of breakthrough is felt as an inner upheaval.

Refusal or avoidance of learning spiritual lessons may precipitate a profound and unsettling "inner earthquake." This tumultuous experience might manifest as illness or a continuous state of exhaustion and energetic depletion. Sometimes, such a jolt is necessary to awaken an individual, compelling them to slow down and cultivate a more profound self-awareness.

This internal earthquake can also be experienced as trauma, leading to soul fragmentation—a state where mental wholeness shatters into fragments, and soul particles detach from the body, leaving one feeling weakened and energetically drained.

Soul fragmentation is a spiritual and metaphysical concept suggesting that difficult life experiences, trauma, or various challenges can cause aspects of one's spiritual essence to become fragmented or disconnected. This fragmentation occurs when we endure traumatic events so painful that a part of ourselves splits off and remains trapped in that specific timeline. The healing process involves, among other strategies, the retrieval or reintegration of these lost fragments to achieve a sense of wholeness—an endeavor further explored in the subsequent letter.

Creational Mind Letter

The letter Peh is a creational mind letter, encapsulating mental and emotional patterns engraved into both personal and collective human consciousness. These patterns, encompassing deep-seated beliefs and aggressive impulses, reside within the base body, transcending from one incarnation to the next. These beliefs tend to activate individuals associated with this letter in a sub-hypnotic manner.

Peh aims to direct a person's attention toward the utilization of the mouth, speech, and language—both toward themselves and those they interact with. Its goal is to transition from hostile to compassionate communication, highlighting the profound impact of verbal expression on personal growth and relationships.

Hard and Soft Sound

The letter Peh can be pronounced with either a hard or soft sound, influencing its characteristics. As a creative mind letter, Peh can intensify or weaken its vibrational frequencies. A hard sound gives the letter a masculine (yang) and more intense tone, while a softer sound imparts a feminine (yin) and gentler tone. When pronounced hard, it suggests difficulty in becoming flexible when needed. Conversely, soft pronunciation represents the ability to be flexible and dissolve the ego.

When Peh is pronounced with a hard sound, as in the word "politica" (meaning "politics"), it exhibits greater strength and presence but also a higher risk of pride and ego-driven actions. Conversely, in its soft form, Peh reduces its vibrational frequency, diminishing the ego's influence and fostering a greater capacity for actions rooted in humility.

When the letter Peh is pronounced softly, it produces a sound similar to the letters "F" or "PH." For example, we encounter the hard sound of the letter in words such as "ptzatza" (bomb), "pur'anut" (disaster), and "pachad" (fear), and the soft sound in words like "afar" (dirt), "efer" (ashes), and "fisfus" (a miss).

Consequential Letter

Peh is a consequential letter that offers insights into the soul lessons an individual has committed to learning in this lifetime—lessons that remain unmastered from past lives. As a consequential letter, Peh carries intense energy that pushes a person to their limits, aiming to awaken within them an awareness of their soul's lessons. This awareness allows them to perceive the hidden outcomes behind their earthly experiences and life events.

The letter possesses powerful energetic abilities. Its vibrational frequencies enable individuals to open doors, break through boundaries, overcome challenges, and transcend the materialistic nature that anchors them to the comfort of material life.

As a consequential letter, Peh guides individuals toward enhanced initiation processes that involve shedding all that does not align with their higher good and soul's purpose. It encourages a focus on introspective processes designed to develop awareness of their conditioned habits and deep-rooted beliefs that tend to control them in a subconscious, hypnotic way and navigate them back to their inner core to uncover their true heart desires and their soul calling. These processes allow them to navigate life with a heart-centered approach, characterized by kindness and compassion toward themselves and others and by following their heart.

Peh is a powerful letter that urges individuals to embrace and surrender to the transformative processes it speaks of.

The Measure of Absolute Judgment

The letter Peh embodies the measure of absolute judgment. This measure restricts and limits the consciousness of the individual, leading them to a state where they judge people and situations harshly and rigorously, holding them accountable and thus distancing themselves from the path it directs them toward.

Redemption Letter

Peh belongs to the group of redemption letters, granting a person the power and opportunity to create significant change in their life and the possibility to cleanse the Qlipoth—the impurities and negative karma accumulated throughout their lifetimes.

The letter Peh is not a simple letter. When it appears as a final letter in a person's name, its energy becomes even more intense and tends to attract individuals toward experiences centered around reliability and control. As a final letter, it implies that the path to authentic self-fulfillment involves, first and foremost, the willingness to let go of the illusory ego and excessive pride, embarking on a journey of renewed self-discovery and transforming one's subconscious operating system that manages them in a subliminal way.

Strengths

The strengths associated with the letter Peh include qualities such as willpower, vitality, sympathy, consideration, responsibility, decisiveness, authority, ambition, mental fortitude, durability, physical stamina, determination, perseverance, resilience, endurance, verbal articulacy, realism, and a readiness to collaborate.

Weaknesses

Conversely, the weaknesses associated with Peh include closed-mindedness, suspicion, rigidity, overreliance on cold intellect, perpetual doubt, fixation, and predispositions toward prejudice, arrogance, pride, jealousy, envy, possessiveness, and excessive materialism. Other inhibiting traits include obsessiveness, conditioned responses, habitual behaviors, attachments, **stagnation**[1], lack of tact, competitiveness, greed, belligerence, and stubbornness—resulting in individuals who are inexorably fixed in their ways and resistant to changing their viewpoints.

The inhibiting aspects tend to foster division and separation, aiming for divide-and-conquer scenarios, often through the use of slander, gossip, and falsehoods. The power of speech linked to Peh can be a double-edged sword, possessing the capacity to either bestow power and wealth or to lead to one's downfall.

---

[1] Stagnation is a psychological term that describes a state in which an individual experiences difficulty moving forward, often remaining stuck in the same situation for an extended period. This term is employed to indicate a lack of self-development, progress, or advancement. In the realm of psychology, it could signify that a person is emotionally or mentally immobilized, failing to progress in various aspects of their life. Stagnation is characterized by a noticeable halt in personal growth, where individuals feel they are not achieving their potential, leading to feelings of dissatisfaction, apathy, and, sometimes, despair.

אבגדההוזחחטיכלמנסעפפ**צ**קרשת

"For the intent of man's heart is evil from his youth."
Genesis, Chapter 8, Verse 21

Uniqueness and Purpose

The letter Tzadi (צָדִי) is the eighteenth letter in the Hebrew alphabet, a letter not commonly used. It represents the energy of hunting, symbolizing the human ability to pursue (hunt) something, whether by speech or action and to control it completely.

The purpose of the letter Tzadi is to awaken spiritual enlightenment and foster soul evolution in individuals. Its vibrational frequencies guide people toward love for the world and humanity, encouraging humanitarian service. This service is intended to be selfless, performed without personal gain, and driven by altruistic motives emanating from a state of pure intentions, integrity, and honesty toward oneself and others. The letter urges individuals to live their daily lives according to the ancient principle: *"Love your neighbor as yourself,"* or, in its alternative interpretation, *"Do not do to your friend what is hateful to you."*

The Letter in Creation Stories

The first encounter with the letter Tzadi in the Biblical creation stories appears in the Hebrew word "be'tzalmenu" (בְּצַלְמֵנוּ), meaning "in our image," coupled with the letter Beth, in the verse, *"Then God said, 'Let Us make mankind in Our image, according to Our likeness; and let them rule over the fish of the sea and over the birds of the sky and over the livestock and over all the earth, and over every crawling thing that crawls on the earth." (Genesis,* Chapter 1, Verse 26)

The phrase "in our image" (בְּצַלְמֵנוּ) suggests that human beings were created following a pattern akin to that of angels and higher beings—in spirit, attributes, and actions. This verse conveys that humans are designed to be active partners in the grand divine plan, equipped with unique qualities that set them apart from other living beings. These qualities include intellectual capacity, rational understanding, creative prowess, moral responsibility, and the ability to feel love, identify, devote, and transcend spiritually.

The metaphysical term "in our image" symbolizes the profound connection between God and humanity. It underscores that humans reflect the divine intellect and embody God's spiritual, intellectual, and moral essence, along with qualities such as spirit and eternal life. These attributes empower humans to think, discern, and differentiate between good and evil and to possess creative capabilities.

The letter Tzadi is first encountered independently in the creation narratives in Genesis Chapter Two, Verse one, within the Hebrew word "tzavaam" (צְבָאָם), meaning "their army." This verse marks the culmination of the creation of the heavens and the earth. The Hebrew word "tzavaam" (צְבָאָם) originates from the word "tzava" (צבא), meaning "army," suggesting an organized and disciplined entity adhering to laws and rules. In this context, "their army" refers to the host of the heavens, encompassing various celestial elements that bring order to our cosmic space and govern it in one way or another.

The verse highlights the completion of our universe's formation, establishing the infrastructure for divine creation. With this foundation, the universe is set to continue functioning in its ordained state. The cosmic order has been achieved, with the heavens, the earth, and a myriad of celestial lights—sun, moon, planets, and galaxies—created to instill order within our cosmic space. These celestial bodies and divine lights provide the created beings with the ability to see and distinguish through the gift of free choice.

Biblical commentators offer two interpretations of the term "their army" (צְבָאָם): Firstly, as the celestial army comprising the sun, moon, planets, galaxies, and all-natural celestial bodies visible to the human eye, and secondly, as invisible battling forces, including angelic beings with distinct roles, engaged in cosmic governance.

Pronunciation

The letter Tzadi is pronounced as "Tza-di" or "Tsa-di" and can be represented in English as Z, TZ, TS, CH, or TCH, depending on its position in a word or name and its hard or soft pronunciation.

The name and pronunciation of the letter Tzadi provide insights into its nature and purpose. Interestingly, the pronunciation of Tzadi sometimes transitions to "Tzadiq", commonly written as "Tzadik" (צָדִיק), meaning "righteous," notably due to its proximity to the letter Qof that follows it. This variation is intentional, signaling the direction Tzadi seeks to lead individuals toward the path of righteousness.

The path of righteousness encompasses a journey of spiritual ascension, mental and emotional refinement, moral purity, and, notably, the development of humility and selfless service to others. It signifies a dedication to continuous self-improvement, where individuals navigate life with steadfast faith in themselves and the divine creation. This path requires humility, integrity, and a seamless alignment between one's words and intentions.

Additionally, it underscores the necessity of preserving the purity of one's eyesight and speech, as thoroughly examined in the letters Ahyin and Peh. Echoing King Solomon's counsel in the Book of Ecclesiastes, "Do not be excessively righteous, and do not be overly wise. Why should you ruin yourself?" (Ecclesiastes, Chapter 7, Verse 16)

A "Tzadik" (righteous) is defined as someone who perceives the world objectively, acting not out of personal gain but driven by a dedication to justice and high moral values, and who adopts altruism and generosity as core life principles. The path of righteousness, given its demanding nature, may account for the infrequent appearance of the letter Tzadi in names.

The second interpretation of the letter Tzadi refers to its spiritual essence, which is "Hunting" (צַיִד). To fully grasp the concept of hunting, we must consider the previous letter, Peh, which discusses the challenge of releasing and letting go of opinions, beliefs, people, relationships, and life events. These challenges often lead individuals to experience significant setbacks, where they feel as though the ground has slipped from beneath their feet, resulting in mental and emotional breakdowns.

When individuals undergo difficult life experiences, trauma, or other challenges, aspects of their spiritual essence can become fragmented. This fragmentation can shatter their mental wholeness and detach soul particles from them, leaving them weakened and energetically drained. In such states, people lose parts of themselves and their life force energy, rendering their incarnated soul incomplete. These scattered particles disperse into various worlds and realms until they are collected in a process known as "Soul Fragment Retrieval" or **"Soul Retrieval."**[1] This act of "hunting" for lost soul particles to return them embodies the essence of Tzadi—enabling individuals to reclaim wholeness and regain control over their mental and emotional well-being.

---

[1] Soul retrieval is a healing concept shared by both shamanism and Theta Healing, aimed at recovering lost parts of the self due to trauma or emotional pain. In shamanism it involves a spiritual journey to retrieve these fragments, while Theta Healing uses meditation and connection to universal energy in the Theta brainwave state for the same purpose. Both practices believe that reintegrating these soul pieces lead to can profound emotional, physical, and spiritual healing, restoring wholeness and balance to the individual. This process facilitates a deep sense of renewal, allowing for healing from past wounds and reconnection with one's complete self.

Tzadi is a consequential letter that symbolizes the consciousness of the Atlanteans, a topic I will delve into extensively in my upcoming books.

The third interpretation of Tzadi focuses on the "hunt of inclinations" (צייד היצרים) and their channeling toward spiritual work. An inclination (יצר) is a deep-seated, subliminal impulse, such as an urge or instinct, that drives a person uncontrollably toward wrongdoing. It acts as a subconscious psychological force, influencing individuals to behave in ways that may contravene divine will. Humans possess two core inclinations, the good and the evil, thoroughly examined in the context of the letter Thet. Without awareness of these inclinations, individuals are prone to being "hunted" by these latent urges.

The letter Tzadi is the final letter in the group of aspiration letters ThLQ'Tz (צלקת), embodying a profound yearning for the ideal—aiming to improve the face of civilization and to amend anything that falls short of this ideal. Additionally, Tzadi is a consequential letter that encapsulates the essence of absolute justice. Its vibrational frequencies, in their inhibiting aspect, may encourage individuals toward the evil inclination by leading them to feign righteousness. Instead of embodying true righteousness, characterized by honesty, decency, and humility, without seeking recognition, individuals might fall into a state of pretentious righteousness. In this state, they are consumed by the illusion of their moral path being the most correct and noble, granting them a sense of moral superiority and a monopolistic grip on justice.

This aspiration for global correction, when mixed with righteousness and a sense of superiority, can lead a person to attempt rectifying the world and others before addressing their attitudes and the necessary self-rectifications. To truly walk the path of righteousness that Tzadi delineates, one must learn to transcend these subliminal inclinations and refine them.

Graphic Shape

The shape of the letter Tzadi is both partially open and partially closed. Its upper part is open, with two arms reaching upward as if to absorb and receive something. These arms function as receptors and antennas, symbolizing, in a spiritual sense, the desire to absorb high spiritual light frequencies. In a material sense, they represent the desire to receive as much as possible for oneself.

The letter is closed downward toward earthly matters and turns its back on the wisdom of the preceding letter, Peh. It stands on a wide and stable base that supports it in maintaining internal balance and equilibrium over time.

By being partly open and closed, the letter Tzadi embodies the ability to understand both the whole and the separate, to "round corners," and to flow with people and the challenges of life. Its upward-reaching antennas suggest a heightened receptivity, enabling the absorption of abstract concepts and theories, envisioning the broader perspective, and encouraging unconventional thinking or thinking outside the box.

The letter Tzadi is represented in two different writing forms, signifying its dual role. At the beginning of a word or name, it is written as a bent letter (צ), while at the end, it transforms into an upright letter (ץ), extending a long leg beneath the line.

Kabbalistic interpretations suggest that the bent shape of Tzadi (צ) merges the letter Nun (נ), which leans forward to represent the feminine principle, with the letter Yod (י) positioned above, symbolizing the masculine principle. This configuration underscores Tzadi's potential to unite two distinct principles, such as the feminine and masculine aspects, demonstrating the potential for two opposing principles to coexist in perfect harmony.

The upright form of Tzadi (ץ) emphasizes masculine qualities, directing energy toward establishing position, strength, control, and impact. This graphic shape, akin to a long stake piercing below the ground (beneath the writing line), also mirrors the slingshot's form, an ancient tool utilized for hunting and warfare.

Diagram 88: Bent Tzadi **Diagram 89: Upright Tzadi**

Gematrical Value

The gematrical value of the letter Tzadi is ninety, a number that resonates deeply with Tzadi's intended purpose.

Ninety symbolizes the cosmic warrior who is dedicated to serving humanity through actions that are aligned with a higher universal purpose. This number is connected to the process of soul initiation—a process through which an individual learns to align their inner light and earthly personality with their "I Am" presence. This initiation aims to encourage individuals to adopt high spiritual principles and qualities such as dedication, loyalty, compassion, humility, a connection to the heart, and service to humanity. This enables them to act as a guiding light that illuminates the darkness for humanity.

Corresponding to Tzadi in the unit's digit is the letter Thet, which has a gematrical value of nine. This number holds significant importance in both spiritual and material realms, symbolizing completion—the closure of a cycle, reaching a destination, the conclusion of a journey, and the onset of a new beginning. Nine embodies transformative power, the capacity to turn the old into the new while maintaining its distinct essence, akin to the metamorphosis of a caterpillar into a butterfly.

The letter Tzadi, thus expanding upon the essence of the letter Thet, amplifies the energy of Thet tenfold. It encourages individuals to transcend their limitations, their illusory ego, excessive self-importance, sense of superiority, and the unconscious inclination to claim divine wisdom as their own.

The Zodiac Sign Associated with Tzadi

Sefer Yetzirah associates the letter Tzadi with the zodiac sign of Aquarius, offering deeper insights into its uniqueness and purpose.

Aquarius is astrologically symbolized by a person holding a water bucket, a container that is open at the top and closed at the bottom, designed for transporting liquids. This symbol highlights the significance of moisture (water) in the air and emphasizes that without feelings and an emotional connection to spirituality, one cannot quench one's thirst for spiritual knowledge.

Diagram 90: Aquarius Zodiac Sign

Aquarius is associated with the air element, characterized by intellect, logic, reasoning, and communication. The sign embodies the desire for distinctiveness and the urge to express creativity and personal abilities outwardly, striving to stand out and, ideally, to take center stage.

The prominent characteristics of Aquarius include aspiration, vision, equality, humanitarianism, nonconformity, and resistance to societal pressures or prevailing cultural norms. The sign endows its individuals with enhanced perception and the ability for abstract, philosophical, and idealistic thinking that goes beyond the realms of logic and imagination. It also enables the ability to grasp the bigger picture, assimilate innovative information, and disseminate ideas across society. The keywords that represent the Aquarians are "I know."

Aquarius exemplifies individuals who value independence, individuality, and active social engagement, demonstrating resistance to limitations and a questioning of authority. It embodies an airy energy with a free-spirited nature, characterizing those who enjoy verbal communication with a wide array of people. A key trait that defines them is their prowess in communication. Individuals born under this sign possess excellent verbal skills and have a knack for using words cleverly to captivate their audience.

This extroverted airy energy, associated with the realm of thoughts, seeks to rise and ascend. In its inhibiting aspect, it tends to create a state where the breadth dimension dominates over depth within an individual, alongside a propensity to roam in the world of imagination among grand ideas or lofty theories. In its unbalanced form, this energy may drive individuals toward grand ambitions, such as saving humanity or the entire world and adopting a detached or "ivory tower" perspective toward life and others.

It is noteworthy that this limiting aspect is more pronounced in names lacking the water element.

Another challenging aspect for individuals born under this sign or associated with Tzadi is a predisposition toward being opinionated. They may believe they possess complete knowledge and that their perspective is the only correct and just one. Such an attitude can cultivate a sense of inflated self-importance, leading to an overestimation of one's capabilities, fantasies of boundless success, and a subconscious desire for admiration from others.

It's essential to understand that spirituality cannot be achieved through logic alone. True spiritual growth requires learning to connect with feelings and emotions, a concept symbolized by the bucket in Aquarius's symbol. This vessel, open at the top to receive and closed at the bottom to contain, signifies the need to merge the logical mind with emotional depth to fulfill the quest for spiritual enlightenment. This understanding is crucial for those associated with Tzadi or this zodiac sign.

The Groups the Letter Tzadi is Associated With

Air Element Letter

The element associated with the letter Tzadi is air—a light and agile element that facilitates energetic connections and the transmission of information through various means. The air element embodies qualities such as communication, ideas, inventions, technology, science, and the need for interaction and social engagement. In Tzadi, these air element qualities manifest as quick thinking, physical and mental agility, speech, conversation, written communication, and persuasive abilities.

Tzadi is a high, light, and airy letter that connects individuals associated with it, or with its zodiac sign, to life, people, and events from an intellectual standpoint.

Aspiration Letter

Tzadi is the final letter in the group of ThLQ'Tz (טלק-צ) letters, embodying the aspirational aspect within individuals. Tzadi symbolizes those who are intellectually driven, believe in ideologies and ideals, do not stick to the common, and strive for freedom, progress, and societal improvement. Such individuals tend to be self-reliant, living by their own rules and expressing their independence.

In handwriting, Tzadi rises above the line, and as a final letter, it descends below the line, beneath the ground, thus disrupting its energetic balance and equilibrium. As an aspiration letter, Tzadi represents the human quest to rise above circumstances, people, and life events, aiming for transcendence.

Practical Letter

The letter Tzadi is practical and is not common in names. Its practical aspect is expressed through its capacity to assimilate information and disseminate it to humanity.

The Measure of Absolute Judgment

Tzadi embodies the measure of absolute judgment, signifying limitation and restriction. This measure operates on the principle of **"measure for measure,"**[2] indicating an acceptance of things as they are without regard for circumstances or mercy.

Tzadi embodies the aspect of elevation alongside harsh and rigid judgment, assessing others—whether consciously or unconsciously—without compromise. When paired with its airy elevation, these traits can lead to opinionatedness, condescension, arrogance, and a sense of superiority.

Consequential Letter

Tzadi is a consequential letter, providing insights into the soul lessons a person has committed to learning in this lifetime, lessons that were not mastered in previous incarnations. As such, it exerts intense energy that pushes individuals to their limits, aiming to foster an awareness of their soul's lessons. This awareness uncovers the hidden meanings behind their experiences and life events.

As a consequential letter, Tzadi guides individuals toward enhanced initiation processes that involve shedding all that does not align with their higher good and soul's purpose. The goal of these

---

[2] The term "measure for measure" implies a principle of justice, where actions or punishments are proportional or equivalent to the offense committed and without considering circumstances.

processes is to guide the person back to their inner core, to uncover their soul's calling and purpose, and to encourage walking this life path in a heart-driven direction. Tzadi is a powerful letter that compels individuals to embrace and commit to the transformative journeys it speaks about.

Redemption Letter

Tzadi is the final redemption letter, and as such, it directs individuals to release what hinders their soul's journey, including the premature ambition to lead others without first achieving authentic self-leadership. It suggests that true reward comes after personal rectification, particularly concerning ego and pride, and after embracing humility, modesty, and loyalty to the highest values of absolute truth.

Strengths

The strengths associated with Tzadi encompass vision, inspiration, intuition, originality, conceptual productivity, brilliant perspectives, profound insights, improvisation skills, agility, cleverness, resourcefulness, wit, technological prowess, scientific acumen, inventiveness, friendliness, communicative ability, hope, and the capacity to connect broadly, build relationships, and collaborate.

Weaknesses

Conversely, the weaknesses linked to Tzadi include superficiality, insensitivity, emotional coldness, detachment, blind allegiance to ideas, opinions and ideals, excessive stubbornness, rigidity, opinionatedness, strict adherence to principles, revolutionary zeal, rivalry, separatism, rebelliousness, and sarcasm.

Its inhibitory aspect can manifest in controlling or manipulating others, overtly or covertly, asserting dominance over situations and people, and distorting material desires through humanitarian gestures.

א ב ג ד ה ה ו ז ח ח ט י כ ל מ נ ס ע פ צ **ק** ר ש ת

*"Everything can be imitated except the truth because
the truth that follows imitation is no longer truth."*

Menachem Mendel of Kotzk

Uniqueness and Purpose

The letter Qof (קוֹף) is the nineteenth letter in the Hebrew alphabet. It is an interesting and unique letter that embodies emotional, sentimental, and instinctual energy, along with good memory and vivid imagination. 'Qof' expresses the point of transition to a high spiritual peak or the fall into the lowest level. It signifies the experiential ability granted to humans to sense and feel the infinite expanse of the divine creation and to understand that the whole is greater than the sum of its parts.

The purpose of the letter Qof is to develop an awareness of the trait of imitation, which reflects a lack of listening to one's authentic self. It aims to guide individuals through a transition from a state of sleep consciousness and conditional and reactive behaviors to conscious awareness and conscious and responsible conduct.

The Letter in the Creation Stories

The first time we encounter the letter Qof in the Book of Genesis is in the word "qara" (קרא), meaning "called." *"God called the light 'Day' and the darkness He called 'Night.'"* (*Genesis, Chapter 1, Verse 5*)

The Hebrew word "called" (קרא) carries several meanings. First, reading the written content; second, announcing loudly, inviting, or requesting someone to come to a specific place, motivating and encouraging one to action; and third, calling a child by its name. The expression "To call by its name" (לקרוא בשמו) implies giving a name to something or someone and thereby determining its essence. In other words, the "call" is a kind of declarative vocal announcement that establishes a specific thing in the earthly domain. One prominent example of this is evident in the biblical creation stories, highlighting that divine creation was accomplished through the power of speech, in the verse, *"And God said, "Let there be light"; and there was light."* (*Genesis*, Chapter 1, Verse 3).

The Hebrew word *"Called"* (קרא) holds multiple linguistic connotations. For instance, the expression "Read him like an open book" (קרא אותו כמו ספר פתוח) signifies knowing the content and interiority of a thing and understanding its essence. The expression "Read the situation" (קרא את המצב) implies a thorough understanding of the situation, and the phrase "Challenged" (קרא תיגר) indicates a state in which a person is ready to engage in a fight.

Pronunciation

The letter Qof tends to be written in various ways, such as "Kof," or "Koph," and is represented in English as C, K, Q, influenced by its position in a word or name.

The pronunciation of the letter Qof mirrors its name, which translates to "monkey." Qof is symbolically linked to the primate animal, the monkey. The monkey is a curious mammal with a developed brain, closely resembling humans. This intelligent creature learns through imitation, and thus, the word "monkey" is metaphorically used to describe someone who mimics behaviors without independent thought.

The letter Qof, in both its name and pronunciation, implies that the primary way of human existence in the earthly realm begins with imitation—through copying and internalizing specific behaviors and automatically and robotically repeating them. Children unconsciously imitate their parents, siblings, environment, and peers, thereby learning various behavioral aspects. The characteristic of imitation is expressed in areas of behavior such as speech and clothing, and it incorporates cognitive, emotional, and motor skills and encodes within it the conditions and rewards received from an act of imitation, including positive and negative reinforcement and punishment.

The trait of imitation has advantages, especially in early childhood, but it can also be detrimental, as it can hinder the development of one's identity and uniqueness and distance them from their authenticity and their unique inner light.

Qof reminds me of the saying of my teacher and rabbi, the holy flame of Kotzk (Menachem Mendel of Kotzk), who stated in his writings: *"Three things I ask of you: that you do not squint from within yourself, that you do not squint into others, and that you do not do this for your own sake. Man is commanded to do two things: not to deceive himself and not to imitate others."*

Graphic Shape

The letter Qof has a unique and captivating shape. It is comprised of two separate and unconnected parts. Among the twenty-two letters of the Hebrew alphabet, only two letters, both in handwriting and in print, share this distinction: the letter Heh and the letter Qof. Yet, unlike the firmly grounded shape of the letter Heh, the form of the letter Qof descends below the line, disrupting its energetic balance and fundamental equilibrium.

As illustrated in the sketch below, one part of the letter Qof rests on the line's border, while the other extends as a long downward leg, breaking through the line and descending beneath the line, which represents the ground. This form symbolizes an energy that descends downward into the shadows, into the hidden factors lying beneath the surface and deep down within the human soul.

Diagram 91: The Letter Heh   **Diagram 92: The Letter Qof**

ה   ק

The letter's shape suggests a desire to delve into the depths of things, exploring the root of various aspects of the soul that lie deep in the personal and collective subconscious. Qof's vibrational frequencies aim to guide individuals to understand the hidden and the unknown, and to bring these unconscious contents into the surface, into the consciousness, to enable their full comprehension. This process aims to descend in order to ascend.

In Jungian psychology, this process of bringing unconscious content into conscious awareness is known as "Shadow Work." It involves individuals becoming aware of the half-dark side within their personality, exploring aspects that may be unfamiliar or consciously and unconsciously masked or concealed. These aspects often deviate from societal expectations or the accepted collective morality of the society and culture in which the person lives.

As it descends, Qof aspires to deepen its wisdom, to grasp the entire whole and the contradictions arising from this whole, and thereby to gain revelation and acceptance. However, the emotional vibrational frequencies contained within Qof can place a person at a crossroads, as dealing with shadows and conditional habitual contents is not simple.

Rabbi Zamir Cohen, one of the well-known commentators of Kabbalah, states that the long leg of the letter Qof symbolizes the descent into the darkness of the abyss, into the realm of the impurity, known in Hebrew as "Sitra Achra" (סיטרא אחרא)—a realm which brings to a person various challenging trials that attempt to fail the person on their path toward enlightenment and examine their resilience against the unconscious inclinations and urges within them.

The shape of the letter Qof is both open and closed, indicating that people associated with the letter possess the ability to see both sides of the coin—the ability to grasp the whole and the separate and exhibit partial openness toward opinions, positions, peoples, and situations. Qof is closed upward toward the matters of the spiritual realm and the consciousness of unity, and it turns its back to the wisdom of the preceding letter, Tzadi. It is open downward toward earthly matters and on her left side toward the wisdom contained in the subsequent letter, Resh. Qof is standing on one long leg, thereby indicating its instability and its challenge to maintain internal balance and equilibrium over time.

Gematrical Value

The gematrical value of the letter Qof is one hundred, a value that represents the completion of a phase or a cycle and the beginning of something new. This number marks a transition from the tens to the hundreds, symbolizing a significant leap in magnitude from the decimal system. This value contains frequencies that push individuals toward independence, exploration of new ideas, and the discovery of new and advanced approaches.

The number one hundred combines two zeros that amplify the characteristics of the number one. Number one is associated with qualities such as primacy, originality, individualism, self-definition, beginning and new creation. It embodies a separatist energy that prefers to decide and determine things on its own. Energy that aims to pause the individual and allow them to assess their situation reflect on the path taken so far, and on their achievements, developmental stages, understandings and what they have learned, contemplating what they wish to learn and become moving forward.

Qof is the first letter in which a leap in magnitude (step jump) is made from the tens to the hundreds, and as such, it signifies the potential for an energetic jump toward ascension or descent downfall. From Qof to Tav (the last letter of the alphabet), or from

Qof onward, the step jumps become increasingly significant, capable of leading a person to a high spiritual peak or dropping them into a deep pit. This is reminiscent of the ancient Aramaic expression, *"From a high peak to a deep pit."* (מֵאִיגְּרָא רָמָא לְבֵירָא עַמִּיקְתָּא)

The Zodiac Sign Associated with Qof

Sefer Yetzirah links the letter Qof to the zodiac sign of Pisces, thus offering us further insights into its qualities.

Pisces, as a water sign, is characterized by emotional feelings, gut instincts, and empathy. The water that Qof represents is the sea waters—water that flows in its free form in nature, constantly changing and exhibiting the characteristics of ebb and flow.

The astrological symbol of Pisces is an aquatic animal. It is represented by two fish facing opposite directions, swimming in a circular pattern, and blending into each other in a way that they form one complete circle. This symbol symbolizes the perpetual nature of the continuous cycle of life, with its ups and downs, which produce situations where a person experiences both highs and lows in their life journey. It also reflects the inherent duality present in individuals associated with the letter Qof and those born under the Pisces zodiac sign.

The fish is an aquatic vertebrate that lives its entire life in water and has difficulty regulating its body temperature independently. The fish possess highly developed reproductive capacity and intelligence, exhibiting complex mental abilities such as short and long-term memory, as well as the ability to sense physical pain and emotions such as fear and depression.

Diagram 93: Pisces Zodiac Sign

The letter Qof, linked to the zodiac sign Pisces, symbolizes sentimental and sensitive individuals who possess creative power, vivid imagination, devotion, and a tendency toward self-sacrifice. They also exhibit a proclivity for keeping quiet and daydreaming, finding it challenging to express their rich inner world and articulate their complex emotional feelings, which sometimes can be even frightening and lead them to situations where they do not always understand themselves.

The areas where they excel are music, art, and creativity, which serve as substitutes for direct communication with others.

Individuals with the letter Qof in their name have a deep longing for love, such as the movie portrayals, and often find themselves in a ceaseless search for an ideal that may not exist. These are sensitive, dreamy, and romantic individuals, highly susceptible to others' emotions, and may struggle with setting boundaries. They tend to be drawn to complex individuals and situations, as well as beliefs, religions, sects, or spiritual practices that push them to the extremes.

The astrological symbol of Qof represents the mental and emotional inclination of individuals with this letter in their name to wander between reality and between the world of dreams and fantasy, swimming in different and sometimes even contradictory directions.

The Groups the Letter Qof is Associated With

Water Element Letter

The element associated with Qof is water, an element that relates to all those emotional aspects within us that we have no conscious control over. The water element grants individuals with emotional intelligence—the ability to identify and contain the emotions of others. Yet, the capacity for containment is challenged in this watery letter due to its graphical shape.

Within the water element resides our inner child, a child trapped within the adult personality and yearning to be loved and accepted. In times of distress, when this inner child does not receive attention and goes unnoticed, it retreats, goes underground, and locks itself away. Given the emotional, dreamy, and vulnerable nature of this letter, it is crucial for individuals who are associated with Qof to recognize this inner child within them, connect with it, and heal it if necessary.

Qof is a watery letter embodies rich imagination and high sensitivity. These qualities can be of great value to individuals who are aware and conscious of these traits, leading them to creative paths such as art, play, music, and therapy. However, in an unaware individual or a personality that has not yet fully developed, these qualities can lead to escapism into a world of daydreaming.

Prolonged escapism, in its inhibiting aspect, dims the consciousness, resulting in inner confusion, lack of grounding, distorted perception of reality, development of unrealistic hopes and irrational fears and anxieties. These can lead to judgment errors, a sense of unconscious helplessness, difficulty being fully present in the here-and-now moment, in the earthly realm, and further into deep escapes toward various addictions, creating openings for external energetic influences.

Practical Letter

Qof is the final practical letter in the group of twelve simple letters that represent the practical and applied aspects of a person. This letter gives a person the ability to establish themselves in the earthly realm through their emotional, creative and artistic powers.

Consequential Letter

The letter Qof is a consequential letter that holds clues about the soul lessons the person's soul has undertaken to learn in this life journey—lessons that remain unlearned from previous lifetimes. As a consequential letter, it carries intense energy, pushing individuals to their limits with the aim of awakening an awareness of their soul's lessons. This awareness allows them to perceive the hidden outcomes behind their life experiences and occurrences.

The letter guides individuals toward advanced initiation processes, encouraging introspection and the elimination of anything that does not serve their higher good or align with their soul's path. As a consequential letter associated with the quality of imitation, it implies the importance of developing high self-awareness, conscious awareness and, most of all, a firm self-identity. This ensures that individuals associated with Qof or its zodiac sign do not fall into a state of blindly imitating various doctrines.

The Measure of Absolute Judgment

The letter Qof embodies the measure of absolute judgment, characterized by limitation, restriction, and adherence to the principle of "measure for measure." As such, it tends to lead individuals toward a zealous and strict attitude toward opinions, ideas, people, and situations, fostering attachment to them.

This mindset can lead to unconscious self-judgment in a harsh and rigid manner and the judgment of others, subsequently extending judgments of other's opinions, ideas, situations, and relationships. The measure of absolute judgment instills in a person irritability, anger, resentment, haughtiness, and difficulty in taking personal responsibility.

Strengths

The strengths associated with the letter Qof include qualities such as sensitivity, devotion, empathy, understanding, identification, therapeutic sense, emotional depth, rich imagination, mediumship, instinctive environmental perception (instinctive ability to sense the external environment), adaptability, loyalty, discretion, sensuality, and sexuality.

Weaknesses

The weaknesses associated with the letter Qof include hypersensitivity, internal conflict between intellect and emotions, immersion in fantasies, excessive daydreaming, self-delusion, mental confusion, and a tendency to see the negative and dark side of things, as well as isolation, moodiness, difficulty in making decisions, love for comfort, treading and stepping on one place for a prolonged period, due to a fear of the unknown, and developing stagnation.

The inhibiting aspect of Qof includes a tendency toward laziness, denial, victimhood, self-pity, frequent mood swings, anxieties, and depression. The inhibiting aspect of the letter is manifested in a tendency toward extremes and being drawn into unhealthy paths, such as substance abuse or falling into cults.

א ב ג ד ה ו ז ח ט י כ ל מ נ ס ע פ צ ק ר ש ת

*"Be grateful for whoever comes your way because each
has been sent to you as a guide from beyond."*

Jalal a-Din Rumi

Uniqueness and Purpose

The letter Resh (רֵישׁ) is the twentieth letter in the Hebrew alphabet, symbolizing **Solar Consciousness**[3]—the vital life force that signifies healing, illumination, and spiritual awakening. This letter encapsulates the inherent healing power within humans, highlighting their capacity for self-recovery and the ability to heal themselves and others.

The sun, our life's source and the sustainer of our mother planet Earth emanates vibrational frequencies of light, color, and sound. These frequencies assist our physical bodies in self-healing. The more effectively our bodies absorb these solar energies, the healthier and more vital our various personality aspects—physical, emotional, mental, and spiritual—become. Self-healing serves as a cornerstone for the expansion of consciousness.

Resh embodies an advanced communicative capability, representing thought at the mind's level. Its purpose is to kindle

---

[3]   Solar consciousness is a spiritual concept that views the sun as a wellspring of consciousness, awareness, healing, illumination, and energy that can be accessed and channeled by humans. Many spiritual traditions regard the sun as a symbol of enlightenment, illumination, and spiritual awakening. It is believed that by tapping into the energy of the sun, individuals can access its transformative power, experience spiritual growth and evolution, and achieve a higher state of awareness and understanding.

spiritual enlightenment within individuals, guiding them toward soul evolution. It leads them through transformative processes that rejuvenate their mental and emotional health, enabling them to create enlightened endeavors.

The Letter in Creation Stories

The first mention of the letter Resh in the *Genesis* creation narratives occurs alongside the formative letter Bet, within the word "b'resheet" (בראשית), translating to "in the beginning." This phrase introduces the foundational concept: "*In the beginning, God created the heavens and the earth*" (*Genesis*, Chapter 1, Verse 1). Here, the letter Bet signifies the commencement of something new—a new entity, state, or cosmic order—challenging the common misconception that nothing existed prior to this "beginning."

Independently, the letter Resh makes its initial appearance in the creation stories within the word "rakia" (רקיע), meaning "firmament" (*Genesis*, Chapter 1, Verses 6-7). This verse holds significant meaning, depicting the creation of a space that separates two types of waters. It reveals a transparent, watery-airy celestial layer that encircles our universe, similar to a dome, which differentiates between the heavenly (upper) waters and the terrestrial (lower) waters.

While "rakia" traditionally denotes the sky or heaven, its biblical context alludes to the atmosphere—an encompassing void enabling material formations, such as life emergence on Earth. This atmospheric envelope is crucial for life, as it filters most of the sun's ultraviolet radiation, balances temperature variations between day and night, and supports water condensation, thereby enabling land to emerge.

However, I believe the significance of this verse extends well beyond its literal interpretation. It portrays the establishment of a "super dome," a vast, expansive, defined, stable, and permanent celestial structure. Composed of solid material, this dome encircles and covers the Earth's space, acting as a barrier that cannot be crossed.

The creation of the firmament, as described in the verse, marks the division of two distinct realms where divine creation unfolds: the space above and the space below. Within these realms, there exist two different types of waters, distinguished not only by their physical locations but also by their essence and nature. Examples include living waters versus dead waters, sweet waters versus bitter waters, and shallow versus deep waters, as well as waters characterized by their vibrational frequencies, both high and low.

In other words, the term "rakia" (firmament) denotes a solid dome enveloping our universe—the cosmos—including the sun, moon, planets, and our planet Earth, thereby creating two distinct spaces. The purpose of "rakia" is to act as a mirror and reflection of the various types of water that the world encompasses on a macro level and humanity on a micro level.

When we reverse the Hebrew letters of the word "rakia" (רקיע), we derive the word "ikar" (עיקר), which signifies "essence," denoting principle, the heart of the matter, and primacy. Furthermore, within "rakia" lies the word "reka" (רקע), meaning "setting" or "scenery"—a term that indicates a collection of elements establishing the tone for the story, encompassing the location, time, and overall setting.

The "setting" typically incorporates historical, cultural, and geographical elements, along with the plot (a sequence of interconnected events following a specific pattern), style (a collection of personal and cultural symbols), characters (both human and non-human entities that are personified within the narrative), and the central idea (the theme or main subject at the heart of the creation). Thus, the setting emerges as one of the fundamental components of the story.

Pronunciation

The name and pronunciation of the letter Resh offer additional insights into its qualities and energetic encoding. The letter is represented in English as R. Resh (רֵישׁ) can be written in full spelling, such as "Rish" (ריש), and alternatively, in a common misspelling, as "Rash" (רש), each variation carrying distinct meanings.

The first interpretation, "Rish" (ריש), relates to the head (derived from the Aramaic word for head), symbolizing the physical organ responsible for thought and mental processes. The head is the human organ that enables elevation to greatness, representing how humans utilize their intellect. For instance, the Hebrew phrase "Rosh Gadol" (ראש גדול), meaning "big-head," implies the ability to adopt a broader perspective and exceed expectations. Conversely, "Rosh Katan" (ראש קטן), meaning "small-head," suggests a tendency to perceive things narrowly and simplistically, doing the bare minimum.

The second interpretation stems from "Rash" (רש), signifying poverty or destitution—a consciousness of scarcity that leads to comprehensive lack. Poverty extends beyond material deprivation to include spiritual scarcity. In a state of spiritual poverty, a person's consciousness gravitates toward survival, pulling individuals energetically downward toward earthly concerns.

The dual pronunciations of Resh suggest that to transcend from destitution ("Rash") to leadership or prominence ("Rosh"), a person needs to cultivate an abundance mindset and a unity consciousness within themselves.

Among the twenty-two letters of the Hebrew alphabet, only two explicitly denote a consciousness of lack: the letter Dalet, derived from "dalut" (poverty), and Resh, from "rash" (destitution/ poverty). The nature of this lack varies between them; Dalet represents emotional poverty, marked by an intense craving for attention, love, affection, and care, whereas Resh symbolizes spiritual poverty, characterized by a desire for material pleasures and physical gratifications, such as food and sex.

A consciousness of lack often manifests as a sense of mental deprivation, leading to inner unrest, a restless spirit, and a reluctance to accept personal responsibility for one's words and actions. This mindset frequently results in placing blame on others for one's suffering and distress. Since the letter Resh embodies the power of speech, its negative aspect tends to emerge as incessant chatter, both mentally and verbally, creating a condition where neither the mind nor the mouth finds a moment of peace.

Resh is characterized by its vibratory nature, exhibiting both internal and external oscillations, and is in perpetual motion. The sound and pronunciation of Resh mimic the buzzing heard near an electrical power pole, symbolizing electrical vibration. Individuals associated with this letter are recommended to practice daily meditation and adopt an attitude of gratitude.

When the letters of Resh's full name (ריש) are reversed, the word "Yarash" (ירש) emerges, connoting the act of receiving or inheriting something from another, be it a characteristic, role, property, or ownership.

Graphic Shape

The letter Resh possesses a graphical shape that is partly open and partly closed. It is closed upward toward matters of the spiritual realm, open downward toward earthly and materialistic concerns, and turns its back on the wisdom of the preceding letter, Qof. The letter stands on one leg, symbolizing a lack of a stable foundation and highlighting the inherent challenge of maintaining balance and equilibrium over time.

The two identical graphical writing forms of Resh, in both handwriting and print, offer us additional insights into its name and the qualities it embodies.

Diagram 94: The Outer Envelope of the Brain/Cerebral Cortex

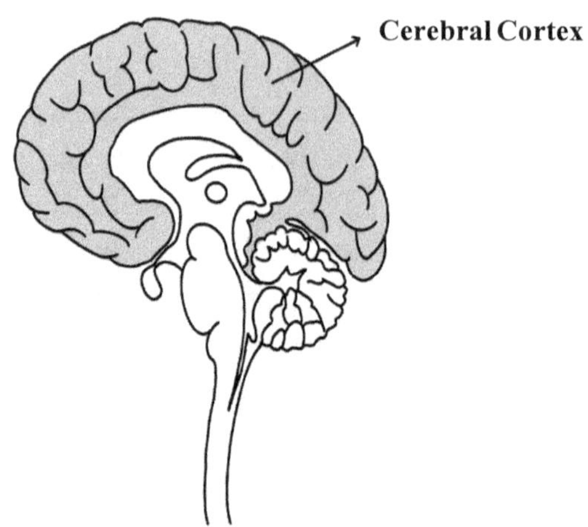

A glance at the structure of the human head reveals a resemblance to the graphic shape of the letter Resh, especially in the upper part of the head within the outer layer known as the "Cerebral Cortex." This region, responsible for protecting the brain, is involved in nearly all bodily processes, including thinking, memory, learning, regulation of physical functions, development, regeneration, and recovery.

The graphical shape of Resh, resembling a curved and hollow tube, acts as a vessel that facilitates connections and forms a solid dome around the head from the forehead to the nape of the neck. This structure serves as a conduit through which thoughts and desires flow downward to various parts of the body, highlighting the significance of being mindful of our thoughts.

Gematrical Value

The Gematrical value of the letter Resh is two hundred. This numerical significance embodies coexistence, addressing themes like cooperation, diplomacy, teamwork, and various relationships—personal, interpersonal, professional, and social—grounded in fairness, established norms, and ethical standards.

It symbolizes qualities such as self-sufficiency, intellectual and practical intelligence, negotiation prowess, as well as strategic and commercial aptitudes. At its core, it seeks to foster peace and coexistence and facilitate conflict resolution among individuals, communities, nations, and peoples.

Resh is far from a simple letter; it is a consequential letter embodying the measure of absolute judgment. It harbors a potent and often restless energy, prone to driving individuals toward extremes. Resh's intense vibrational frequencies encourage individuals to shed conditioned behaviors and habits that obstruct personal and spiritual growth. It urges individuals to surrender to a higher inner source within and radiate their true inner essence to those around them.

Corresponding to Resh in the unit digit is the letter Bet, with a gematrical value of two, and in the tens digit is the letter Kaf, valued at twenty. The number two hundred represents a synthesis of the qualities of the number two, amplified by two zeros, further emphasizing the theme of coexistence.

Resh's gematrical value is illustrated in the biblical narrative of Jacob and Esau, particularly through the dynamics between the two brothers following acts of deceit and theft by one against the other. After twenty years of barrenness, Rebekah, the mother of Esau and Jacob, is informed that she carries two sons (**gentiles**[4]) in her womb. *"And the Lord said to her, 'Two nations are in your womb, and two peoples from within you shall be divided."* (Genesis, Chapter 25, Verse 23)

This biblical story highlights the two distinct forces present within every individual engaged in an internal struggle and

---

[4]   The term "gentiles" traditionally signifies a distinction between those who belong to a specific religious or cultural group (in this case, Jews) and those who do not, encompassing a wide range of nationalities and ethnic backgrounds without regard to their specific beliefs or practices. It is often used in religious texts, particularly in Judaism and Christianity, to denote individuals of other nationalities or foreign origins outside the Jewish people.

underscores the challenges of accepting differences. At its simplest level, the story of Rebekah's pregnancy carries two significant implications: First, the internal conflict within Rebekah prefigures the external conflict that will manifest with the birth of her sons. Second, it predicts the rise of two unique foreign nations from her womb.

Jacob and Esau, the rival twins, symbolize this dichotomy. Mercury, associated with the letter Resh, rules the zodiac sign of Gemini (the twins), further emphasizing this theme. Esau, the hunter, epitomizes the carnal, extroverted, and impulsive aspects of human nature, while Jacob, the tent dweller, embodies introspection, calculated thought, and a focus on spiritual and personal development. This contrast highlights the divergence between physical and spiritual pursuits, impulsivity versus strategic planning, and a present-focused versus future-oriented outlook.

Esau's emergence as the firstborn, with Jacob following closely, clutching his brother's heel, sets the stage for their lifelong rivalry. The narrative progresses to a pivotal moment when a famished Esau trades his birthright for sustenance from Jacob, indicating a disregard for the spiritual significance of the birthright in favor of immediate physical needs.

Years later, as Isaac nears death, Rebekah orchestrates a deceit whereby Jacob, following her guidance without question, impersonates Esau to receive Isaac's blessing. This act of deception leads Esau to contemplate fratricide, prompting Jacob to flee to Haran, as advised by his mother.

Upon God's command to return to Canaan, Jacob initiates a strategic, diplomatic approach to reconcile with Esau, symbolized by sending gifts of two hundred female and two hundred male goats, representing an offer of peace and coexistence.

The Planet Associated with Resh

"He made the letter Resh king, and He bound a crown to it, and He combined one with another, and with them, He formed the star..." (*Sefer Yetzirah*, Chapter 4, verse 10)

Sefer Yetzirah connects the letter Resh to the planet Mercury, which he names as "Star," thus providing us with an understanding of the qualities the letter contains.

Mercury is one of the five planets known in Western astrology as personal planets, which represent a person's characteristics, tendencies, personal needs, and desires. Mercury is a fast and small planet, and it is the closest to the sun and our Earth. Due to its speed, its vibrational frequencies tend to have a significant influence on a person's character. Mercury symbolizes a person's personal needs and desires, their approach to life, and how they gain experience in earthly matters. According to the Kabbalistic teachings, Mercury represents the area in which one's personality requires clarity, purification, and redemption.

Mercury is associated with movement, kinetic energy, rapid changes, and everything related to business activities, practical studies (not necessarily spiritual), trade, and commerce. Mercury governs communication, intelligence, memory, thinking ability, data analysis, decision-making, sophistication, and cunningness.

Mercury is a communicative planet that symbolizes in a person cognitive skills, spatial awareness and coordination, technological and communication abilities, linear thinking through intellect and logic, and the ability to classify (categorize), sort, and communicate information to others through spoken or written word. This planet is linked to physical and mental movement, the power of speech, conversation, and clever persuasion.

The planet Mercury is dual-natured and rules over two zodiac signs, which astrologically represent humans: Gemini and Virgo. In the sign of Virgo, a person has one head, while in the sign of Gemini, a person has two heads. Thus, this symbol emphasizes the two main mental functions that the letter Resh represents. One is the ability for internal communication—thinking and logical analysis of things, represented by Virgo. The other is external communication—verbal, speech, information exchange, and trade, represented by Gemini. One possesses introverted characteristics, and the other possesses extroverted characteristics.

In Egyptian mythology, Mercury is associated with the god Thoth, the god who invented writing and hieroglyphs for humanity, giving humans knowledge, language skills, and the ability to speak.

The Groups the Letter Resh is Associated With

Air Element Letter

The letter Resh is associated with the air element, symbolizing energetic connections and the transmission of information through various means. This element is linked to communication, ideas, inventions, technology, and science, as well as the necessity for social interaction. Among other air letters, Resh is considered the densest, emphasizing its compact nature.

Creational Mind Letter

Resh is a creational mind letter, encapsulating mental patterns that are deeply ingrained in both personal and collective human consciousness. These patterns, which contain deeply rooted beliefs carried from one incarnation to another, tend to activate individuals in a sub-hypnotic manner. The purpose of Resh is to direct attention to these fundamental beliefs, encouraging awareness and transcendence through its creative power, thereby facilitating their permanent release.

Hard and Soft Sound

The letter Resh can be pronounced with either a hard or soft sound, influencing its characteristics. As a creative mind letter, Resh can intensify or weaken its vibrational frequencies. A hard sound gives the letter a masculine (yang) and more intense tone, while a softer sound imparts a feminine (yin) and gentler tone. When pronounced hard, it suggests difficulty in becoming flexible when needed. Conversely, soft pronunciation represents the ability to be flexible and dissolve the ego.

When Resh is pronounced with a hard sound, it exhibits greater strength and presence but also a higher risk of pride and ego-driven actions. Conversely, in its soft form, Resh reduces its vibrational frequency, diminishing the ego's influence and fostering a greater capacity for actions rooted in humility.

Consequential Letter

Resh is a consequential letter, revealing the soul lessons that an individual has committed to learn in this life journey—lessons not yet mastered in past lifetimes. As a consequential letter, Resh embodies intense energy that challenges individuals, aiming to awaken their awareness of these soul lessons. This awareness helps them perceive the hidden outcomes behind life's experiences and events.

The letter Resh possesses powerful, energetic abilities. Its intense vibrational frequencies guide individuals toward introspection and enhanced initiation processes, which involve shedding all that does not align with their higher good and soul's purpose. It focuses on developing awareness of conditioned habits and deep-rooted beliefs that subconsciously control them. Resh encourages a heart-centered approach to life, characterized by kindness, compassion, and following one's heart.

Resh is one of the most challenging consequential letters. It contains high energetic power and a wealth of abilities. However, its intense and compressed vibrational frequencies can lead individuals associated with it toward stubbornness, imbalanced ego, pride, harsh judgment, and rigid critical attitudes. They may also experience jealousy, high self-importance, and a conviction that their perspectives are the only correct ones.

The Mind Trap and Accumulation of "Qlipoth"

Resh is one of the prominent letters that tend to trap individuals in the "maze of the mind," a Kabbalistic concept known as "malcodet da'at" (mind trap), where individuals believe they understand something with absolute certainty, becoming overly assured of themselves. This unconscious trap hinders the necessary change in attitude toward people, life, and relationships, highlighting the crucial need for this transformation.

Resh is also prone to accumulating "Qlipoth" (impurities and negativity). Kabbalistic interpreters suggest that Resh embodies elements of opacity, wickedness, and evil. These negative aspects of thinking and behavior unconsciously aim to inflict suffering on others, underscoring the complex challenges associated with this letter.

The Measure of Absolute Judgment

The letter Resh embodies the measure of absolute judgment. This measure restricts and limits the consciousness of the individual, leading them to a state where they judge people and situations harshly and rigorously, holding them accountable and thus distancing themselves from the intended path.

Resh stands on one leg, symbolizing instability and a loss of inner balance more quickly compared to letters with a base or legs. As the letter of absolute judgment, it represents in a person a possessive attachment to ideas and opinions and a high level of judgment that obligates judging others. This state involves harsh and critical judgments and criticisms of others, adhering to the principle of "measure for measure."

In its constructive aspect, Resh's vibrational frequencies encourage social engagement, enabling individuals to connect with and open the hearts of those who are emotionally guarded. However, its various combinations also attract people toward beneficial interactions, with a mindfulness of cost-benefit analysis and commerce, showcasing its dual nature in facilitating connection and consideration.

When this energy is imbalanced, it can become violent in thought, speech, or action, leading to conflicts, control issues—either controlling others or being controlled—and engaging in slander. Resh urges individuals to develop a heightened awareness of judgmental tendencies and negative speech to prevent experiencing the very things they judge and criticize in others.

Kabbalistic teachings highlight that Resh, blessed with the characteristic of speech, has the power to elevate individuals through compassionate, caring, and considerate speech, potentially making them leaders who guide themselves and others positively. Conversely, misuse of speech can lead them to experience material and spiritual challenges, as it is stated in Proverbs, *"Life and death are in the power of the tongue."*

Strengths

The strengths associated with the letter Resh include qualities such as vitality, vigor, vigilance, dynamism, movement, strength, magnetism, good health, curiosity, communicativeness, sociability, as well as talent in speaking and teaching. It includes logic and the ability to express oneself both in writing and verbally.

Resh imparts the capacity to transform potential into action, facilitating breakthroughs, advancement, and leadership. When its energy is balanced, it bestows reliability, responsibility, spirituality, a desire to help and serve others, and an aptitude for working with healing energies and medicine.

Weaknesses

Conversely, the weaknesses associated with Resh include rigidity, excessive stubbornness, intellectualism, detachment from emotions and the heart, opinionatedness, self-centered, an unrealistic sense of self-importance, harsh criticism, unwillingness to compromise, jealousy, arrogance, haughtiness, anger, hot temper, and impatience. Its inhibiting aspects may manifest as blame-shifting, excessive materialism, greed, exploitation of others, sophistry, trickery, and long-term grudges.

The shadow side of Resh is characterized by hyperactivity, impatience, intolerance, restlessness, ignorance, false wandering, quickly ignited thoughts, unsettled energy, an inability to focus on defined goals, arrogance, distrust, suspicion, skepticism, and tendencies toward overt or covert control and dominance.

א ב ג ד ה ו ז ח ט י כ ל מ נ ס ע פ צ ק ר שׁ ת

*"The soul has been given its ears to hear things
the mind does not understand."*

Jalal a-Din Rumi

Uniqueness and Purpose

The letter Shin (שִׁין) stands as the twenty-first letter in the Hebrew alphabet, embodying the spiritual essence of the fire element in our world. It functions as a generative dynamic force, propelling individuals into action and symbolizing the divine power behind transformative changes in traits, forms, or phenomena.

Shin is a mystical, spiritual, earthly, intuitive and creative letter. It possesses spiritual heights and, in its constructive aspect, represents holiness. Among the twenty-two letters of the Hebrew alphabet, Shin is distinguished by its intense energy and power. It drives the dismantling of the old, prompting individuals to redefine their conduct and self-perception. This transformative change fosters self-renewal and rebirth.

The purpose of the letter Shin is to catalyze fundamental shifts in behavior and personality, steering people toward decisions made from a position of free choice, free from external pressures and internal constraints. It accelerates personal transformation, facilitating a renewal of self-identity.

The letter Shin is not simple energetically, as the mental and emotional processes it directs are far from easy. Nevertheless, individuals who commit to its path are rewarded with profound, core-level renewal and transformation at a nuclear level.

Shin also embodies the energy of glory and heroism—the energetic force that grants individuals remarkable survival abilities, such as the ability to overcome challenges in ways that astonish and inspire others.

Decorating the doorposts of Israelite homes, Shin is featured on the **Mezuzah**[1] and within the word "Shaddai" (ש-די), conveying a powerful message of protection: "Evil forces shall not pass this door." As a guardian, Shin symbolizes the "Shekhinah"—the divine feminine's ultimate celestial shield, establishing barriers against certain energetic frequencies.

Additionally, Shin plays a vital role in the **"Tefillin,"**[2] worn on the heads and left arms by the Israelites each morning. This practice channels divine energy from the head to the heart, ensuring a harmonious balance between intellect and emotion.

In esoteric teachings, Shin is seen as the driving force behind human power struggles. It embodies the element of fire—a dynamic force that requires careful navigation; while it can provide warmth and motivation, uncontrolled fire may lead to destruction and chaos in the world and the human soul.

Shin symbolizes a clear, purposeful fire aimed at uncovering and purifying deep-seated karmic and hereditary burdens accumulated in the evolving soul through various life incarnations. It seeks to burn these factors to the core, facilitating a transformative rebirth reminiscent of a phoenix rising from its ashes or a snake shedding its skin and being resurrected.

---

[1] Mezuzah is a small case attached to the doorframes of Jewish homes. Inside is a special parchment with verses from the Torah. It's a symbol of faith and protection. Placing and touching the Mezuzah is a ritual practice, inviting the celestial forces to protect the home and its inhabitants.

[2] Tefillin is a pair of black leather boxes containing Hebrew parchment scrolls with specific verses written on them. A set includes two boxes, one for the head and one for the arm, to represent the connection between the heart and the head and the submission of one's mind and heart and actions and implies recognition of the Almighty God Shaddai. Tefillin serves as a tangible reminder of the wearer's commitment to God's commandments.

Shin marks a critical point in the human journey, whispering the need to heed the voices of reason and the soul. As the penultimate letter, it heralds the final steps toward enlightenment, urging individuals to awaken, transcend material illusions, and surpass the confines of ego to breach the barriers of consciousness.

With Shin, compromise is not an option. It demands a choice: to actively pursue the profound changes it prescribes or face them as inevitable consequences. It emphasizes the urgency of embracing transformation at this moment, without delay, highlighting the urgency of personal evolution.

The Letter in Creation Stories

The letter Shin first appears in the creation stories with the word "shamayim" (שמים), meaning "Heaven." *"Then God said, 'Let there be an expanse in the midst of the waters, and let it separate the waters from the waters. God made the expanse, and separated the waters that were below the expanse from the waters that were above the expanse; and it was so. God called the expanse heaven."* (*Genesis*, Chapter 1, Verses 6-8)

In the biblical narrative, "shamayim" signifies not only physical and spiritual distance but also outer space—the layer of the upper atmosphere where water forms as clouds, steam, rain, and snow. This celestial space, lying at a considerable physical distance from Earth, encompasses different galaxies referred to in creation stories as the "host of heaven." This layer symbolizes the abode of divinity, a spiritual height far removed energetically from human beings, yet one they are destined to reach.

The letter Shin makes its second appearance in the creation narratives with the word "sheretz" (שרץ), meaning "swarming creatures." (*Genesis*, Chapter 1, Verse 20) This term encompasses aquatic creatures—mammals, reptiles, and vertebrates—known for their capability to reproduce.

Pronunciation

The name and pronunciation of the letter Shin shed light on its nature and purpose. It is articulated in two distinct forms, determined by the placement of the punctuational dot above it. In English, it is represented as SH or S, varying with its word or name position and the dot's placement above its head.

Diagram 95: Shin with a Right Dot

Diagram 96: Shin with a Left Dot

When the dot is positioned above the right side of Shin, it is pronounced as "shin" (שׁ), symbolizing the forces of grace active in the world and humans. This pronunciation is found in Hebrew words such as "shekinah" (divine presence), "sheket" (quiet), "shalom" (peace), and "shlemut" (wholeness). Its articulation is used as a soothing sound, "shhh-shhh-shhh," to calm a baby.

When Shin is written in its misspelling form with a dot above its right side (שׁן), it spells "shen," meaning "tooth," symbolizing the bone that grinds and breaks down substance (food), thus fundamentally altering it. The tooth, mirroring the shape of Shin, consists of three main parts: the crown (the visible part), the root (the hidden part), and the neck (the part connecting the crown to the root).

Conversely, with a dot above its left side (שׂ), it spells "sin," representing the law of judgment operating in the world and within the human soul. This pronunciation is found in words like "sin'ah" (hate), "sechel" (mind), "mishak" (play) and "satan" (devil). This sound, akin to a snake's hiss, symbolizes dormant Kundalini energy in yoga philosophy, the coiled life force at the spine's base, awaiting awakening for spiritual enlightenment.

The letter Shin, in its dual manifestations, illustrates the profound balance between grace and judgment, encapsulated in its visual and phonetic diversity.

Kabbalistic teachings state that the various forms of writing Shin symbolize the two main inherent forces it contains—the force of destruction and renewed creation. These are a constructive (positive) force and a hindering (negative) force, reflecting the dual roles Shin embodies: to enlighten the mind and to awaken the base of the spine.

The term "destruction" might sound ominous, but it denotes the essential elimination that paves the way for new beginnings, both internally and externally. For instance, the destructive power represented by Shin is crucial for completely dismantling negative traits within ourselves and eradicating malevolent forces to their very core, ensuring their absolute cessation.

Graphic Shape

The letter Shin features a unique graphical shape with a narrow base, from which three lines emerge—right, left, and center—resembling three flames ascending. While Shin's base is narrow, its arms are tall and elongated, stretching from the base (representing the root chakra) toward the head, the realm of human consciousness.

These three arms are rich in symbolism, representing the three creative forces in the world and within humans: creation, preservation, and destruction. These forces shape our personalities and lives through thought, emotion, and action, whether expressed physically or verbally. Additionally, they embody the three main paths to personal and spiritual development: the philosopher and theologian, who explore the self and the divine; the spiritual seeker, who pursues mysticism and spiritual practices; and the servant, who dedicates themselves to others and humanity.

Stam Scribes, also known as **Sofer Stam**[3] (סופר סת״ם), craft the letter Shin in two ways: Some begin with three Yods (י״ד) and connect them with lines to the base, symbolizing Shin's triangular wisdom. Others start with three Vavs (ו״ו) and connect them, representing the gematrical value of eighteen, a number that Kabbalistic teachings associate with "chai" (חי), meaning "life" or "to be alive," symbolizing protective life energy.

In my lectures, I am often asked about the significance of Shin's three Vavs, which together create the number 666—a number linked with the devil. While this number can be used negatively, its spiritual interpretation encourages focus, structural change, and foundational reorganization. The number 666 represents stagnation, illusion, passive surrender, and a survival mindset that obscures the broader truth. To understand the full picture, one must transcend superficial appearances, much like the three flames of Shin suggest.

Diagram 97: Letter Alef

Diagram 98: Letter Shin

---

[3] Sofer Stam is a Jewish scribe trained to transcribe holy scrolls, including Tefillin (phylacteries), Mezuzahs, and other ancient religious texts.

Among the twenty-two letters of the Hebrew alphabet, only two, Shin and Alef, comprise three parts. This signifies three distinct channels through which the supreme creation communicates with its creations: through positive, negative, and neutral forces and three measures: compassion, mercy, and judgment.

The letter Shin is enclosed on three sides, with an opening at the top that allows light frequencies to enter through two channels. Closed on its right and left sides, it turns away from the wisdom symbolized by the preceding letter, Resh, and from the wisdom of the letter that follows, Tav. Positioned on a narrow base, it symbolizes a lack of a stable foundation, highlighting the inherent challenge of maintaining balance and equilibrium over time.

Gematrical Value

The gematrical value of Shin is three hundred, associated with sharp and high intuition, inexhaustible creative energy, wisdom, knowledge, spiritual vision, and multi-level communication. This value represents a high spiritual potential, embodying qualities such as spiritual inspiration, liveliness, vitality, optimism, and enthusiasm. It holds an energetic resonance potent enough to awaken someone from a deep slumber.

Shin's corresponding letter in the tens is Lamed, with a gematrical value of thirty, and in the units, Gimel, with a value of three. The letter Shin multiplies their energy by ten and a hundred times, enhancing the traits they represent.

In the Bible, Shin's gematrical value is linked to heroism, a courageous spirit, warfare, and divine supervision. The virtue of heroism, symbolized by Shin, is epitomized in Samson (Shimshon in Hebrew), whose name twice includes the letter Shin. Samson, a warrior and judge, was endowed with immense strength, enabling extraordinary feats. His heroism aligns with the seven virtues in Christian theology.

The concept of divine providence associated with Shin is illustrated in the biblical story of the Israelites' battle against Amalek, led by Gideon ben Yoash, the fifth judge of Israel. This narrative highlights the power of divine providence during the Israelites' conflict with Midian, Amalek, and other ancient enemies.

It recounts a period of low spiritual frequency, leading to the oppression of the Israelites by the Midianites and Amalekites. Guided by an angel, Gideon assembled an army seeking divine signs for battle success. With faith in God's power, he selected three hundred valiant warriors, ultimately achieving victory. This biblical story highlights that victory is not solely dependent on numerical strength but is achieved through courage, faith, and trust, enabling divine intervention and guidance.

The Planet Associated with Shin

The letter Shin is linked to Pluto, a small yet powerful celestial body distant from the Sun. Its distance and invisibility from Earth give Pluto a secretive and mysterious character. Pluto symbolizes themes of death, purification, regeneration, violence, and healing, representing unseen processes occurring beneath the surface. It destroys and eliminates impurities, paving the way for new emergence.

As a generational planet, Pluto represents transformation and **transmutation**[4], embodying primal drives and energies that seek change and growth. Its vibrational frequencies delve into the depths of things, breaking down unsuitable structures and unveiling the concealed.

---

[4]   Transmutation represents the profound and comprehensive transformation of something at its core level, typically into a higher state. This term signifies a deep and all-encompassing shift in the essence of an individual's being. In psychological terms, it involves a deliberate and complete change in mindset, behavior, or character, leading to positive growth, self-improvement, and fulfillment. Biologically, this process mirrors the metamorphic stages seen in various organisms, encompassing essential cellular and structural changes that propel the organism toward a more advanced and elevated state.

Pluto's effect on the human soul is intricate and challenging. When individuals resist the transformative processes Pluto directs, it can profoundly shake their foundations. The goal of Pluto's vibrational frequencies is to surface suppressed karmic residues accumulated over lifetimes, residues shaped by education, culture, and socialization that mask a person's authentic self. By exposing these layers for thorough examination and transformation, Pluto facilitates deep self-awareness and complete self-recognition.

Every change, whether minor or significant, encounters resistance, as it necessitates departing from the familiar and secure, regardless of its benefit. Change often triggers fear, especially when it leads to confronting unpleasant aspects like negative traits or harmful habits that need alteration.

Individuals hesitant to embrace the new may prefer the comfort of the old, isolating themselves and building barriers, potentially living within these confines indefinitely. However, with Pluto's influence, persistent resistance is futile. This celestial entity disrupts and demolishes established patterns. In cases of strong resistance, it can provoke a psychological crisis, forcing a reassessment and openness to the necessary transformation.

The Groups the Letter Shin is Associated With

Fire Element Letter

The letter Shin is associated with the element of fire, representing a powerful and essential force that instills courage, strength, self-confidence, motivation, progress, enthusiasm, and a zest for life in humans. It symbolizes the fire element in its purest form—a vibrant, warm, and radiant flame that is essential for our existence. The presence of the fire element in one's name encourages action, while its absence might leave a person struggling to find motivation and discover their soul's purpose.

We emerge into the world carrying a divine spark that may either increase and expand or diminish and extinguish throughout our life journey. From early childhood, we are subject to various forms of programming that shape our thoughts and beliefs. Flaws in this programming, such as negative mantras like "You are not good enough, worthy, or valued," lead to inauthentic behaviors that distance us from our uniqueness.

The Bible, serving as an ancient history book, provides numerous examples, such as the stories of Cain and Abel, Isaac and Ishmael, and Joseph and his brothers, illustrating how feeling unworthy in the eyes of authority figures can lead to feelings of inadequacy.

These influences might cause us to surrender our inner fire and personal strength to subconscious internal programming that plays within us like a broken record or external forces such as religious teachers, gurus, or politicians. In such a state, we become conditioned beings, forgetting our uniqueness and walking through life similar to programmed robots. Shin symbolically dismantles these barriers, advocating for a return to core individuality.

Spiritual Letter

Shin belongs to the group of AMSh letters—three spiritually significant letters embodying nobility, faith, wisdom, understanding, spiritual power, vision, and the capacity to create a new reality from nothing. As such, Shin encourages individuals to transcend everything that inhibits their uniqueness and freedom, urging them to start anew, even from ground zero, when needed.

Consequential Letter

As a consequential letter, Shin directs individuals toward processes of self-empowerment. It urges them to release anything that does not serve their higher good or the path of their soul.

Absolute Judgment Letter

The letter Shin is extremely intense, embodying the measure of absolute judgment. This measure is harsh, zealous, judgmental, and challenging, implying restriction and limitation and adhering strictly to the principle of "measure for measure." Those associated with Shin must fully comprehend this aspect to channel their energy toward positive and constructive ends.

Prefixes/Formative Letter

Shin, one of the seven prefix letters, creates relations between words when added to them. As a formative letter, it links words, functioning as a conjunction for "Asher" (אשר), meaning "that," "which," "who," and "whom." When used this way, it is pronounced SH-EH. For example, "hasefer asher karati" (the book I read) becomes "hasefer she'karati," and similarly, "hasipur asher siparty" (the story I told) becomes "hasipur she'siparti."

Strengths

Strengths associated with the letter Shin include energy, dynamism, liveliness, vitality, bravery, courage, prowess, independence, resourcefulness, enthusiasm, spontaneity, wit, inspiration, self-confidence, assertiveness, drive, self-efficacy, vigor, and movement. These attributes reflect Shin's vibrant and forceful nature, empowering individuals with a broad spectrum of positive qualities.

Weaknesses

Conversely, the weaknesses associated with Shin encompass restlessness, inner tensions, lack of focus, suspicion, secrecy, skepticism, obsessiveness, lust, anger, victimhood, conditional behavior, and acting from a place of automatic pilot. Further, it includes power and control games, uncontrolled ambition, difficulty channeling desires into positive outlets, arrogance, haughtiness, envy, and excessive pride. The inhibiting aspects of Shin may also manifest in tendencies toward politics, intrigue, corruption, and crime, highlighting the challenges inherent in managing such a powerful force.

אבגדהוזחטיכלמנסעפצקרשת

"It is never late to ask yourself "Am I ready to change my life, am I ready to change myself?". However old we are, whatever we went through, it is always possible to reborn. If each day is a copy of the last one, what a pity! Every breath is a chance to reborn. But to reborn into a new life, you have to die before dying."

Shams Tabrizi

Uniqueness and Purpose

The letter Tav (תָּו) is the twenty-second and final letter in the Hebrew alphabet. It symbolizes the ultimate goal and end result toward which the evolving soul aspires by the conclusion of its life journey. This journey encompasses gaining wisdom and life experience through various experiential circumstances, learning pivotal life lessons, undergoing developmental processes, rectifying one's approach to life and interactions with others, aligning with heartfelt desires, and ultimately attaining enlightenment and self-mastery. Such processes enable individuals to ascend to a higher developmental stage.

The letter Tav is far from simple; it ranks among the most challenging and complex letters. It carries the energy of all preceding letters and embodies **lunar consciousness**[1]—a watery,

---

[1]   Lunar consciousness refers to a metaphysical and spiritual concept symbolizing the awakening of human emotional and intuitive abilities. It associates the moon with feminine energy, intuition, emotions, subconscious aspects, and the hidden dimensions of the self, suggesting that the moon's various phases significantly impact human emotions and mental

emotional consciousness characterized by fluctuation and cycles of ebb and flow. This consciousness fosters associative thinking, which is essential for both individual and societal transformation. It facilitates profound, transformational change within individuals and social systems alike. Together with solar consciousness, introduced by the preceding letter, Resh, lunar consciousness drives individuals toward transformation and transmutation, enabling significant changes at the DNA level.

The vibrational frequencies associated with the letter Tav aim to guide individuals toward authentic self-development. This involves reaching a state where they possess a profound and intimate understanding of various aspects of their personality, including mental, emotional, physical, and spiritual dimensions. It also involves engaging in the diverse developmental processes described by the twenty-two letters. By mastering these processes, individuals become experts, capable of serving as guides for others.

The Letter in the Creation Stories

The letter Tav makes its initial appearance in the creation narratives through the words "tohu" (תֹהוּ), meaning "formless," and "tehom" (תְהוֹם), meaning "the surface of the deep." *This is evident in the verse, "And the earth was a formless and desolate emptiness, and darkness was over the surface of the deep, and the Spirit of God was hovering over the surface of the waters." (Genesis* Chapter 1, Verse 2)

The literal meaning of the word "tohu" conveys emptiness, desolation, nothingness, or primordial chaos, representing a chaotic state before the establishment of order or destruction, leading to a

---

awareness. This concept proposes that connecting with lunar consciousness fosters internal reflection, emotional exploration, and the healing of emotional wounds. Engaging with this consciousness leads individuals to a deeper understanding of themselves, promoting personal growth and self-discovery.

state of pre-existence. Biblically, Tohu signifies the universe's initial state—a formless, infinite void where the Earth was shapeless and desolate. From this chaos, the world was created.

According to Kabbalistic teachings, The World of Tohu is considered a supreme and sacred realm, containing divine revelation and a powerful light emanating from the highest divine source. Kabbalistic teachings propose that before the formation of our world, God created a realm known as "The World of Tohu." This world is characterized by much divine spiritual energy, high spiritual souls, and few vessels representing physical bodies. Due to the vessels' incapacity to contain the intense divine powers, they shattered, causing divine light fragments to scatter. In other words, The World of Tohu broke and collapsed. Subsequently, our world was created, referred to in Kabbalistic terms as "**Olam Asiyah**[2]" or "The World of Action," known as a realm of rectification.

"The World of Action" is the lowest of the four spiritual levels of reality and is linked to physical and material existence, representing the tangible reality perceived through our senses. This world is constructed with numerous vessels and few lights, a balance that enables its existence. The process of gathering the divine fragments and reconstructing them into an ordered, balanced, and harmonious world is symbolized in Kabbalistic teachings as the rectification process—a process that humans are entrusted with.

The term "tehom" (תְּהוֹם) encompasses a rich tapestry of meanings, traditionally referring to the "primordial sea" before the world's creation, known in Hebrew as "mei b'resheet" (מֵי בְּרֵאשִׁית). It symbolizes an abyss or water of unfathomable depth, including subterranean waters. In biblical and Sages literature, "tehom" is frequently paired with descriptors like "many" and "deep waters."

---

[2]   According to the Kabbalistic teachings, the universe is comprised of four worlds or levels of reality. The names of these worlds are Atzilut (emanation), Briyah (creation), Yetzirah (formation), and Asiyah (action).

Genesis recounts that at creation's dawn, tehom's waters enveloped the Earth until God commanded their congregation, unveiling the land. Tehom, residing deep within the Earth, is the primary source of the world's springs.

A notable Hebrew linguistic application of "tehom" is found in "tehom haneshiyah" (תְּהוֹם הַנְּשִׁיָּיה), which signifies a state of oblivion or profound forgetfulness. This biblical concept metaphorically represents, among other things, the psychological and spiritual journey that one must undertake from chaos and darkness toward personal rectification. Intriguingly, reversing the letters in the Hebrew word for "forgetfulness" (שכחה) forms the word "darkness" (חשכה), highlighting the deep interconnection between these states.

As previously discussed, Western religions rooted in patriarchal traditions predominantly highlight a male deity, often overlooking the feminine divine. This focus largely sidelines feminine divine power, and so does the Bible. Such an approach reflects a significant imbalance between masculine and feminine energies, manifest in the world as we see it today. The letter Tav is considered a feminine letter, embodying the feminine divine power, especially as articulated through the concept of Tohu.

Biblical scholars suggest that the Bible was composed at various times throughout history, with its texts being edited from older sources, including Sumerian and Babylonian texts. These scholars, along with experts in ancient myths, establish a link between the term "tohu" and the ancient water goddess—the primordial goddess of the abyss, known in the Bible's creation stories as "Tohu and Tehom" and in Babylonian creation myths as "Tiamat."

The Abyssal Goddess Tiamat

The figure of Tiamat, the ancient goddess of the abyss, emerges from the Babylonian epic poem **Enuma Elish**[3], discovered in 1849 in

---

[3] Enuma Elish, or "The Epic of Creation," is an ancient Babylonian mythological poem narrating the tale of the world's creation and the struggle between the gods for power. It is

Nineveh (modern-day Iraq) across seven clay tablets. These texts reveal Tiamat as reigning over the universe's deepest realms—the primordial waters of creation.

Tiamat, revered as the mother of all gods, birthed divine beings by merging her salty waters with the sweet waters of the god Apsu. Amidst a conflict among the gods, Tiamat summoned water monsters for aid but was ultimately defeated. Her body was split into two, giving form to the heavens and the earth. The tears she shed during her dismemberment birthed the rivers Euphrates and Tigris, as well as the Milky Way, our galaxy.

Pronunciation

The letter Tav is pronounced as "Tav" and is represented in English as T or TH.

The name and pronunciation of the letter Tav have multiple interpretations, including "musical note" and "sign," —an indicator for action and potential event. It is also seen as a "symbol" for communication, a "landmark" for navigation, a "label" for additional information, and a "seal" reflecting personal impact.

Rabbi Akivass Midrash interprets the pronunciation of Tav as "Taev" (תאיו), meaning "desire." The Midrash suggests that the letter embodies a strong desire that is wished to be fulfilled, a desire that originates from a sense of emptiness or lack. This unconscious feeling may lead those associated with the letter to inner distress due to the inability to understand the meaning of this inner emptiness and, consequently, to a state of chasing something that is often linked to material achievements. This reflection underscores the profound emotional and spiritual implications of longing represented by Tav, emphasizing the inner journey to comprehend and address this foundational emptiness.

---

a story first written by the ancient Sumerians thousands of years ago and one of the oldest stories known to mankind.

Diagram 99: Musical Note   **Diagram 100: Seal**

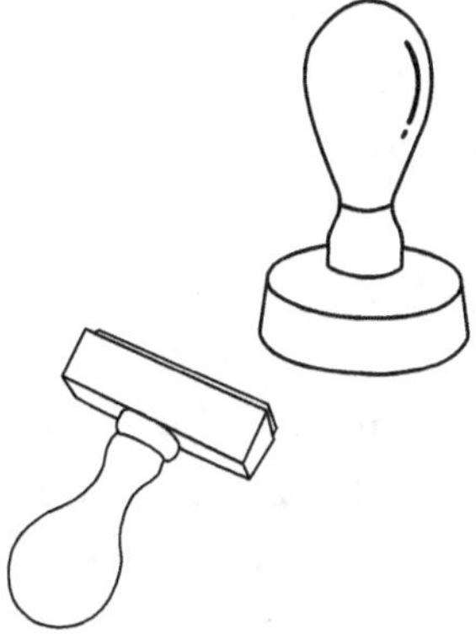

Graphic Shape

The letter Tav possesses a closed form from three sides. It is sealed at its top, symbolizing its closeness to unity consciousness and the matters of the spiritual world, and it is open at its lower part, indicating openness to the matters of the material world. Tav is enclosed on the left and right, distancing itself from the wisdom of the adjacent letters, Resh and Alef. Standing on two firm legs, Tav symbolizes stability and the ability to maintain balance and equilibrium over time.

Tav's design is akin to a house with walls and a roof, featuring a lower opening that represents a gateway. This opening may lead one toward spiritual enlightenment or draw them into the material world's complexities, fostering an excessive preoccupation with earthly matters.

Diagram 101: The Handwritten and Printed Tav

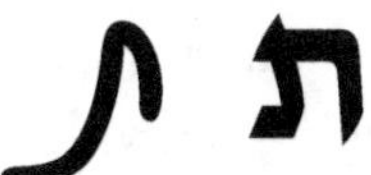

Due to its enclosed form on three sides, Tav embodies boundaries and limitations, potentially narrowing perspectives and distorting perceptions of self and the world, challenging individuals to see life's full scope and leading to fragmented consciousness and feelings of inadequacy.

Gematrical Value

The gematrical value of the letter Tav is four hundred, embodying qualities that guide an individual toward the successful completion of their journey or goal. This value symbolizes systematicity, pragmatism, productivity, responsibility, initiative, and a focused approach toward tasks and goals. It reflects the energy of duty, leading to the construction of a stable material foundation, assessed by the outcome. This foundation, built on conscientiousness, emotional stability, and authenticity, enables success, growth, and flourishing.

Diagram 102: DMT Letters

דמת

The corresponding letter to Tav in the tens digit is Mem, with a gematrical value of forty, and in the units digit, the letter is Dalet, with a gematrical value of four. The number four hundred, amplifying the qualities of the number four, signifies structure, systematicity, and process orientation, influencing how one interacts with one's environment, institutions, and frameworks.

As the ultimate creative mind letter, Tav marks the completion of a life stage or cycle. Its gematrical value encourages introspection—assessing one's journey, achievements, growth, lessons learned, and future aspirations. This numerical significance prompts a shift toward deliberate action, urging individuals to take responsibility, concentrate on objectives, delay instant satisfaction, adhere to ethical standards, and contemplate before acting physically or verbally, encapsulating the adage "think before you act."

The gematrical value of Tav appears multiple times in the Bible, particularly in the context of "slavery." One notable example is found in God's prophecy to Abraham about the future enslavement of his descendants for four hundred years in a land not their own, as detailed in *Genesis*, Chapter 15, Verse 13. *"Then God said to Abram, know for certain that your descendants will be strangers in a land that is not theirs, where they will be enslaved and oppressed for four hundred years."*

This verse indicates two distinct degrees of suffering. The first pertains to feelings of alienation and rejection, as expressed through *"your descendants will be strangers."* The second degree involves oppression and mental anguish, characterized by being under someone else's control. *"they will be enslaved and oppressed."*

The Bible, among its diverse themes, delves into the events of the Israelites descent into Egypt and their subsequent exodus, shedding light on the causes behind a notable decline in their collective consciousness. This deterioration is linked to a shift away from spirituality and faith toward materialism, power, and control, coupled with the exploitation inherent in patriarchal hierarchies. To transition from a narrow, emotional (watery) consciousness to higher vibrational frequencies, the Israelites had to undergo a transformational process. This process was essential for them to elevate beyond the low emotional frequencies that clung to them during their years of exile. Notably, in Hebrew, the words for "Egypt" (מצרים) and "narrow waters" (מי צרים) share the same full spelling, symbolizing the confinement they had to transcend.

One manifestation of patriarchal hierarchy's exploitation is observed in societal dynamics where men possess dominant power, establish norms, and engage in practices like polygamy. Following Jacob's death, the biblical narrative transitions from a previously emotional and feminine tone to one that underscores the patriarchal dominance. This significant change marks the beginning of the descent into a state of narrow emotional consciousness characterized by a low vibrational frequency. Within this context, the letter Tav emerges as a pivotal symbol, representing the necessary processes and actions for individuals to embark on a journey toward redemption and liberation from such narrow-mindedness.

Another example of the gematrical value of the letter Tav is highlighted in the story of Sarah's burial. Abraham purchases a burial plot for her, paying four hundred silver shekels for the land. (*Genesis*, Chapter 23, Verse 16)

The Planet Associated with Tav

"He made the letter Tav king, and He bound a crown to it, and he combined one with another, and with them, He formed the moon in the universe..." (*Sefer Yetzirah*, Chapter 4, Verse 11)

Sefer Yetzirah associates the letter Tav with the moon, thus offering us a deeper understanding of its qualities. The moon, a significant celestial body, exerts a profound influence on human life, symbolizing power and centrality across cultures and nations. Governing the night, the moon's light enables nocturnal creatures to navigate. As the closest celestial body to Earth, it plays a crucial role in our lives, accompanying our planet in its orbit as part of Earth's sphere.

Our lives are deeply intertwined with the moon's cyclical nature. Throughout history, numerous civilizations have celebrated the full moon ceremony, a symbol of releasing the old and embracing the new. The full moon night, a time of power, beauty, and healing, facilitates this transition. Each lunar month introduces unique energy, with thirteen different moon phases representing various cycles of release and renewal throughout the year.

The moon symbolizes the depth of the human soul, the feminine and maternal aspects responsible for the realm of feelings, home, family, and basic needs essential for proper functioning. The aspect that signifies the need for belonging and offers security, peace of mind, and a desire for assimilation. With its waxing and waning cycles, the moon influences a woman's fertile cycle, contributing to the fertility from which earthly life emerges.

The moon, with its watery aspect, manifests power through cycles, rhythms, regularity, periodicity, fluctuations, fertility, renewal, and transformation. Understanding the role of water is crucial for complete self-development, as it embodies a purifying aspect. Without recognizing the full spectrum of their emotional nuances—shades, forms, rhythms, and fluctuations—humans cannot grasp the true purpose and meaning of earthly life.

Water is formless, seamlessly adapting its shape to the container that holds it. It merges, blends, and transforms, assuming qualities that may not always reflect its true essence. Water symbolizes moisture, waves, fluctuation, and the cyclical ups and downs of life, touching upon the unconscious aspects deep within the soul. It resonates with both the personal and collective unconscious of human beings, capturing memories, dreams, and instincts.

As the sun sets, the moon becomes our primary light source. It harbors a distant side, unseen by us, often referred to as the "hidden side" or the "dark side." Throughout each month, the moon reflects light in eight recurring phases, including four primary stages: new moon, first quarter, full moon, and last quarter; and four secondary phases: waxing crescent, waxing gibbous, waning crescent, and waning gibbous.

The letter Tav, linked to the moon, represents the emotional imprints absorbed during early childhood. These imprints often exert a strong influence over a person until they reach a full understanding of them. Similarly to the moon's phases, Tav illustrates the dynamic nature of human emotions—the ebb and flow. This analogy extends to suggest that individuals reactions to different circumstances are influenced by the vibrational frequencies of their "internal waters" and intuitive feelings.

The Groups the Letter Tav is Associated With

Water Element Letter

The element associated with the letter Tav is water. This element is linked to the emotional aspects within us and all those parts over which we have no control. A significant characteristic of water is its ability to retain molecular memory. The water element contains ancient emotional memories that are deeply embedded in the personal consciousness of individuals, not necessarily related solely to their current life incarnation.

The virtue of memory that water endows helps humans recall their spiritual essence and the divine aspect pulsating within them—to remember that they are divine entities experiencing human life and learning from it.

Tav is not only the last alphabetical letter but also the last letter in the series of watery letters (choking-dead letters), and as such, its watery energy works more strongly in a person. It prompts individuals to address and heal their inner child and all those painful memories that tend to pop up unexpectedly and manage them unconsciously. It encourages individuals to learn how to regulate and manage their emotions.

Creational Mind Letter

Tav is a creational mind letter, encapsulating emotional patterns that are deeply ingrained in both personal and collective human consciousness. These patterns, which contain deeply rooted beliefs carried from one incarnation to another, tend to activate individuals in a sub-hypnotic manner.

Tav is a creational letter with a closed pattern from three directions and contains judgments that tend to manifest as narrow-mindedness and mental and emotional restrictions, drawing individuals into a state of duality. The purpose of Tav is to direct attention to these fundamental beliefs, encouraging awareness and transcendence through its creative power, thereby facilitating their permanent release.

Hard and Soft Sound

The letter Tav can be pronounced with either a hard or soft sound, influencing its characteristics. As a creative mind letter, Tav can intensify or weaken its vibrational frequencies. A hard sound gives the letter a masculine (yang) and more intense tone, while a softer sound imparts a feminine (yin) and gentler tone. When pronounced hard, it suggests difficulty in becoming flexible when needed. Conversely, soft pronunciation represents the ability to be flexible and dissolve the ego.

When Tav is pronounced with a hard sound, it exhibits greater strength and presence but also a higher risk of pride and ego-driven actions. Conversely, in its soft form, Tav reduces its vibrational frequency, diminishing the ego's influence and fostering a greater capacity for actions rooted in humility. Examples include hard sound Hebrew words like "desire" (תַּאֲוָה), "abyss" (תְּהוֹם), and "understanding" (תְּבוּנָה), compared to softer sound words such as "kindness" (אֲדִיבוּת) and "devotion" (מְסִירוּת).

Consequential Letter

In Kabbalistic teachings, the letter Tav signifies the completion of rectification or the risk of becoming overly rigid. It is one of the letters that highlight emotionally unresolved karmic connections, often with a key figure in the life of the letter's holder, typically representing the mother but not exclusively—it can also be a sister, aunt, or dominant grandmother figure. This situation can lead to the accumulation of unconscious anger toward this figure, resulting in an unstable relationship dynamic.

As a consequential letter, Tav carries intense vibrational frequencies and energetic imprints of a mental and emotional nature, pulling individuals toward extremes. It urges individuals to develop a high level of self-awareness regarding their deep-seated beliefs, emotional spectrum, and the internal programs that subconsciously guide them. This self-awareness allows individuals to identify, understand, and manage these aspects in a balanced way.

The vibrational frequencies of the letter guide individuals toward achieving wholeness within themselves and in all aspects of their life journey, encouraging them to transform into a new, pure, innocent, and virtuous energetic entity, akin to a newborn baby. Upon reaching this state, individuals embody a "Messiah consciousness," embracing the principle of "Love your neighbor as yourself" in every moment of their lives.

The Measure of Absolute Judgment

The letter Tav is an interesting letter that contains many gifts. However, the path it indicates is not easy to implement, as it encompasses the measure of absolute judgment. This measure restricts and limits an individual's consciousness, leading to harsh and rigorous judgments of people and situations. This tendency can distance individuals from the transformative path the letter directs them toward.

Strengths

Strengths associated with the letter Tav include sensitivity, understanding, gracefulness, sympathy, wit, independence, curiosity, inquisitiveness, responsibility, purposefulness, ambition, cleverness, moderation, and a structural, systematic, practical, and methodological approach. Individuals characterized by this letter tend to be task and goal-oriented. The letter characterizes sensitive individuals who often require emotional, intimate experiences, pampering, and indulgence. It also represents those who are connected to frameworks, home, work, partners, and children.

Weaknesses

The weaknesses related to the letter Tav encompass rigor, excessive caution, excessive stubbornness, high self-importance, attachment, clinginess, skepticism, distrust, victimhood, controlling behavior, compulsiveness, possessiveness, competitiveness, over-stubbornness, dependency, a demanding need for personal attention, and attraction to dominant partners, sometimes resembling parental figures. Other weaknesses include a tendency to be opinionated, to indulge in self-pity, and to be judgmental. The inhibiting aspect of the letter manifests in restlessness, frequent mood swings, outbursts of anger, self-deprecation, belittling others, closed-off emotions, and the tendency to store memories, possessions, and anger. Emotional complications and difficulty in forgiving, releasing, and letting go are also common challenges associated with Tav.

CHAPTER 8

Practical Implementation of the Wisdom of Alphabet Letters in Everyday Life

Now, we have reached the most exciting part: the section where you can practically apply the knowledge you have gained throughout the reading. In this chapter, you will learn about situations where changing a name is advisable or not, what criteria make a name strong and powerful, the timeframe for the impact of a new or additional name, and how to establish its earthly validity.

It is important to note that this book is the first in a series exploring the secret power of letters and names. As such, it provides initial and basic information. Nevertheless, I am confident that even this preliminary information will offer you a wealth of practical insights.

Before detailing the circumstances in which changing a name is desirable or undesirable, I wish to highlight an important and even crucial point: there are nearly fifteen Gematria methods for evaluating a name. Successful naming is determined using at least twelve different Gematria methods, ensuring that the name aligns well with the person's date of birth, at least in most calculations.

Consulting someone who has not specialized in various numerological systems and Gematria calculations and who has not extensively studied the ancient alphanumeric cipher code can be limiting. In my experience and knowledge, a name given by such individuals might assist in one specific area but cause challenges in others.

Therefore, when seeking advice for a name change, it is crucial to ensure that the numerologist is well-versed in the ancient knowledge of Kabbalah and the alphanumeric cipher codes and possesses comprehensive knowledge of various numerological methods.

As you will see later in this chapter, I often use examples to illustrate the practical application of the material. These examples are primarily based on classical numerology and the short Hebrew Gematria.

The Significance and Importance of Selecting an Appropriate Name

The full name of an individual—including their first name, middle name, and surname—carries immense importance. It serves as the source of energetic power that enables a person to fulfill and actualize their soul's potential. The full name mirrors the array of abilities and skills available for the person's complete self-realization. Moreover, it acts as a shield, safeguarding the individual and providing the strength necessary for success. Conversely, an unsuitable name could, unfortunately, impede their fortune and become a significant obstacle.

A name that harmoniously aligns with a person's date of birth bestows upon them a life marked by happiness, fulfillment, and success. It ensures a smooth flow of life, accompanied by robust physical and mental health, and empowers them to achieve their desires, aspirations, and heartfelt wishes.

The importance of an individual's given name—be it their birth name or the name they currently use—cannot be overstated. It exerts a profound influence over their life. Therefore, it is crucial for a person to genuinely love their first name, to feel that it accurately represents who they are, and to maintain a deep connection with it, encapsulated in the sentiment, "This is my name." Such identification is essential, as the first name serves as the link to our essence, our spirit, and our spiritual purpose in this incarnation.

Nicknames and affectionate names also play a role and can either support or hinder. It is vital to recognize that even if one changes their first name, the birth-given name continues to wield influence. Changing a name can shift a person's fortune and destiny but does not modify the spiritual lessons their soul is meant to learn in this lifetime. If an individual changes their name without assimilating and embracing these spiritual lessons, the energy of the old name will persistently accompany them on their earthly journey.

In What Situations Should Someone Consider Changing Their Name?

Frequently, individuals facing various life challenges swiftly contemplate changing their name, harboring the belief that such a change will bring about the desired transformation. However, this is not always the case. Without having learned the spiritual lessons conveyed through their given name and birth date and lacking awareness of their spiritual potential, significant life changes are unlikely to occur. Furthermore, changing or adding a name without substantial justification could potentially exacerbate the individual's circumstances.

Thus, it is crucial to underline that hastily changing a name due to immediate challenges is generally not advisable. At times, fostering comprehensive self-awareness and embracing the transformative processes indicated by one's current name can yield benefits, eliminating the necessity for a name change. Nevertheless, for those who have attained profound self-awareness, assimilated and applied their spiritual lessons, and engaged in transformative processes yet continue to encounter persistent difficulties, considering a name change could be extremely helpful.

The will to change one's name often originates from the soul's deep-seated desire for it. If an individual does not feel a strong, internal urge to change their name, even after facing numerous challenges and setbacks, it is important to honor this feeling. Some people might choose a path filled with obstacles and see through adversity and pain as opportunities for personal growth and resilience. Ultimately, the decision to change one's name is a deeply personal choice guided by one's own free will.

In specific instances, a name change is strongly recommended and, at times, imperative. These scenarios will be elaborated upon in subsequent sections.

Situations Where Changing One's Name is Highly Recommended

A Name with a History

Consider changing your name if it was given in honor of someone who experienced significant misfortune, suffered greatly, was severely ill, or had a tragic or nefarious reputation. Additionally, if you wish to sever ties with your past and embark on a new journey, changing your name can symbolize a fresh start and liberation from negative historical associations.

Lack of Connection

An immediate name change is advisable if you feel no connection or identification with your current name. If your discontent stems from social acceptability, adding a supportive second name could enhance your confidence in social settings. Should dissatisfaction arise from the name's meaning or sound, changing or adding letters to achieve a more pleasing resonance or significance is beneficial. Should these adjustments still not resonate with you, a complete name change is strongly recommended.

Lack of Support

If your first and full name does not harmonize with your date of birth, it may suggest that your name does not support your life's path and destiny. A name that fails to provide support can lead to obstacles, delays, financial difficulties, relationship challenges, and even health issues. In situations where there is no compatibility, a person's ability to fulfill themselves and live a life full of satisfaction and success is compromised. In such cases, renaming can realign and strengthen your journey toward success and fulfillment.

Divorce

Family names carry energies and vibrations stemming from ancestral experiences, which include hereditary conditions or karmic ties. Sometimes, these energies are tied to challenging histories, such as hereditary illnesses or the burdens of generational karma. These energies can subtly influence the consciousness of those bearing the name, often without their awareness, thereby hindering their progress in life.

Therefore, for women post-divorce, reevaluating the family name is recommended, as retaining an ex-spouse's surname might inadvertently continue the energies associated with their ex-husband and his family legacy.

This change is designed to facilitate a fresh start, enhancing mental and emotional well-being after divorce. It allows women to embark on their life's journey with revitalized energy, a renewed identity, and an enhanced sense of empowerment.

Here are some examples where these incompatibilities can be identified:

- Persistent challenges in health, relationships, work, and finances.
- Recurring instances of setbacks. A person manages to progress in various areas of their life, but just before achieving significant success, an unforeseen and unexpected event occurs, causing things to fall apart.
- Extended periods of despondency, lack of motivation, physical and mental lethargy, or an unwillingness to actively engage in life.
- Difficulties in establishing stable, long-term relationships, failure to marry until the age of forty, or experiencing repeated marriages and divorces.

- Awareness of the necessary changes for happiness but a lack of inner strength to initiate these changes—understanding that the change would be beneficial but lacking the mental fortitude to act, thereby remaining stuck and enduring unnecessary prolonged suffering for years.
- Fertility challenges, in the absence of health issues, such as extended periods of unsuccessful attempts to conceive.

If you recognize one of these situations, before changing your name, consider the possibility of adding or removing letters in your name before opting for a complete change. This adjustment can provide better support and help align your name with your life path and destiny.

Guidelines for Naming or Name Change

For the energies of a new name to start working effectively, it is beneficial to connect with the wisdom of its letters, understanding their uniqueness and purpose.

It is crucial to remember that a name change should stem from the individual's free will, made from a place of autonomous choice, without any coercion. The final decision on the new name should solely belong to the individual, not their advisor.

The Name and the Date of Birth

A name change must align with the person's date of birth, ensuring that the numerical value of the name and its constituent letters balance harmoniously with the birth date, thereby supporting it.

As discussed in previous chapters, letters act as electromagnetic pulses influencing our psycho-physiological system. Certain letters can enhance or restrict energetic flow, evoke energies of kindness, compassion, and generosity, or, conversely, foster self-centeredness, criticism, and judgment. Some letters attract a consciousness of unity, while others may lead to a sense of separateness.

A mismatch between a person's name and their date of birth can lead to stagnation, rejections, repeated setbacks, conflicts, and illnesses. These negative influences can sometimes be mitigated by changing one or two letters, adding another name, or adopting a new name, be it a first name or a surname.

The full date of birth symbolizes a person's life path, akin to the peak of a high mountain that the soul aspires to climb. The first and full name serves as an energetic vehicle empowering them to reach this peak. This vehicle can vary from a high-powered, efficient means, like a Mercedes jeep or a flying apparatus, to a limited and malfunctioning one, like a slow-moving car. An appropriate name acts as a high-powered vehicle, aiding the individual in reaching the mountain's peak in the safest and most efficient manner.

When a name change is accurately tailored to a person's date of birth, the impact is positive and beneficial. Conversely, an inaccurate name change that does not align with the person's soul essence can introduce additional challenges and delays in their life journey.

The Name and Place of Residence

A person's name impacts not only their career, relationships and health but also their success in their current place of residence. Occasionally, relocating to a new country can unexpectedly influence one's fortunes, either positively or negatively.

If relocating results in a downturn in success, where achievements become elusive despite considerable efforts, this may indicate that the person's name is incompatible with the new locale. In such instances, adding a name that harmonizes with both the individual's date of birth and the vibrational energy of the new country may be beneficial. Alternatively, considering a change in the family name could provide a solution.

The Criteria for a Strong and Powerful Name

When selecting a name, there are several criteria to consider. This section will focus on the key criteria that guide the choice of a strong and powerful name.

Vowel and Consonant Balance in a Name

The balance between vowel and consonant letters in a name is another indicator of its strength. As detailed in Chapter Two, consonant letters provide stability and grounding, while vowel letters offer fluidity and expansion.

An imbalance where consonant letters significantly outnumber vowel letters can result in stagnation and resistance to change. This may obstruct adaptation to new circumstances, hinder the ability to embrace change, and make releasing from certain situations and people difficult, ultimately impeding smooth life navigation. Conversely, a surplus of vowel letters over consonants may pose challenges in grounding and solidifying one's identity, leading to unattainable aspirations that lack practical foundations.

To emphasize the importance of this balance, imagine consonants as the external walls of a house and vowels as its windows. While walls provide safety and structure, windows allow light and air to enter. A house with too few windows can feel enclosed, stifling, and dark. In contrast, a house with an excess of windows might compromise security, leading to restlessness due to external noise and diminished privacy. It is all a matter of balance.

Consecutive and Continuous Vowel Letters in a Name

Vowel letters, symbolizing higher aspirations, spirituality, and elevation, can present challenges when positioned consecutively in a name. Names with three or more consecutive vowel letters, such as Aaliyah, Auriela, Juliana, Alayah, Aeleen, Louie, and Raoul, may result in unrealistic aspirations, difficulties in staying grounded, constant mental restlessness, or a pervasive sense of inadequacy. It is thus advisable to avoid names with three consecutive vowel letters.

This issue is particularly pronounced in individuals who are practical, goal-oriented, and down-to-earth, as determined through a comprehensive analysis of their full date of birth. For these individuals, consecutive vowel letters might lead to ambivalence, uncertainty about their desires, and challenges in remaining grounded and present. A common sign of this struggle is the duration it takes to fully connect to the present moment upon waking, which can range from an hour to several hours, indicating a fundamental issue with orientation.

Multiple Names

The practice of using multiple names, such as being named Michael at birth but called Misha (in Russian) or Mikel (in French) by parents, Miko by friends, and Mike at work or school, should be avoided to prevent energetic dispersion. Utilizing a consistent name, whether a nickname or a term of endearment, that best aligns with the individual's identity and supports their fortune is recommended. For instance, while the given name Michael might enhance the person's luck, the name Mike could potentially detract from it.

Syllables, Rhythms, and Sound Intensities

An important aspect of naming involves considering the syllables, sound strength, and rhythm created by the syllables of a person's full name. An ideally harmonious full name would have an equal number of letters, syllables, or matching sound rhythm in the first name, middle name (if applicable), and last name. Examples of such balanced names include Julia Roberts, Michael Jackson, Bruce Willis, Ayn Rand, and Mason Parker.

Conversely, names like Tal Troskovchikovitz or Ann Fetherstonehaugh demonstrate a lack of balance in letters, syllables, or sound rhythm. In these instances, adding letters to the first name, introducing a middle name, or opting for a more harmonious name change might be considered.

Giving a Birth Name

The name given to a newborn significantly influences their life journey. It can shape whether they lead a healthy, happy, and fulfilled life or encounter challenges, frustrations, and obstacles. A name that resonates with the child's soul path and supports their development can have a positive impact on their life, while an unsupportive name may lead to difficulties, including health issues. This influence also extends to the parent's journey.

It is recommended to name the child as soon as possible after birth. Promptly calling the child by their name fosters a deep connection with their spiritual essence. Delaying the naming process can hinder the child's ability to embrace their strengths and destiny.

In instances of parental disagreement over a name, Kabbalistic teachings suggest giving precedence to the mother's intuition, as women often possess a more profound intuitive connection to the child and their soul's desires. Although the child's umbilical cord is physically cut, the energetic connection between the child and the mother remains strong for a long time.

Choosing a name that clearly aligns with the child's gender is highly recommended. It is recommended to avoid names that are ambiguous or could be interpreted as belonging to either gender.

It is crucial to recognize that a name bestows upon the child a distinct personal identity and shapes their character. A well-defined and clear identity from early childhood is instrumental in the development of self-perception, and it positively influences their emotional development and self-image. A delayed formation of self-identity may cause the child to experience anxiety, doubts, and fears.

When selecting names for children, opting for names with positive or spiritual meanings is advisable. A second name is always beneficial as it acts as a protector, shielding the individual from negative influences. In Judaism, a second name, known as a "cradle name," is traditionally kept within the family, known only to the individual and their parents, to protect and maintain its energy.

Dos and Don'ts Guidelines for Choosing a Child's Name

It is advisable to give a child a name with a positive and empowering meaning, avoiding names with dual or negative implications.

Ideally, a child's name should consist of four to seven letters for Hebrew names and four to nine letters for English names to provide balance and energetic strength.

It is best to avoid names with only two letters, as such names might not offer the necessary energy and spiritual support for the child's life path.

Avoid naming a child after someone who passed away from a serious illness or under tragic circumstances, as this may carry unintended, energetic consequences.

Refrain from giving the child a peculiar or unusual name that could lead to misunderstandings or unfair treatment by others.

Avoid names with complex or ambiguous meanings, such as Sue (which can imply "to prosecute"), or names like Dick, Barbie, Rebel, and Sea, which carry potentially negative or unstable connotations. Similarly, Hebrew names like Din (judgment), Aya (a cry of pain), Mazal (luck), and Levanah (moon) should be chosen with care due to their meanings.

Changing a child's name without their consent is considered inappropriate. If parents believe a name adjustment is necessary, they should opt to add or modify the name in a way that supports the child, respecting the child's connection to their identity. Avoid changing a name that the child identifies with or is unwilling to change. Children often have a strong sense of self and intuition, even before they can articulate it, and usually know what is best for them.

In cases involving very young children who cannot yet speak or express their desires, and if parents genuinely believe a name change or addition is in the child's best interest, the decision should be made with the child's well-being as the primary concern.

Changing a Name After Marriage

An important issue primarily affecting women is the change of one's name due to marriage. In discussing this topic, I will use the term "spouse" (בן זוג) instead of "husband" (בעל), which in Hebrew suggests connotations of possession and ownership. We women are not anyone's property.

Many women choose to adopt their spouse's family name after getting married, adhering to societal norms and traditions. This decision introduces new energies into their lives, which can either support and enhance the flow of positive energy or create obstacles and challenges.

In some instances, adopting a new family name may lead to energetic incompatibility between the name numbers of the couple's full names. Consequently, the new surname a woman takes may disrupt the frequency of love, appreciation, and admiration that existed between the couple before the name change. This could explain why some couples experience behavioral changes, leading to increased arguments, with remarks such as, "She was different before the marriage."

Granting Validity to a Name

When deciding to change one's name, it is crucial to update all official documents, including ID cards, passports, driver's licenses, bank records, and work documents. Changes should also extend to social networks, email accounts, and business cards. Informing family, friends, and colleagues about the new name is essential for ensuring they address you by your updated name. Consistent use and signing with the new name help to establish and validate it.

Using both the new and old names simultaneously may delay the transition. It can take a significant amount of time for the new name's energy to integrate fully. Thus, fully committing to the new name is recommended to experience its effects more effectively.

The Length of Time for the Influence of the New Name to Take Effect

In general, the energies of a new name take time to start influencing a person's life. According to Judaic tradition, this period can vary, ranging from several months to several years, with some suggesting it could span from nine months to nine years.

However, I firmly believe that when a person aligns themselves with the energy of their new name, the impact can be felt in as little as three months. This alignment involves developing a deep awareness of their life path, as indicated by their full date of birth, and engaging in spiritual learning, which includes studying both their given name and new names. By doing so, the energy begins to work more rapidly. As electromagnetic beings, the energy we emit interacts with similar energies in our surroundings, accelerating the influence of the new name.

It is important to note that simply changing a name on official documents like passports or ID cards is not enough to activate the new name's energy significantly. Active steps are necessary to set this energy in motion. The new name should be consistently used across various platforms, including emails, business cards, and social media channels such as LinkedIn, Facebook, Instagram, Telegram, WhatsApp, and others. The more the new name is firmly established in different contexts—such as with family, friends, and at work— the stronger and quicker its energetic effect will be.

Before concluding this chapter, I want to emphasize the power of the subconscious mind. When the subconscious mind is presented with an idea or intention, it mobilizes all its resources toward achieving that goal. To expedite the impact of the new name, it is crucial to implant this new name in the subconscious mind with love, warmth, and joy. The subconscious responds quickly and positively to such emotional investments.

The Implementation of the New Name

Throughout history, ancient cultures have practiced the ritual of a naming ceremony when giving a name to a newborn. During this ceremony, close family and friends would gather for a festive meal to celebrate the revelation of the chosen name- a word (name) that symbolizes the child's identity, and to bless the newborn with their newly given name and grant the name its validity.

However, the act of giving a new name is not limited to birth. People change their names for various reasons, which I will elaborate on further. It is important to know that when a person changes or adds a new name, it is advisable to conduct a ceremony in order to give the new name validity. It is advisable to invite close family and friends to this ceremony to bless the person with their new name and new path, introduce the new name to the community and society, and thereby give the new name validity.

Naming ceremonies are an ancient tradition widely practiced in different cultures around the world. These ceremonies hold significant cultural, religious, and social importance, with their contents varying according to different traditions. Some cultures hold elaborate naming ceremonies, while others have simpler, more informal practices. The meaning and significance behind these ceremonies make them vital and meaningful events.

The primary purpose of these naming ceremonies is to bestow upon a person a sense of identity and belonging, to confer blessings for their new journey, and to acknowledge them within the community and society under their new identity. Another objective is to celebrate the new name and mark the commencement of a new chapter in the individual's life, to offer blessings, to provide family and social support, and to grant official validity to the chosen name.

There are different types of ceremonies, generally divided into two main categories: religious and social or secular. A religious ceremony is deeply rooted in the beliefs and customs of a specific religion. In this ceremony, the new name is declared, and religious scriptures or texts related to names and blessings are read, such as Psalms in Judaism. The second type, a social or secular ceremony, is usually personalized for the individual and their family, reflecting their values, beliefs, and desires.

During the naming ceremony, whether religious or secular, it is considered desirable to have at least ten people present as witnesses for the name change. If assembling a full **minyan**[1] (a group of ten) proves challenging, a smaller number of attendees may be deemed acceptable. However, according to Jewish tradition, the presence of at least three individuals is required.

It is also recommended to decorate the space with white candles and flowers, symbolizing purity and new beginnings, along with pomegranates and grapes to represent fertility and abundance. The custom of wearing white garments, indicative of holiness and purity, is also encouraged.

In Judaism, fasting on the day of the naming ceremony, akin to fasting on a wedding day, is a practice observed to prepare the individual's body for the sanctification accompanying the blessing of the new name.

During the name integration ceremony, before announcing the new name, expressing gratitude for the journey thus far is desirable. This includes acknowledging the past and blessing the future. Ideally, the person announcing the new name should be spiritually inclined and possess pure intentions.

---

[1]   In Jewish practice, a minyan is defined as a group of ten Jewish adults gathered to fulfill communal religious duties and participate in ceremonies. This quorum is essential to nurture a sense of communal connection and shared responsibility. It underscores the value of togetherness in the Jewish faith, highlighting the greater power and importance of communal prayer compared to individual prayer.

Religious Ceremony for a Name Change

In this section, I present an example of a Jewish religious ceremony for a name change, illustrated through the case of a young woman named Danah, daughter of Lea, who desires to add the name Naamah to her existing name.

Please note, that the text offers insights into a religious ceremony and is directly translated from Hebrew. It is important to understand that the translation may not fully capture the nuances of the original Hebrew blessings.

The Announcement

At the beginning of the ceremony, it is customary to announce:

> "We have gathered today on this festive day to give Danah, daughter of Lea, an additional name, Naamah. May the additional name Naamah added to Danah, daughter of Lea, bring her good fortune, an abundance of blessings, light and love, good health, kindness, compassion, peace, and complete harmony of the soul."

At this stage, additional blessings can be added to bless the girl, concluding with, "Amen, so may it be, and so it is."

Reading Psalms

Immediately after the declaration, it is recommended to read several chapters from the Book of Psalms, specifically Chapters 20, 130, 142, and 121.

Blessing Related to the Name Change

Following the reading of the Psalms, it is customary to say:

> "May the name of the Lord be blessed from now and forevermore. He who blessed our holy and pure matriarchs Sarah, Rebecca, Rachel, and Leah, Prophet Miriam, Abigail, and Queen Esther, daughter of Abihail, may He also bless, safeguard, and protect Danah Naamah, daughter of Lea. The King of Kings, in His compassion, shall guard and preserve her, deliver her from all sorrow and harm, and grant her a long and fruitful life."

At this stage, a personalized blessing may be added according to the individual's circumstances:

- For a young girl: "May God grant her a long life with her father and mother."
- For a married woman: "May God bless her with daughters and sons."
- For a mother: "May God protect her children and grant her additional children in her life" (if the woman desires more children).
- For an ill woman: "May God bestow complete healing upon her, among all the other sick individuals of Israel, through the skillful hands of physicians and the compassionate care of nurses. Please, God, heal her. We fervently pray for her healing, and may she be restored to her original strength. Let us all say, Amen! So shall it be, and so it is."

After the personal blessing, we continue as follows:

"Creator of all that is, King of the universe and bellowed Shekinah, merciful and gracious God, whose kindness extends to thousands and who forgives iniquity, transgression, and sin, we lift our eyes upward and seek the blessing of divine providence upon Danah Naamah, daughter of Lea. "In fulfilling the wisdom of our ancestors, sages, and holy matriarchs, we understand that a change of name can alter one's decree. Therefore, we declare that from this moment forth, the name of Danah, daughter of Lea, shall be Danah Naamah, daughter of Lea.

"May it be your divine will to accept this new name and shower Danah Naamah, daughter of Lea, with kindness, mercy, and protection. May any strict judgment, harsh decrees, curses, or ill fortunes upon her be annulled, and may she be regarded as a newborn infant in your eyes. If any severe decree or misfortune has been destined for Danah, daughter of Lea, we beseech that it shall not be enforced on Danah Naamah, daughter of Lea.

"And let there be that Danah Naamah, daughter of Lea, will experience rectification and healing, reflecting the hope that 'The Lord will remove from you all sickness; and He will not inflict upon you any of the harmful diseases.' 'Then your light will break out like the dawn, and your recovery will spring up quickly; and your righteousness will go before you; the glory of the Lord will be your rear guard.' 'For length of days and years of life and peace they will add to you.' Amen, Selah." (Deuteronomy, Chapter 7, Verse 15; Isaiah, Chapter 58, Verse 8; Proverbs Chapter 3, Verse 2).

After the Blessings

Upon concluding the blessing, it is customary to recite a specific set of eight verses from Psalm 119, with each verse corresponding to a letter in the person's new name. The verses are recited in the order of the letters in the name. For instance, using the name provided in the example (Dana Naama), the recitation of the verses would follow this sequence:

D   (Dalet) – eight verses referring to this letter
A   (Alef) – eight verses referring to this letter
N   (Nun) – eight verses referring to this letter
AH (Heh) – eight verses referring to this letter
N   (Nun) – eight verses referring to this letter
A   (Alef) – eight verses referring to this letter
A   (Alef) – eight verses referring to this letter
M   (Mem) – eight verses referring to this letter
AH (Heh) – eight verses referring to this letter

Some also have the practice of reciting Psalm 27 and Psalm 29 from the Book of Psalms, adding to the spiritual depth of the ceremony.

A Secular (Non-Religious) Ceremony

In this section, I present an example of a secular (non-religious) ceremony for a name change.

Throughout my extensive professional experience, I have observed that a significant portion of individuals do not feel a profound connection to religious ceremonies. They often find these ceremonies tiresome, lacking in excitement and joy, and struggle to relate to ancient scriptures. As a result, I have explored non-religious rituals practiced worldwide, embraced by people celebrating important milestones that signify the beginning of a new chapter in their lives.

The secular ceremony, which is becoming increasingly popular, is characterized by its flexibility and lack of standardization. This allows it to be customized to each individual's preferences. Its main purpose is to announce the new name to family, friends, and the community and to bless the person on their new journey.

This secular ceremony involves the official bestowal of the new name, affirming the person's identity and uniqueness. It also provides emotional support from loved ones and the community, marking a significant milestone in their life that symbolizes a fresh and exhilarating beginning.

During the ceremony, well-wishes, expressions of love, and care are shared, and blessings are bestowed upon the individual in a way that makes the event unforgettable, leaving a lasting memory for the individual and their family.

In the secular ceremony, multiple elements come together to foster an uplifting and joyful atmosphere, offering family members and friends an active role in the proceedings. Some of these engaging activities may include:

- Officially introduce and present the new or chosen name to the family and community.

- Lighting candles and announcing the new name while emphasizing its significance.
- Reading empowering songs or short quotes that symbolize new beginnings and personal growth.
- Giving meaningful speeches about life, love, and new beginnings.
- Dedication of beloved songs or instrumental pieces that create a joyful ambiance.
- Playing favorite songs of the name holder, ones that invite dancing.

Activities that leave tangible memories can also be included, such as:

- Planting a tree or flowers or sowing seeds in honor of the name holder.
- Signing a certificate with the new name, with guests serving as witnesses, bestows official recognition upon the new name. The certificate can then be preserved as a cherished keepsake.
- Offering written blessings to be hung on a "Blessing Tree"—a creatively arranged tree with many branches in a vase—allows participants during the ceremony to share their good wishes by attaching them to the tree. These blessings can be gathered after the event and compiled into an album, creating a lasting memento of the occasion.
- Creating a video where loved ones congratulate the person with their new name.
- Taking group photos to document the event.
- Involving children in activities such as blowing bubbles, creating artwork or greeting cards for the guests, and so forth.

Diagram 103: New Name Certificate   **Diagram 104: Blessing Tree**

Choosing how to commemorate your new name should be a reflection of your personality; celebrating this change is crucial for lending it official validity.

Now, armed with an understanding of the wisdom, power, and purpose behind the letters, as well as guiding principles and practical tools, we are ready to explore the most vital aspect: conducting a practical analysis of a name. This next chapter promises an exciting journey, guiding you step by step to analyze your name or those of your loved ones. Let's embark on this fascinating exploration together!

CHAPTER 9

Basic Principles for Analyzing a Person's Name

When analyzing a name, start with the **full birth name—first, middle (if applicable), and last name**—before examining the current name.

Important:

It is recommended to use the letters of the native language for name analysis to ensure accuracy within its original linguistic context.

Note that there are over twelve gematria calculations for name analysis. Therefore, I am presenting two different tables of Gematria calculations below. For clarity, the vowel letters in both tables are presented in bold. The first table is for Hebrew short Gematria calculations, tailored for my Hebrew readers, and the second is for simple Gematria calculations designed for my English readers.

Diagram 105: Short Hebrew Gematria

1	2	3	4	5	6	7	8	9
א	ב	ג	ד	ה	ו	ז	ח	ט
י	כ	ל	מ	נ	ס	ע	פ	צ
ק	ר	ש	ת					
	ך		ם	ן			ף	ץ

Diagram 106: Simple Gematria

Number	Letter
1	**A**, J, S
2	B, K, T
3	C, L, **U**
4	D, M, V
5	**E**, N, W
6	F, **O**, X
7	G, P, **Y**
8	H, Q, Z
9	**I**, R

Eight Steps for Basic Analysis of a Person's Name:

1. Understanding Each Letter's Uniqueness and Significance

Analyzing a name starts with comprehending the unique role and purpose of each letter. This foundational knowledge not only ensures a thorough and accurate analysis but also reveals the layers of an individual's human self, including their essence and potential.

Similar to how DNA shapes your physical being, your name encodes a blueprint of your incarnated soul. For an in-depth understanding of the letters in your name, refer to dedicated chapters in this book.

2. Identification of the Heart's Desire

After understanding the energetic power and direction of the letters in your name, it is essential to identify your true heart's desire. This desire mirrors your deepest motivations and passions, emanating from your spirit and soul. Recognizing your heart's desire is crucial, as it unveils what you genuinely seek in life—beyond superficial appearances. It highlights your profound motivations, joys, and sources of fulfillment, steering you toward your soul's purpose. Recognizing the heart's desire is vital since it propels you into action and, whether consciously or unconsciously, influences the choices you make in life.

As mentioned in Chapter Two, the vowel letters are considered the core of a person's name, and they contain significant energy. By converting these vowels to numerical values, we can quantify and analyze their energetic impact. Each number correlates with specific qualities and traits, and reducing these numbers to a single digit unveils the main energy of a person's heart's desire.

Names without vowel letters hint at a pronounced focus on life's practicalities and suggest that an individual might not be in touch with their true heart's desires. Such individuals subconsciously tend to prioritize the desires of their loved ones over their own, potentially overlooking their souls' true intentions. Acknowledging this distinction is crucial.

Diagram 107: Four Dynamics of Motive Force

Hebrew Letter	Hebrew Letter Name	The Motive Force the Letter Represents
א	ALEF	Ability to navigate through all directions, possibilities, and situations.
ה	HEH	Ability to move forward with a focus on practicality and tangible application.
ו	VAV	Ability to move outward to either connect with people and situations or to detach from them.
י	YOD	Ability to cultivate and enhance spiritual aspects.

As shown in the table, each vowel letter contains a unique energetic movement. To reveal the ultimate purpose and goal that your spirit and soul aspire to, you need to convert the vowels in your name into numbers and then combine these numbers into a single digit, following the examples provided below.

For example, the name **Rona** includes two vowels: O and A. When combined, these vowels create a spiritual movement, symbolized by the simple gematria value of six: O + A = 6 + 1 = 7. Therefore, Rona's heart desire is represented by the number seven.

The name **Paul** includes two vowels: A and U. These vowels, when combined, create a spiritual movement, symbolized by the simple gematria value of four: A + U = 1 + 3 = 4. Therefore, Paul's heart desire is represented by the number four.

The name **Antony** includes three vowel letters: A, O, and Y. These vowels, when combined, create a spiritual movement, symbolized by the simple gematria value of five: A + O + Y = 1 + 6 + 7 = 14; 1+ 4 = 5. Therefore, Antony's heart desire is symbolized by the number five.

An important consideration is the integration of both first and middle names in cases where the person's birth name comprises both. For illustration, if the person's name is Paul Antony, the combined heart's desire is represented by the number nine (4 + 5 = 9), showcasing the necessity of a holistic approach to name analysis.

Once you have determined the numerical value representing your hidden and authentic heart's desire, proceed to the following explanation for a deeper understanding.

Heart's Desire Number One

Individuals with this number wish to express their uniqueness and personal individuality. They are drawn to leadership, independence, and innovation. This heart's desire fosters a penchant for trailblazing and being at the center of action. These individuals do not enjoy sitting in the backseat or remaining behind the scenes; they aspire to be at the forefront of affairs and leadership rather than mere bystanders. Additionally, this heart's desire cultivates a longing for a comfortable material life, as these individuals view wealth and material possessions as symbols of success.

Heart's Desire Number Two

For those with this heart's desire number, the goal is to find peace, balance, and a deep connection with a significant other, fostering harmony in partnerships. This heart's desire nurtures a yearning for emotional intimacy and relationships based on reciprocity and collaboration, embodying the essence of "you and me together." This number reflects a strong longing for true love, relationships, togetherness, friendship, and companionship. They are more inclined toward supportive roles than being in the spotlight.

Heart's Desire Number Three

Individuals with this number strive for authentic self-expression in this lifetime. They seek to flow with life, enjoy, have fun, and express themselves artistically through activities like playing music, writing, speaking, performing, writing poetry, and engaging in architecture, sculpting, and cosmetics. This heart's desire revolves around craving sensory pleasure and creative self-expression in various aspects of life.

Heart's Desire Number Four

The heart's desire of individuals with this number is to establish stability, order, and security, grounding themselves in material life by developing roots and anchors for a firm grasp on the present. Their aspirations include a desire for family life and a supportive framework, the fulfillment of material goals, and a life built upon system and structure. They also aspire to be reliable, responsible, loyal, self-disciplined, and strong, serving as dependable figures for others.

Heart's Desire Number Five

The heart's desire for individuals with this number is to experience freedom, explore new things, and take risks. They find joy in diversity, freedom, movement, traveling, and connecting with new people while embarking on different and diverse adventures. The essence of their heart's desire is the ability to be constantly in motion and to visit exotic, faraway places.

Heart's Desire Number Six

Individuals with this number long for love, romance, rest, peace of mind, and a warm, loving, and harmonious home and family life. They seek relationships based on reciprocity and intimacy, embodying the spirit of togetherness and mutual support. Their heart desires to create a nurturing environment, help others through nurturing, healing, or counseling, establish a deep emotional connection with a soulmate, and dedicate their lives to loving and caring for their loved ones.

Heart's Desire Number Seven

Individuals with this number aim to establish a connection with their spirit and higher self in this life. They aspire to deeply understand life, acquire wisdom and knowledge, and experience profound insights. Their heart's desire is driven by the quest for truth, a deep understanding of life's mysteries, the expression of inner wisdom, and the comprehension of the unseen and profound. These individuals often value their privacy, being introspective and reflective, and spending time alone to contemplate life's deeper questions.

Heart's Desire Number Eight

For individuals with this heart's desire, the focus is on experiencing power, strength, wealth, success, and, importantly, material comfort and self-gratification in this life. They strive to showcase their skills, demonstrate their talents, engage in significant projects, and earn substantial rewards. Ambitious and goal-oriented, they have a strong desire for success and material abundance. To fulfill their heart's desire, they are often willing to work tirelessly, sometimes expressing frustration over the sacrifices made in pursuit of their goals.

Heart's Desire Number Nine

Heart Desire Number Nine radiates exceptionally high energy, which often prevents those bearing this number from fully grasping their heart's desires due to its supremely high vibrational frequency. This frequency directs individuals toward a path that is rich in spiritual and humanitarian pursuits but can also obscure personal desires beneath layers of intense energy.

Those with this number seek a meaningful and authentic life, aiming to understand the deeper meanings of life and the universe and to achieve personal and social growth and enlightenment. This heart's desire manifests as a quest for freedom, exploration, and expanding consciousness, alongside a selfless commitment to bettering the welfare of others through volunteering and humanitarian deeds. People with this number have a strong inner desire to connect with a higher purpose, aspiring to make a positive impact in the world.

However, when they are not conscious of these elevated spiritual goals, they may encounter inner turmoil, a sense of restlessness stemming from their soul's quest for more profound fulfillment and purpose.

3. Identification of Personality and Outer Appearance

The subsequent step, following the unveiling of the "inner content"—which is often hidden from others and sometimes even from the individual—is to discern the "outer appearance." This concept pertains to the "external you," encompassing the persona and characteristics that an individual comfortably displays to the world. Essentially, it delves into how others perceive individuals based on the qualities they openly exhibit in societal interactions.

Each personality number is associated with distinct traits and characteristics, shedding light on the image a person projects, their public persona, their engagements with others, and the overall impression they leave on people.

Consonant letters imbue an individual's character with strength, structure, and stability. Every consonant in a name is linked to specific traits and characteristics. By translating these letters into numerical values, we are able to quantify and analyze this energy, providing insights into a person's personality and the outward image they typically project.

To reveal the outer appearance or personality, it is necessary to convert the consonant letters in your name into numbers. These numbers are then combined into a single digit, as demonstrated in the examples below.

For example, the name **Alina** contains two consonant letters: L and N. When these two consonants are combined, they project an outer image symbolized by the simple gematria value of eight: L + N = 3 + 5 = 8. Thus, Alina's personality is represented by the number eight.

The name **Judy** contains two consonant letters: J and D. When these two consonants are combined, they project an outer image symbolized by the simple gematria value of one: J + D = 3 + 7 = 10; 1 + 0 = 1. Therefore, Judy's personality is represented by the number one.

Now that you have the numerical value representing your personality or your "external you," you can read the abbreviated explanation concerning it.

Consonant Number One

A person with this personality number is characterized as independent, pleasant, unique, original, determined, assertive, courageous, confident, and ambitious. They project an image of someone who is clear about their desires and expectations from themselves and others. They value being perceived as authoritative and powerful figures, embodying impressive leadership qualities and garnering respect for their organizational and managerial skills. This includes the capability to lead both people and projects effectively.

Individuals with this personality number have a preference for leadership roles over background positions.

Consonant Number Two

A person with this personality number displays sociability, friendliness, pleasantness, kindness, serenity, reliability, and magnetic attraction. They project an image of someone who can be trusted and relied upon, both in times of trouble and in general. They tend to be kind and caring and are often good listeners who can understand the emotions and needs of others. It is important for them to feel loved and appreciated and let others know they can be trusted and relied on.

People with this personality number generally prefer to be behind the scenes rather than in a leadership position. When there is a tense atmosphere, it negatively affects them and throws them off balance.

Consonant Number Three

A person with this personality number displays a high level of lightheartedness, sociability, friendliness, creativity, and, most importantly, a high level of optimism. People with this personality number tend to be optimistic, social, outgoing, and have a good sense of humor. Others perceive them as a "relentless optimist." They are often charming and persuasive, able to use their words and charisma to influence others, and are generally well-liked with a large circle of friends.

They are beloved and engaging individuals who are enjoyable to be around. They tend to spread love and sympathy to those around them and inspire others.

Consonant Number Four

A person with this personality number displays a high level of seriousness, practicality, conservatism, and responsibility. It is important for them to convey punctuality, reliability, diligence, and purposefulness and to be perceived by others as serious, grounded, disciplined, and practical individuals who can be trusted.

Those with this personality number are seen as reserved, hardworking, and rigorous, someone who pays attention to details, which is evident in their attire as well. They demonstrate great dedication and concern toward others, whether it's within their family, work, or community.

Consonant Number Five

A person with this personality number exhibits charm, high charisma, versatility, and a love for adventure. They are witty, persuasive, and possess good communication skills. With an optimistic and vibrant personality, they emphasize the importance of freedom—freedom of speech, action, and dress. People with this personality number tend to be curious, energetic, sociable, charismatic, and entertaining, with a love for new experiences and meeting new people.

They have a zest for life, particularly indulging in sensory experiences, which may lead to a tendency to engage in various addictions such as sex, drugs, and alcohol. These individuals often prioritize quantity over quality.

Consonant Number Six

A person with this personality number exhibits sympathy, kindness, calmness, attentiveness, personal responsibility, understanding, heartfelt generosity, fairness, and protection. They are willing to help, reliable, and often seen as caretakers, healers, and protectors. They are empathetic and have a natural ability to make others feel comfortable and safe in their presence.

Individuals with this personality number are often family-oriented and possess a strong sense of responsibility toward their loved ones. They are also known for their strong sense of justice and desire to create harmony and balance in their environments. People with these qualities tend to attract two types of individuals into their lives: those in need of support, security, stability, and protection or those who may take advantage of their open hearts and willingness to help.

Consonant Number Seven

A person with this personality number displays friendliness, pleasantness, wisdom, and an attraction to mysticism in all its forms but also to a certain type of secrecy and obscurity. They are perceived as analytical and intelligent individuals, wise, conservative, and introverted, with strong intuition and a natural inclination toward understanding the mysteries of life.

People with this consonant number may appear as reserved or even aloof to others, as loners or outsiders, even outside the norm, but this is often because they are constantly engaged in deep thought and contemplation.

Consonant Number Eight

A person with this personality number displays confidence, friendliness, and optimism but primarily strength, authority, power, and success. They are individuals who have an innate inclination toward power, control, and authority and enjoy making an impressive impression. They project to others a presence of status and prestige. This impression is often expressed through attention to detail in their attire, conveying luxury with items such as briefcases, ties, expensive watches, keychains, cufflinks, and other similar accessories.

Consonant Number Nine

A person with this personality number displays gracefulness, elegance, friendliness, sociability, loveliness, kindness, generosity, and charisma. They are often empathetic and caring toward others and are driven by a desire to make the world a better place.

They are individuals who value space and freedom and have a deep desire to understand the mysteries of the universe and to use their talents to make a positive impact on the world.

4. Understanding the Basic Nature and Personal Temperament

Now that you have identified your inner wishes, aspirations, and the outer image you tend to project to those around you, the next essential step is to delve into another significant factor: your basic nature and personal temperament. This analysis will provide you with a profound understanding of whether your basic nature is intuitive (represented by fire), emotional (water), analytical (air), or practical (earth).

To achieve this, it is first necessary to identify the elements from which your name is composed based on the following examples:

Let us take the name **Gibran** as an example. This name contains three air letters (G, R, and A), two earth letters (B and I), and one water letter (N). Thus, the analysis reveals that Gibran possesses an analytical, emotional, and practical nature, with his fundamental inclination leaning toward the intellectual domain (air element).

Diagram108: Letters and Elements

Another example is the name **Shlomi.** This name incorporates a letter associated with the fire element (SH), a letter linked to the air element (L), two letters representing the earth element (O and I), and one letter connected to the water element (M). This name presents a unique combination of all four elements. Therefore, it reveals that Shlomi embodies the qualities of these elements within his name: the intuitive and entrepreneurial spirit of fire, the emotional depth of water, the practicality and grounded nature of earth, and the intellectual prowess associated with air.

Now that you have identified the elements from which your name is composed read the brief explanation about the basic nature that your name reveals.

Fire People

Those aligned with the element of fire exude a passionate and dynamic nature, often driven by intuition and creativity. They possess an innate ability to lead and inspire, radiating warmth and enthusiasm that ignites the spirits of those around them. Determined and independent, they carry the fire of creativity within them. Warm and courageous, they allow their inner fire to guide them, making them visionary people who can perceive their path through their intuition, which acts as their third eye.

The positive and constructive aspects of fire people lie in their ability to transform fear into a driving force, their relentless pursuit of goals, their capacity to achieve great heights, and their willingness to take responsibility and lead. However, the inhibiting aspects of fire include impatience, impulsive desires, a tendency to be often self-centered, and a propensity to act from an unconscious and impulsive place.

Air People

Individuals dominated by the element of air showcase an analytical and intellectual temperament. They are characterized by their curiosity, quick wit, and rational thinking, excelling in tasks that demand problem-solving and strategic planning.

They tend to be independent, connected to their intellect, and driven by logic and analytical analysis. Intellectual and capable, they can elevate the spirit of the world through the development of advanced new theories. The positive and constructive aspect of air people is their aspiration for ideals and absolute truth, alongside the desire to understand themselves and the surrounding world. The unbalanced aspect of air is overthinking, where the same thoughts keep spinning in the mind.

Water People

Individuals dominated by the element of water tend to be deeply in touch with their emotions and possess remarkable empathy. They are nurturing and highly attuned to the feelings of others, making them natural caregivers and devoted friends. These individuals exhibit emotional intelligence, sensitivity, internal strength, and the ability to sense the emotions of those around them. The positive and constructive aspect of water people is their propensity for understanding, empathy, and nurturing.

However, the inhibiting aspects of the water element include vulnerability, a constant need for reassurance, difficulty in maintaining emotional stability, a tendency toward emotional dependence, fluctuating moods, and emotional overflows.

Earth People

Individuals dominated by the element of the earth represent practicality and groundedness. Those influenced by this element tend to be reliable, patient, and methodical in their approach to life. They excel at creating stability and security, making them excellent organizers and providers. They are pragmatic, calculated, cautious, and balanced and approach life proactively and responsibly, relying greatly on a safe and stable framework in both their personal and professional lives. The positive and constructive aspect of earth people is their practicality and purposeful action.

The unbalanced aspects of the earth element include rigidity, stubbornness, resistance to change, a preference for material comfort, and a tendency to stick to routines. They also desire safe, cautious, and measured progress, taking steps one at a time.

Identifying Personal Temperament

One aspect that enhances our understanding of the essence of a person's temperament is the presence of an excess element in their name. When a specific element is repeated excessively within a person's name, it reveals two important aspects: First, it highlights the individual's inherent temperament, and second, it indicates the energy that tends to drive them, which can sometimes also cause inner restlessness.

Let us take the name **Aliza:** A + L + I + Z + A = Air + Air + Earth + Air + Air.

As you can see, the name Aliza comprises four letters representing the air element (A, L, Z, A) and one representing the earth element (I). The prominence of the air element indicates a dominant influence of its energies. Therefore, Aliza's fundamental temperament is represented by air, signifying traits such as thoughtfulness and analytical reasoning, and by earth, signifying traits such as practicality and reliability.

However, Aliza's name lacks the elements of water and fire. Water embodies qualities that foster emotional depth and sensitivity, enhancing connections with others on an emotional level. Fire connects a person to passion, vitality, and inner motivation, fueling drive and ambition. The absence of water and fire in Aliza's name might suggest a potential imbalance in her energy makeup, possibly lacking in emotional depth and inner motivation. Balancing these elements can lead to a more holistic and well-rounded personality, encompassing both intellectual capacities and emotional intelligence.

Stability of the Personality

Another aspect that arises here concerns the stability of the personality, a topic which I have expanded upon in Chapter Six.

Upon examining the Hebrew name Dudu (דודו), it is observed that all letters stand on one leg, suggesting difficulties in maintaining stability and equilibrium. Similarly, in the Hebrew name Aliza (עליזה), four out of the five letters stand on one leg, indicating a propensity toward losing stability quickly.

It is important to emphasize that the topic of elements is broad and complex. Consequently, in this book, I provide only a foundational explanation to aid in understanding.

Diagram 109: The Names Dudu and Aliza in Hebrew

5. The Level of Openness and Closeness

Another valuable insight we uncover from a person's name is their predisposition toward openness or closed-mindedness in relation to changes, processes, people, situations, and life events. This aspect is significant, as the trait of openness plays a crucial role in one's life, enabling individuals to forge profound emotional bonds, enhancing their overall satisfaction and fulfillment, and promoting mental and physical well-being. If someone's name analysis indicates a tendency toward closed-mindedness, awareness of this trait allows them to cultivate greater openness through learning and growth.

To determine the predisposition toward openness or closeness, we must examine each letter in the name.

For example, let us consider the name **Bob** (בוב). The Hebrew name Bob contains two letters that are closed from three sides, B (Bet), and one letter that is half open and closed from two sides, O (Vav). Thus, the name suggests that Bob's natural tendency leans toward closeness.

Another example is the name **Ain** (אין). The name Ain contains one completely open letter, Alef, and two letters that are partly open, I (Yod) and N (Final Nun). Therefore, the name suggests that Ain's natural tendency is toward openness.

A detailed explanation of open and closed letters is provided in Chapter Two.

6. The Measure of Compassion, Mercy and Judgment

Once the assessment of a person's degree of openness and closeness is complete, it becomes crucial to gauge their level of compassion. This examination will unveil their overall approach to life, interactions with others, and responses to various situations.

By conducting this analysis, we can discern whether individuals naturally lean toward forgiveness and compassion, embracing a tendency to let go and release negativity, or if they tend to accumulate anger and resentment, habitually judging and blaming others while nurturing grudges. To fulfill this objective, we examine each letter in the name.

Diagram 110: Two Forms of the Letter N

נ   ן

As mentioned previously, in the Hebrew language, some letters appear in two different groups due to their position in a name or word. For instance, the letter N demonstrates this phenomenon.

When it is written at the beginning or in the middle of a name, it indicates the measure of mercy. Conversely, when the letter N appears at the end of a name, it signifies the degree of absolute judgment. An example of this can be seen in the name Ronen (רונן), where the letter N embodies both the energy of mercy and the energy of absolute judgment.

For example, let us consider the name Din (דין). The name comprises letters associated with judgment (D), mercy (I) and absolute judgment (final N). The name lacks letters that signify kindness and compassion. As a result, the name inherently suggests a natural inclination toward judgment, indicating a difficulty in forgiving and letting go.

Another example is the name Anna. The name includes two letters associated with the measure of compassion (AA) and two letters associated with the measure of mercy (NN). Therefore, the name inherently suggests a natural inclination toward kindness, compassion, and mercy.

The details about the letters of compassion and judgment are mentioned in Chapter Six.

7. Identifying the Weaknesses

One of the additional important aspects of analyzing a person's name is identifying missing energy in their daily functioning. The absence of a specific element in a person's name signifies a particular weakness and a lack of certain qualities in their everyday life.

For example, a lack of the water element points to difficulty in connecting with the emotional world. A lack of the fire element indicates a deficiency in internal drive, passion, and initiative. A lack of the air element suggests a shortfall in awareness, akin to a blind spot, as well as in analytical and logical thinking. A lack of the earth element signifies impatience, practical difficulties, and a struggle to be grounded and fully present in the moment.

To identify the energy lacking in a person's daily functioning, we analyze the elements in their name to determine which are absent.

Let us consider the name **Manana**. This name contains three letters (M, N, and N) associated with the water element and three letters (A, A, A) associated with the air element. The name lacks both the earth and fire elements. The absence of these elements might suggest a potential imbalance in the individual's energy composition, potentially lacking in practicality, patience, grounding, and inner drive. Balancing these elements can foster grounding and practicality, leading to a more harmonious and complete expression of energy.

8. Identifying the Unique Present

As mentioned in Chapter Three, according to Kabbalistic teachings, each soul descends into the present incarnation, bearing a distinctive gift destined to enrich humanity. To unveil this special endowment, we must delve into the individual "soul root" (שורש נשמה).

This is achieved by calculating their soul root, considering their first name (birth name) along with their mother's first name (birth name). Through this process, the inherent gift that the soul carries can be revealed.

These calculations are performed using both small and large Hebrew gematria. The tables for both are included in the appendix.

Small gematria represents the reduced numerical value of each letter. For example, the letters Alef, Yod and Q = 1, the letters Bet, Caf and Resh = 2, the letters Gimel, Lamed and Shin = 3, and so on.

Large gematria represent the full numerical value of each letter. For example, the letter Alef = 1, Yod = 10, the letter Qof = 100, the letter Bet = 2, the letter Caf = 20, the letter Resh = 200, and so on.

The calculation is performed as follows:

Step 1: Calculate the person's first name in full gematria.

Step 2: Calculate the mother's first name in full gematria.

Step 3: Add the two names together.

Step 4: Divide the total sum obtained from the two names by twelve.

Step 5: Take the result obtained after the division, without the remainder, and multiply it by twelve.

Step 6: Take the number obtained by adding the two names in Step 3 and subtract the number obtained in Step 4.

For example, let us take the Hebrew name, Yitzhak son of Sarah (יצחק בן שרה).

1. **Step A:** Yitzhak (יצחק = 208)
2. **Step B:** Sarah (שרה = 505)
3. **Step C:** 208 + 505 = 713
4. **Step D:** Divide 713 by 12 = 59.416666
5. **Step E:** Take the result without the remainder, which is 59, and multiply it by 12 = 708
6. **Step F:** Take the value of Step C, which is 713, and subtract the value from Step E, which is 708 = 5 (713-708). Therefore, the soul root of Yitzhak, the son of Sarah, is five.

Kabbalistic teachings describe twelve soul groups. The source of all of us is the divine light, the infinite light that fills all of existence. We come from the infinite, and to it, we shall return. We descend into the here-and-now moment, to the earthly realm, through a process of "detachment" (ניתוק).

This detachment involves disconnecting from the unity of the infinite light to descend to the physical plane as an "infant" (תינוק) to perform rectification and return. This concept is concisely explained in the Hebrew word for "detachment" (ניתוק), which, when its letters are reversed, equals "infant" (תינוק) and "rectification" (תיקון)—the same letters in different arrangements. The rectification begins at the time of detachment—at the time of leaving the womb.

When we detach from the source and descend into the physical material world, we become enveloped in layers that conceal the divine light and our spiritual potential. The Kabbalistic term "soul root" refers to different aspects of the divine self, with each soul root representing spiritual qualities that form the basis of the human experience. Thus, the twelve soul roots signify twelve soul archetypes from which all human souls emanate.

By identifying their soul root, individuals can gain a deeper understanding of their spiritual potential, aligning their actions and intentions with their higher self or divine self.

Here is the breakdown of the twelve soul roots.

Soul Root Number One – The Pioneer Soul

Individuals with soul root number one are trailblazers responsible for initiating projects and introducing new methods to the universe. Those with this soul root have come to teach that love equals trust and that actions performed from a place of unconditional love bring success to any project. The lesson they are here to learn in this incarnation is the value of delaying gratification.

Soul Root Number Two – The Gatheringand Preserving Soul

Individuals with soul root number two are highly spiritual people connected to cosmic knowledge. They are tasked with gathering, preserving, and organizing knowledge in the universe in its most practical and functional form. These individuals are characterized by perseverance, talent, and skill in collecting and organizing knowledge uniquely. Those with this soul root teach that love equals patience and perseverance. The lesson they are here to learn is to release emotions rather than accumulate them internally.

Soul Root Number Three – The Communicating Souls

Individuals with soul root number three are highly curious and capable of understanding things intellectually. They are responsible for the communication and exchange of knowledge. Those with this soul root have come to teach that love equals awareness. The lesson they are here to learn is that love encompasses not only intellect but also emotion.

Soul Root Number Four – The Caring Soul

Individuals with soul root number four are highly emotional and sensitive. They are the "mother" of everyone. Those with this soul root have come to teach that love equals nurturing. They are souls who came to impart the essence of true care. The lesson they are here to learn is not to overwhelm them with excessive love and nurturing.

Soul Root Number Five – The Royal Soul

Individuals with soul root number five are charismatic. They are here to teach that love equals enthusiasm and open-heartedness.

The lesson they are here to learn is the importance of humility and meekness.

Soul Root Number Six – The Serving Soul

Individuals with soul root number six are dedicated to purity, spiritual refinement, and selfless service. They have come to teach that love equals purity. The lesson they are here to learn is the importance of releasing control.

Soul Root Number Seven – The Balancing Soul

Individuals with soul root number seven focus on balancing opposing forces and creating harmony in the universe. They have come to teach us that love equals balance and encompasses both inner and outer harmony. The lesson for them in this incarnation is acceptance—to accept things as they are.

Soul Root Number Eight – The Transformative Soul

Individuals with soul root number eight are passionate and driven, tasked with the alchemy of the universe. They are seekers of understanding the depths beneath the surface, with the potential to be great psychologists and mystics. These souls are responsible for transformational processes and deep change. They have come to teach us that love equals passion and zeal. The lesson for them is that love also embodies profound transformation, enabling them to bring the gift of alchemy and transformation to the world.

Soul Root Number Nine – The Philosophical Soul

Individuals with soul root number nine are philosophical, searching for the meaning of life and responsible for upholding truth in the universe. They have come to teach us that love equals spiritual truth or absolute truth. The lesson they are here to learn is the value of grounding and practicality.

Soul Root Number Ten – The Ambitious Soul

Individuals with soul root number ten are focused on laws and achievements in the universe. Determined and goal-oriented, they are concentrated on success and accomplishments, descending into this world to fully realize themselves and reach the pinnacle of success and fulfillment in their earthly lives. They have come to teach us that love equals wisdom, emphasizing that true wisdom requires goal orientation and dedication. The lesson they are here to learn is personal responsibility, including the ability to release and let go.

Soul Root Number Eleven – The Information Distributor Soul

Individuals with soul root number eleven are tasked with disseminating knowledge in the universe for the purpose of promoting social justice. They have come to teach us that love equals unity. The lesson they are here to learn in this incarnation involves avoiding arrogance and establishing heartfelt connections with others rather than relying solely on intellectual connections.

Soul Root Number Twelve – The Compassionate Soul

Individuals with soul root number twelve are here to teach us that love equals wholeness and the merging or communication with all aspects of life: minerals, plants, animals, and humans. Merging signifies a deep connection. The lesson for them in this incarnation is the acceptance of things and situations and fostering compassion, especially toward themselves.

Final Thoughts on the Journey of Name Analysis

As we conclude our exploration of name analysis, I hope this journey has unveiled new insights about your name that you can embrace as valuable tools for personal growth.

It is important to note that if someone has changed their name during their lifetime and now goes by a different name, they should analyze their current name after completing the analysis of their birth name, following all eight steps previously outlined.

Furthermore, it is crucial to remember that these guidelines provide a basic understanding of a person's name analysis but not a complete and comprehensive one. For a thorough, complete, and professional analysis, there are many additional parameters that, due to space limitations, I will expand upon in future books.

CHAPTER 10

Welcome to Your New Lives

If you are reading these lines, I want to congratulate you. You've made it! You have already made significant progress on your journey. This journey, undoubtedly fascinating, life-changing, and impactful, is also profound and sometimes challenging to understand. I assure you that as long as you continue to contemplate and delve into the materials, they will become clearer and provide you with new insights each time. This is the amazing aspect of our creation, where development is infinite, and there are always more depths and realizations that unfold within us as we continue our process of growth, development, and ascension.

The time we live in is special. In the year 2012, we entered a unique period in human history. On December 21, 2021, planetary changes began occurring in the universe, and our planet Earth entered a new era where the gates of heaven were open, allowing abundant light to enter. This light accelerates the opening of our hearts and helps awaken our emotional and mental bodies. It is a high-frequency light that awakens all karmic, personal, and collective lessons from our past lives—including those related to emotional wounds—and grants us the power to heal these wounds. This light enables our bodies to undergo molecular and physiological changes that align our biology with the emerging divine energies intensifying on our planet Earth.

A vibrating and purified body allows high frequencies of light to descend into it, intensifying deep healing processes and awakening the **remembrance**[1] of the divine light within. This remembrance brings with it a renewed connection to our higher aspects, such as the "I am" presence. All we need to do is open ourselves to this new learning, develop high self-awareness, deeply understand the different aspects of our personality, and allow these light-informing frequencies to generate changes within us.

There are no shortcuts in life. The foundation for personal and spiritual growth begins with self-awareness. To fulfill our soul's desire, we must first acquaint ourselves with our complete personality and its psycho-physiological structure. The responsibility for our lives is in our hands; whether we choose to develop our consciousness or remain in ignorance is up to us.

If you feel the energy of stagnation in your personal or professional life, or if you are discouraged by the current state of the world, please let the information presented in this book serve as inspiration and a source of hope for you. Allow the words you have read and the Hebrew letters to guide you on a journey of growth and personal empowerment.

I hope this information awakens in you a higher self-awareness and a clear understanding of your authentic nature. I hope it helps you become familiar with your "soul's script" and accelerates your personal and spiritual development, thus assisting you in breaking free from the survival loop. Above all, I hope the words written in this book ignite in you the courage and willingness to embrace change, enabling you to create a world of love, compassion, awareness, and abundance for yourself, your loved ones, and those dear to you.

---

[1]   Remembrance is a process through which a person, via various spiritual practices, recollects their true nature and divine essence. This remembrance enables one to shed self-imposed limitations and the distractions of the material world, thereby reconnecting with their authentic essence. These spiritual practices include, among others, meditation, yoga, conscious breathing, mindfulness, connection with nature, and music. Music, in particular, serves as an effective pathway because it has the power to bypass our rational consciousness, directly connect us to our hearts, and facilitate access to deeper levels of awareness and recognition.

Now that you are aware of the powers and strengths inherent in the letters of your name, you can transform your earthly journey into a magnificent voyage of limitless choices, self-evolution, and full self-fulfillment. You have every right to do so.

We are at a point in human history where we no longer need religious figures, political leaders, or academic authorities as our guides. There is no need for an external "Messiah." We are the ones we have been waiting for. The Messianic aspect, the consciousness of the Messiah, resides within each of us. The path to manifesting this Messianic potential depends on our free choice.

Today, sacred knowledge is becoming increasingly accessible with each passing day. All we need to do is open our hearts to it. These teachings aim to remind us of what we have forgotten, the lessons imparted by great teachers like Moses, Jesus, and Buddha. As long as we do not awaken the remembrance of our Messianic essence, the consciousness of unity within us, we will continue to be slaves to the system and the divisive, conditional social structures designed to control us.

Before we part, I would like to mention that this book serves as an "introduction," providing beginner readers with an understanding of the structure of the Hebrew language and the energetic power of each Hebrew letter.

Despite being an introductory book, it provides insights into important spiritual issues such as awakened consciousness and dormant consciousness, karma, the power of the human mind, remembrance, lost soul particles, soul contracts, and more. It connects these spiritual and philosophical concepts to the Hebrew letters.

My next books will expand our understanding of the power of Hebrew letters by addressing the biological, psychological, and physiological processes associated with them. They will deepen our understanding of the structure of the human soul and explore how we think, our thinking styles, the relationships we aspire to and attract, and our reactions in different life situations. They will reveal our fears through the letters of our names and the defense mechanisms we unconsciously employ.

Furthermore, the books will establish connections between the letters and sacred geometry, as well as between spiritual and philosophical concepts such as recognition, akashic records, the wounded healer, generational karma, and more. They will also provide insights into psychological concepts like containing, holding, the authentic self, the false self, energetic cords, emotional regulation, internal and external motivation, and much more.

The motivation to bring this information to light stems from a strong desire to share it widely, to offer my gift to the world, and to assist humanity in its blessed awakening process. I believe that the insights contained in this book and those that will follow have the potential to cultivate love and great compassion in readers, both for themselves and for those around them, thus enabling active participation in building a new world based on love, compassion, and kindness.

Blessings upon you.
May all beings of the divine creation be happy.

With love and humility,
Angela Robyinson

SOURCES AND BIBLIOGRAPHY

1. Idel, Moshe. *Prophetic Kabbalah Chapters*. Jerusalem: 1990.
2. Epstein, Abraham. *The Antiquities of the Jews*. Jerusalem, 1957.
3. Kaplan, Aryeh. *Meditation and Kabbalah*. Jerusalem, 1995.
4. Kaplan, Aryeh. *Sefer Yetzirah: The Book of Creation with Commentary and Explanation*. Yedioth Ahronoth, 2011.
5. Ben Shlomo, Yosef. *The Teachings of Godliness by Rabbi Moshe Cordovero*. Jerusalem, 1964.
6. Gottlieb, Ephraim. *Studies in Kabbalistic Literature*. Tel Aviv, 1986.
7. Scholem, Gershom. *Basic Principles in the Understanding of Kabbalah and Its Symbols*. Jerusalem, 1976.
8. Scholem, Gershom. *The Origins of Kabbalah*. Jerusalem, 1947.
9. Ibn Tibbon, Dunash. *Commentary on Sefer Yetzirah*. London, 1902.
10. Rabbi Yosef Kapach. *The Guide for the Perplexed by Maimonides*. Mosad Harav Kook, 1972.
11. Luzzatto, Moshe Chaim. *Path of the Just*. Orot Chaim, 1987.
12. Wertheimer, *Letters of Rabbi Akiva*. Jerusalem, 1914.
13. Zhitomir, *Sayings of the Righteous*. 1900.
14. Ashlag, Yehuda. *The Book of Introductions*. Kol Yehuda, 1987.
15. Liebes, Yehuda. *The Theory of Creation in the Book of Creation*. Schocken, 2000.
16. Aviv, Yosef. *The Kabbalah of the Ari*. Ben Zvi Institute, 2008.
17. Naveh, Yosef. *Letters and Their History*. Keter, 1979.
18. Tishby, Isaiah. *Studies in Kabbalah, Jewish Philosophy, and Ethical Literature*. Jerusalem, 1986.

19. Leibowitz, Yeshayahu. *Conversations on the Path of the Just by the Ramchal*. 1997.

20. *The Holy Scriptures*.

21. Goodman, Linda. *Sun Signs*. Erez, 1979.

22. Margaliot, Reuven (Edition). *The Zohar*. Jerusalem 1975.

23. Margaliot, Reuven (Edition). *Sefer HaBahir*. Jerusalem, 1975.

24. Helzer, Michael. *The Tradition of Hebrew Names Outside the Bible*. University of Haifa, 1978.

25. Ramchal Institute. *The Way of the Wisdom of Truth by the Ramchal*.

26. Shapiro, Nathan. *Megaleh Amukot*. Krakow, 1637.

27. Hawking, Stephen. *A Brief History of Time: From the Big Bang to Black Holes*. Tel Aviv, 1990.

28. Saadia Gaon. *Commentary on Sefer Yetzirah*, translated by Yosef Kapach. Jerusalem, 1972.

29. *Sefer Yetzirah*. Jerusalem Edition, 1965.

30. *Sefer Yetzirah*. Mantua, 1562.

31. Nachmanides. *Commentary on Sefer Yetzirah*.

32. Cassuto, Moshe David. *The Book of Genesis and Its Structure*. Magnes Press, Hebrew University, 1990.

33. Zondag, Karen Hamaker. *Astro-Psychology*. Mixam, 1997.

34. Rabbi Abraham Abulafia. *Gan Na'ul*. Grimoire website.

35. Rabbi Chaim Vital. *Sefer HaGilgulim*. Przemyśl, 1875.

36. Rabbi Chaim Vital. *Etz Chaim*. Mekor Chaim, 1989.

37. Rabbi Chaim Vital. *Etz Chaim*. Warsaw, 1891.

38. Rabbi Chaim Vital. *Shaar HaGilgulim*. Jerusalem, 1912.

39. Rabbi Chaim Vital. *Lev David*. Livorno, 1789.

40. Rabbi Chaim Vital. *Etz HaDa'at Tov*. Zhovkva, 1871.

41. Rabbi Judah Halevi. *The Kuzari*, translated by Rabbi Judah ibn Samuel. Tel Aviv, 1973.

42. Rabbi Menachem Azariah of Fano. *Asarah Ma'amarot*. 1597.

43. Rabbi Menachem Recanati. *Biur HaTorah*. Jerusalem, 1961.

44. Rabbi Moshe de Leon. *The Wise Soul*. Basel, 1608.

45. Rabbi Moshe Cordovero. *Pardes Rimonim*. Jerusalem, 1960.

46. Rabbi Moshe Cordovero. *Shi'ur Qomah*. Warsaw, 1883.

47. Rabbi Saadia Gaon. *Emunot ve-Deot*. Slutsk, 1984.

48. Rabbeinu Bahya ibn Paquda. *Duties of the Heart*, translated by Yosef Kapach. 1973.

49. Cohen, Rimona. *The Language of the Stars*. Graphaur-Deptal, 1995.

50. Rumi, Jalal ad-Din. *The Orchard*. Translated by Gil Ron Shama. Inspiration House: One Horn Publishing, 2022.

51. Rumi, Jalal ad-Din. *The Well*. Translated by Gil Ron Shama. Inspiration House: One Horn Publishing, 2021.

52. Rumi, Jalal ad-Din. *The Dance of Love for God*. Inspiration House: One Horn Publishing, 2012.

53. Rumi, Jalal ad-Din. *The Divan - Collection of Shams Tabrizi's Poems*. Translated by Alexander Feigin. Little World / One Horn Publishing, 2005.

54. Rumi, Jalal ad-Din. *One Song*. Translated from English by Gil Ron Shama and Coleman Barks. Or Yehuda: Kinneret-Zmora-Bitan, Dvir, 2007.

55. Hafiz. *I Heard God Laughing: Selections of Soul Poetry by the Great Sufi Poet*. Original translation by Daniel Ladinsky, Hebrew by Nimrod Borosh. Holon: Orion, 2011.

56. Selected poems from the Divan-e Shams-e Tabrizi, by Jalaluddin Rumi, Reynold Alleyne Nicholson, Ibex Publishers, 2001

57. Kahlil Gibran, The Prophet, The Original 1923 Edition With Complete Illustrations, Amazon, 2023

58. The Love Poems of RUMI, translated by Nader Khalili, Wellfleet Press, 2020

59. Love Poems From God, Twelwe Sacret Voices from the East and West, Daniel Ladinsky, Penguin Books, 2002

60. The Essentials Rumi, translated by Coleman Barks with Reynold Nicholson, A.J. Arberry & John Moyne, Harper One, 1995

61. The Gift, Poems by Hafiz, translated by Daniel Ladindky, Penguin Compass, 1999

Electronic Versions:

1. https://www.sefaria.org/Sefer_Yetzirah_Gra_Version.1.1?ven=Sefer_Yetzirah_The_Book_of_Creation&vhe=Sefer_Yetzirah,_Warsaw_1884&lang=bi&with=all&lang2=en
2. https://www.sefaria.org/Sefer_Yetzirah_Gra_Version.1.3?ven=Sefer_Yetzirah_The_Book_of_Creation&vhe=Sefer_Yetzirah,_Warsaw_1884&lang=bi&lookup=with%20a%20singular%20covenant&with=Gra&lang2=en
3. https://www.yumpu.com/en/document/view/12305486/a-depth-of-beginning-colins-hermetic-kabbalah-page
4. https://www.abrahamicstudyhall.org/2021/12/05/sefer-yetzirah-the-book-of-creation-full-text-commentary/#Chapter_1
5. https://sophian.org/forum/viewtopic.php?t=206
6. https://ellimalki.wordpress.com/2020/09/09 /ספר-יצירה-סיפורו-של-היקום/
7. https://www.hayadan.org.il/lancet-221102
8. https://www.sefaria.org/Midrash_Tanchuma%2C_Vayakhel.1.1?lang=bi&with=all&lang2=en
9. https://humanists.uk/ceremonies/humanist-namings/
10. Cohen, Rimona. *Fundamentals and Methods in Astrology for Advanced Students.* Fischer, 1985.
11. Horodetzky, S.A. *Judaism of the Intellect and Judaism of the Emotion.* 1947.
12. *Shulchan Aruch of the Ari.* 1681.
13. Moshe Zacuto. *Roots of Names.* Jerusalem: [No publisher], 2009.
14. Sperling, Abraham Isaac. *The Reasons for the Customs.* Jerusalem, 1957.

APPENDIX

The diagrams following are designed to make the insights offered in this book accessible to English-speaking readers through the study of Hebrew letters. They draw parallels between the Hebrew and English alphabets, enabling you to uncover the hidden treasures within your name. This exploration taps into the ancient wisdom of Hebrew letters, allowing for a profound understanding without requiring prior knowledge of the Hebrew language.

A Comparison Between the Hebrew and the English Alphabet

The Hebrew alphabet does not have a direct one-to-one correspondence with the English alphabet. Some Hebrew letters can be represented in English in multiple ways, depending on pronunciation or the context of the word. The diagram below shows how Hebrew letters may be transliterated into English, illustrating the diversity in representation.

English Letter	Hebrew Letter
A	א
B	ב
C	כ
D	ד
E	א
F	פ
G	ג
H	ה
I	י
J	ג
K	ק, ח
L	ל
M	מ
N	נ
O	ו, ע
P	פ
Q	ק
R	ר
S	ס
T	ט, ת
U	ו
V	ו
W	ו
X	כ+ס
Y	י
Z	ז, צ

Hebrew to English Letter Correspondence

The below diagram presents the twenty-two Hebrew letters, their names, pronunciation, and corresponding letters in the English alphabet. The corresponding English letters may change depending on pronunciation.

Hebrew Letter	Hebrew Letter Name	Pronunciation of the Hebrew Letter	Corresponding English Letter (s)
א	ALEF	A-LEF	A, E
ב	BET	BHET, BET	B, V
ג	GIMEL	GHI-MEL, GI-MEL	G, J
ד	DALET	DHA-LET, DA-LET	D
ה	HEH	HEH	H, AH, EH
ו	VAV	VAV	V, W, O, U
ז	ZAYIN	ZA-YIN	Z
ח	KHET	KHET	KH, CH
ט	THET	THE-T, TE-T	TH, T
י	YOD	YOD	I, Y
כ	CAF	CA-F, CHA-F	C, X, CH, KH
ל	LAMED	LA-MED	L
מ	MEM	MEM	M
נ	NUN	NUN	N
ס	SAMECH	SA-MECH	S, C
ע	AHYIN	AH-YIN, A-YEEN	O, AE, AH, AY, EY
פ	PEH	PHEH, PEH	P, PH, F
צ	TZADI	TZA-DI, TSA-DI	Z, TZ, TS, CH, TCH
ק	QOF	QOF	Q, K
ר	RESH	RHESH, RESH	R
ש	SHIN	SHIN	SH, S
ת	TAV	THAV, TAV	T

Hebrew Letters and Their Essence and Meaning

The below diagram presents an overview of the Hebrew alphabet, detailing each letter's name, associated meanings, and the corresponding English letters that approximate its sound. Understanding these associations can provide deeper insight into the symbolic and phonetic connections between Hebrew and English.

Hebrew Letter	Hebrew Letter Name	Meaning or Essence of the Hebrew Letter	Corresponding English Letter(s)
א	ALEF	WONDER, LEADER, COMMANDER, CHAMPION, EXPERT, TAMING, THOUSAND	A, E
ב	BET	HOUSE, DWELLING PLACE, INSIDE, WITHIN, AMID	B, V
ג	GIMEL	CAMEL, RECOMPENSE, GIVER, PAY OFF, HELPED TO STOP A HABIT, GAVE VALUE, WEANING	G, J
ד	DALET	DOOR, PORTAL, PASSAGE, PULL OUT, MEAGER	D
ה	HEH	ECHO, RESONANCE, HALLWAY, THE	H, AH, EH
ו	VAV	HOOK, PIPE, AND	V, W, O, U
ז	ZAYIN	WEAPON, NURISHMENT	Z
ח	KHET	SIN, FEAR	KH, CH
ט	THET	CLEY, MUD, DIRT	TH, T
י	YOD	YODIN, ARM, HAND	I, Y

ך	CAF	SPOON, SCALE, PALM OF HAND	C, X, CH, KH
ל	LAMED	LEARNING, TEACHING, EDUCATING, GUIDING, COACHING, STAFF	L
מ	MEM	WATER, MOTHERHOOD	M
נ	NUN	FISH, SOUL, SPIRIT	N
ס	SAMECH	TRUST, SUPPORT, PROTECTION, COVER, SCREEN, MASK, DISGUISE	S, C
ע	AHYIN	EYE, OBSERVATION, EYESIGHT	O, AE, AH, AY, EY
פ	PEH	MOUTH, SPEECH, PRESENCE	P, PH, F
צ	TZADI	RIGHTEOUS, HUNT, HUNTER, HUNTING	Z, TZ, TS, CH, TCH
ק	QOF	MONKEY, IMITATION	Q, K
ר	RESH	HEAD, POVERTY, DESTITUTION	R
ש	SHIN	TOOTH	SH, S
ת	TAV	SIGN, SYMBOL, LANDMARK, LABEL, SEAL, MUSICAL NOTE	T

Groups of Hebrew Letters by Openness and Closeness

The diagram below categorizes the twenty-two Hebrew letters, along with the five final letters, based on their levels of openness and closeness and their corresponding letters in the English alphabet, as discussed in Chapter Six. The corresponding English letters may vary depending on pronunciation.

Group	Hebrew Letter Name	Hebrew Letter	Corresponding English Letter(s)
Group A: **Completely Open**	ALEF	א	A, E
Group B: **Completely Closed from All Sides**	SAMECH FINAL MEM	ס ם	S FINAL M
Group C: **Both Open and Closed from Two Sides**	GIMEL DALET HEH VAV ZAYIN YOD AHYIN TZADI RESH SHIN FINAL NUN FINAL CAF FINAL TZADI	ג ד ה ו ז י ע צ ר שׁ ן ך ץ	G, J D H V, W, U Z I, Y O TZ, TS R SH FINAL N FINAL CH, KH FINAL TCH
Group D: **Closed from Three Sides**	BET KHET THET CAF LAMED MEM NUN PEH QOF TAV FINAL PEH	ב ח ט כ ל מ נ פ ק ת ף	B KH, CH TH C, X L M N P, F Q, K T FINAL P, F

Hebrew Vowel Letters & Corresponding English Letter

The diagram below presents the Hebrew vowel letters and their corresponding letters in the English alphabet, as discussed in Chapter Two.

Hebrew Vowel Letter	Hebrew Vowel Letter Name	Corresponding English Letter (s)
א	ALEF	A, E
ה	HEH	H, AH
ו	VAV	V, O, U, W
י	YOD	I, Y

Hebrew Vowel Letters & Corresponding English Letter

The diagram below presents the Hebrew vowel letters and their corresponding letters in the English alphabet, as discussed in Chapter Two.

Hebrew Consonant Letter	Hebrew Consonant Letter Name	Corresponding English Letter (s)
ב	BET	B
ג	GIMEL	G, J
ד	DALET	D
ז	ZAYIN	Z
ח	KHET	KH, CH, H
ט	THET	TH
כ	CAF	C, X
ל	LAMED	L
מ	MEM	M
נ	NUN	N
ס	SAMECH	S, C
ע	AHYIN	O
פ	PEH	P, F
צ	TZADI	Z
ק	QOF	Q, K
ר	RESH	R
ש	SHIN	SH, S
ת	TAV	T

Hebrew Letters, Elements, & Corresponding English Letter

The diagram below presents the Hebrew letters, the elements associated with them, and their corresponding letters in the English alphabet, as discussed in Chapter Four. The corresponding letters may vary depending on pronunciation.

Element	Hebrew Letter	Hebrew Letters Name	Corresponding English Letters (s)
FIRE	ד	DALET	D
	ה	HEH	H
	ט	THET	TH
	כ	CAF	C, X
	ס	SAMECH	S
	ש	SHIN	SH
AIR	א	ALEF	A, E
	ג	GIMEL	G, J
	ז	ZAYIN	Z
	ל	LAMED	L
	צ	TZADI	Z, TZ
	ר	RESH	R
WATER	ח	KHET	KH
	מ	MEM	M
	נ	NUN	N
	ק	QOF	Q, K
	ת	TAV	T
EARTH	ב	BET	B
	ו	VAV	V, W, U
	י	YOD	I, Y
	ע	AHYIN	O
	פ	PEH	P, F

Soul, Rectification, and Outcome Letters:
Hebrew Letters & Their Corresponding English Counterparts

The diagram below categorizes the twenty-two Hebrew letters, along with the five final letters, into three groups: Soul Letters, Rectification Letters, and Outcome Letters. It provides their names, symbols, and corresponding English letters as discussed in Chapter Six. The corresponding English letters may vary depending on pronunciation.

Category	Hebrew Letter Name	Hebrew Letter	Corresponding English Letter(s)
Soul Letters	ALEF	א	A, E
	BET	ב	B
	GIMEL	ג	G, J
	DALET	ד	D
	HEH	ה	H
	VAV	ו	V, W, U
Rectification Letters	ZAYIN	ז	Z
	KHET	ח	KH
	THET	ט	TH
	YOD	י	I, Y
	CAF	כ	C, X
	LAMED	ל	L
	MEM	מ	M
Outcome Letters	NUN	נ	N
	SAMECH	ס	S
	AHYIN	ע	O
	PEH	פ	P, F
	TZADI	צ	TZ, TS
	QOF	ק	Q, K
	RESH	ר	R
	SHIN	ש	SH
	TAV	ת	T
	FINAL CAF	ך	FINAL CH
	FINAL MEM	ם	FINAL M
	FINAL NUN	ן	FINAL N
	FINAL PEH	ף	FINAL P, F
	FINAL TZADI	ץ	FINAL CH, TCH

The Degree of Kindness, Mercy, and Judgment Measure in Hebrew Letters & Their Corresponding English Letters

The diagram below categorizes the twenty-two Hebrew letters, along with the five final letters, by the levels of kindness, mercy and judgment associated with them, as well as their corresponding letters in the English alphabet, as discussed in Chapter Six. The corresponding English letters may vary depending on pronunciation

Degree of Kindness	Hebrew Letter Name	Hebrew Letter	Corresponding English Letter(s)
Compassion Letters	ALEF	א	A, E
	GIMEL	ג	G, J
	HEH	ה	H
Mercy Letters	ZAYIN	ז	Z
	KHET	ח	KH, CH
	THET	ט	TH
	YOD	י	I, Y
	LAMED	ל	L
	MEM	מ	M
	NUN	נ	N
Judgment Letters	DALET	ד	D
	VAV	ו	V, W, U
Combination of Mercy and Judgment Letters	BET	ב	B
	CAF	כ	C, X
	SAMECH	ס	S
	AHYIN	ע	O
Absolute Judgment Letters	PEH	פ	P, F
	TZADI	צ	TZ, TS
	QOF	ק	Q, K
	RESH	ר	R
	SHIN	ש	SH
	TAV	ת	T
	FINAL CAF	ך	FINAL CH, KH,
	FINAL MEM	ם	FINAL M
	FINAL NUN	ן	FINAL N
	FINAL PEH	ף	FINAL P, F
	FINAL TZADI	ץ	FINAL Z, CH, TCH

Hebrew Redemption Letters, Their Gematrical Values & Corresponding English Letters

The diagram below presents the final Hebrew letters, also known as "Sofit," and their corresponding letters in the English alphabet, as discussed in Chapter Six.

Hebrew Letter	Hebrew Letter Name	Gematrical Value	Corresponding English Letter
ך	FINAL CAF	500	CH, KH
ם	FINAL MEM	600	M
ן	FINAL NUN	700	N
ף	FINAL PEH	800	P, PH, F
ץ	FINAL TZADI	900	Z, TS, TZ, CH, TCH

Energetic Stability in Hebrew Letters & Their English Counterparts

The diagram below categorizes the twenty-two Hebrew letters, along with the five final letters, by the level of energetic stability associated with them and their corresponding letters in the English alphabet, as discussed in Chapter Six. The corresponding English letters may vary depending on pronunciation.

Degree of Energetic Stability	Hebrew Letter Name	Hebrew Letter Shape	Corresponding English Letter (s)
Letters with Stable Base	BET	ב	B
	CAF	כ	C, X
	NUN	נ	N
	PEH	פ	P, F
	TZADI	צ	TZ
	FINAL MEM	ם	FINAL M
Letters with Stable Legs	ALEF	א	A, E
	GIMEL	ג	G, J
	HEH	ה	H
	KHET	ח	KH, CH
	MEM	מ	M
	TAV	ת	T
Letters with Unstable Base	DALET	ד	D
	VAV	ו	V, W, U
	ZAYIN	ז	Z
	THET	ט	TH
	YOD	י	I, Y
	LAMED	ל	L
	SAMECH	ס	S
	AHYIN	ע	O
	QOF	ק	Q, K
	RESH	ר	R
	SHIN	ש	SH
	FINAL CAF	ך	FINAL CH, KH
	FINAL NUM	ן	FINAL N
	FINAL PEH	ף	FINAL P, F
	FINAL TZADI	ץ	Z, TZ, TS, TCH

Hebrew Letters and Their Gematrical Values

The diagram below lists the Hebrew letters along with their traditional gematrical values, which are numerical equivalents assigned to each letter, as mentioned in Chapter Two.

Value	Hebrew Letter	Value	Hebrew Letter	Value	Hebrew Letter
1	ALEF	10	YOD	100	QOF
2	BET	20	CAF	200	RESH
3	GIMEL	30	LAMED	300	SHIN
4	DALET	40	MEM	400	TAV
5	HEH	50	NUN	500	FINAL CAF
6	VAV	60	SAMECH	600	FINAL MEM
7	ZAYIN	70	AHYIN	700	FINAL NUN
8	KHET	80	PEH	800	FINAL PEH
9	THET	90	TZADI	900	FINAL TZADI

Short Hebrew Gematria

The diagram below categorizes the twenty-two Hebrew letters, along with the five final letters, and their gematrical values in the short gematria system, as mentioned in Chapter Nine. The vowel letters in short Hebrew gematria are: א, ה, ו, י.

1	2	3	4	5	6	7	8	9
א	ב	ג	ד	ה	ו	ז	ח	ט
י	כ	ל	מ	נ	ס	ע	פ	צ
ק	ר	ש	ת					
	ך		ם	ן			ף	ץ

Simple English Gematria

The diagram below presents the English letters and their gematrical values according to the **simple gematria** system, as mentioned in Chapter Nine. The vowel letters in this system are: A, E, I, O, U, and Y.

Number	Letter
1	**A**, J, S
2	B, K, T
3	C, L, **U**
4	D, M, V
5	**E**, N, W
6	F, **O**, X
7	G, P, **Y**
8	H, Q, Z
9	**I**, R

Motive Force: Hebrew Letters and Their Corresponding English Counterparts

The diagram below presents the Hebrew vowel letters, their motive force, and the corresponding letters in the English alphabet, as discussed in Chapter Nine.

Hebrew Letter	Hebrew Letter Name	Motive Force	Corresponding English Letter
א	ALEF	Ability to navigate through all directions, possibilities, and situations.	A, E
ה	HEH	Ability to move forward with a focus on practicality and tangible application.	H, AH
ו	VAV	Ability to move outward to either connect with people and situations or to detach from them.	V, O, U, W
י	YOD	Ability to cultivate and enhance spiritual aspects.	I, Y

ABOUT THE AUTHOR

 **Angela Robyinson** is a renowned scholar of Kabbalah, numerologist, author, and international speaker with over 23 years of experience in numerology, nameology (onomastics), and Kabbalistic teachings. She holds an honors degree in Behavioral Sciences with specializations in Psychology, Holistic Psychotherapy, and Life and Career Coaching, as well as a master's degree in Sociology and Anthropology with a focus on Organizational Consulting. Angela is certified in numerology, the secret power of letters, the 72 Names of God, Theta Healing, Reiki, and guided imagery.

Angela began her professional journey in human resources and finance. After achieving significant success in the corporate world, she chose to leave it behind to pursue a spiritual path. She settled in Mount Shasta, California, where she dedicated seven years to deep spiritual practices. During this transformative period, she wrote books exploring the mystical and practical aspects of letters, names, numerology, and Kabbalistic teachings.

In her book, *The Hidden Power of Names*, the first in the "22 Codes of Creation" trilogy, Angela shares profound insights from *Sefer Yetzirah* (The Book of Creation) and offers advanced onomastic analyses. This book provides readers with practical tools to decipher the hidden messages and codes within their names.

Angela is a mother and a grandmother. She continues to consult, lead international workshops, and guide individuals worldwide. Her work helps people uncover their true selves and realize their soul's potential through profound insights into the power of their names and birth dates.

INSIGHTS THAT CAN CHANGE YOUR LIFE

I hope the knowledge you have gained from reading this book has helped you uncover the power hidden in your name and understand its impact on your life's path.

I wish you great success on your journey and invite you to continue deepening your knowledge in the fields of numerology, nameology, onomastics, gematria, and Kabbalistic name analysis. For more resources, visit the NOMENUMERICS website: www.nomenumerics.com, where you can expand your reading, stay updated with new content, and explore additional services.

If you wish to further deepen your self-awareness and uncover the various layers of your higher and human selves, please feel free to contact me. I am here to assist you with professionalism and dedication.

What Will You Gain from This?

This consultation offers you the chance to better understand yourself, discover your soul's potential, and find the path to fulfilling it. In a personal session, we can discuss the topics that concern you and identify precise strategies that can lead to significant changes in your life.

I invite you to a Numerological Reading and Kabbalistic Name Analysis Consultation (The Comprehensive Holistic Analysis of Your Name and Birthdate). This session will help you understand the actions you need to take to align with your higher self, equipping you with the tools and guidance to maximize your inherent potential and natural talents. These insights will make your earthly life journey more enjoyable, fascinating, and rewarding.

Key Points Emphasized in This Analysis

- A deep understanding of your human self and higher self.
- Identification of thought, emotion, and behavior patterns.
- Insight into how your name influences and guides your destiny.
- Recognition of your personal temperament and unique communication style.
- Discovery of your spiritual, intellectual, emotional, and physical potential.
- Understanding the life path and overall direction your life is guiding you towards.
- Clarity on your true heart's desires and the types of relationships you are naturally drawn to.
- Unveiling the challenges and opportunities that await you on your earthly journey.
- Identification of the mental energy that drives you and brings you the greatest success in life.
- Awareness of the fears that tend to control you and your unconscious responses to people and situations.
- Understanding your strengths, powers, and weaknesses.
- Discovery of the karmic rights and obligations that shape the course of your life.
- Understanding the soul lessons you came to learn in the present, and the corrections required for authentic self-fulfillment.
- Gaining insights to make more informed choices in various life areas, such as relationships, personal development, education, and career.

The consultation is conducted via Zoom or phone in two sessions, each lasting up to 60 minutes (for a total of 120 minutes), and costs $600.

However, since you have taken the first step toward improving your life by reading my book, I am offering this consultation **at a special price of**

Only $500!

To take advantage of this unique offer, I invite you to schedule our meeting directly through the NOMENUMERICS website **using the barcode provided.**

Enter the coupon code:

Comprehensive Holistic Analysis 888

At checkout to receive a one-time discount of $100 for reading this book.

If you prefer, you can also book a consultation by contacting me directly via email or WhatsApp:

✉ **Email:** info@nomenumerics.com

☎ **Phone:** +1 (530) 859-1061

Stay Updated and Join Our Community

To receive updates on upcoming books in the series, activities, lectures, workshops, promotions, and discounts, and to join my followers' community, please sign up via the form at this link:
https://nomenumerics.com/mailing-list/

You can also follow me on the following social networks:

Facebook:

LinkedIn:

Instagram:

YouTube:

WhatsApp:

Nomenumerics Website:

About NOMENUMERICS

NOMENUMERICS is a consulting and coaching institute founded with a clear vision: to empower and guide individuals, parents, students, and professionals toward self-realization. Our mission is to free people from doubt, confusion, and uncertainty, helping them confidently move toward a life full of meaning, personal growth and professional success.

Some of the institute's services include:

- **Naming Newborns:** Assisting in choosing a name that bestows health, luck, and supports your child's life path and destiny.

- **Numerology Reading:** Uncovering your higher self, understanding your true purpose, and revealing the karmic influences shaping your life. Gain insights into your life path, strengths, innate abilities, and the energy that drives your success.

- **Kabbalistic Name Analysis:** Exploring the layers of your human self to reveal your spiritual, intellectual, emotional, and physical potential. Understand the patterns guiding your destiny and the compatibility between your name, birth date, and place of residence to support your life path and luck.

- **Discovering the Power of Your Name:** Checking the compatibility between your name, birth date, and place of residence, to understand how it supports your luck and life path.

- **Name Change Consultation:** Assisting in finding or adjusting a name to enhance your health and fortune.

- **Optimal Timing for Life's Biggest Decisions:** Advising on the best timing for major life changes such as moving, career shifts, marriage, pregnancy, divorce, starting a business, and more to ensure success and positive outcomes.

- **Educational and Career Guidance:** Discovering the professional direction and career path that will bring you the most success.

- **Lectures and Workshops:** Offering public and organizational workshops on self-awareness, numerology, nameology, and Kabbalistic name analysis.Gaining insights to make more informed choices in various life areas, such as relationships, personal development, education, and career.

Why Wait?

The universe is waiting for you to take the leap forward with confidence and clarity to fulfill your soul potential. Visit www.nomenumerics.com, or contact us for personal consultations, lectures, and workshops, and start your journey of self-fulfillment today!